Prehistorians Round the Pond

Prehistorians Round the Pond

REFLECTIONS ON AEGEAN PREHISTORY AS A DISCIPLINE

Papers presented at a workshop held in the Kelsey Museum of Archaeology, University of Michigan, March 14–16, 2003

Edited by
John F. Cherry
Despina Margomenou
Lauren E. Talalay

Kelsey Museum Publication 2

Ann Arbor, Michigan, 2005

Published by
Kelsey Museum of Archaeology
The University of Michigan
434 South State Street
Ann Arbor, MI 48109-1390
USA

ISBN 0-9741873-1-3

Cover image:
Terracotta group of three dancers in a ring
Mycenaean, ca. 1300 BC
(British Museum GR 1996.3-25.1)
Reproduced by permission of
The Trustees of the British Museum

This book is available direct from
The David Brown Book Company
PO Box 511, Oakville, CT 06779, USA
(Telephone 860-945-9329; Fax 860-945-9468)

and

Park End Place, Oxford OX1 1HN, United Kingdom
(Telephone 01865-241249 Fax 01865-794449)
www.oxbowbooks.com

Contents

Figures

Tables

About the Authors

Stelios Andreou is Associate Professor of Prehistoric Archaeology in the University of Thessaloniki, Greece. He has worked in Crete and in Northern Greece and directs the excavation of the Bronze Age site of Thessaloniki Toumba. He is the author or coauthor of a number of articles, focusing mainly on the prehistory of Northern Greece, that have recently included: 'Macedonian politics and Aegean encounters: the social context of Mycenaean and Protogeometric pottery in Central Macedonia, Greece,' *Bulletin of the Institute of Classical Studies* 46 (2002/03); (with M. Fotiadis and K. Kotsakis) 'The Neolithic and Bronze Age of Northern Greece,' in T. Cullen (ed.), *Aegean Prehistory: A Review* (*American Journal of Archaeology* supplement 1, Boston, 2001), 259–327; and 'Exploring the patterns of power in the Bronze Age settlements of Northern Greece,' in K. Branigan (ed.), *Urbanism in the Aegean Bronze Age* (Sheffield Studies in Aegean Archaeology 4, Sheffield, 2001), 160–73.

Byran E. Burns is Assistant Professor in the Classics Department at the University of Southern California. He has participated in field projects in the Peloponnese, the Cyclades, and Crete, as well as Italy, Tunisia, and Cyprus. He is currently completing a book manuscript on the consumption of foreign items and materials in Bronze Age Greece. Forthcoming publications include 'Life outside a Mycenaean palace: elite houses on the periphery of citadel sites,' in *Building Communities* (British School at Athens supplementary volume, in press), and (with Y. Kourayos) 'Exploration of the Archaic sanctuary at Despotiko Mandra,' *Bulletin de correspondance hellénique* 128 (2004).

John F. Cherry is Professor of Classical Archaeology and Greek in the Department of Classical Studies at the University of Michigan, Curator of Prehistory and Publications at the Kelsey Museum of Archaeology, and has been Director of the Interdepartmental Program in Classical Art and Archaeology since 1994. He has directed or codirected archaeological survey projects on Melos and Kea and in the Nemea Valley and has also been involved in fieldwork in the United Kingdom, the USA, Italy, and Armenia. He has published more than 100 papers and coauthored or edited 11 books, the most recent of which are *Side-by-Side Survey: Comparative Regional Studies in the Mediterranean World* (with Susan E. Alcock, ed.; Oxford, 2004) and *Explaining Social Change: Studies in Honour of Colin Renfrew* (with Chris

Scarre and Stephen Shennan, eds.; Cambridge, 2004). He has been coeditor of the *Journal of Mediterranean Archaeology* since 1990.

Tracey Cullen is currently the Editor of *Hesperia: The Journal of the American School of Classical Studies at Athens*. She has participated in excavations and regional surveys on Cyprus, Crete, in the Peloponnese, and on Euboea. Recent publications include (editor) *Aegean Prehistory: A Review* (Boston: Archaeological Institute of America, 2001); (with L. E. Talalay) 'Sexual ambiguity in Early–Middle Cypriot plank figures,' in D. Bolger and N. Serwint (eds.), *Engendering Aphrodite: Women and Society in Ancient Cyprus* (Boston: American Schools of Oriental Research, 2002), 181–95; and (with L. E. Talalay, D. R. Keller, and E. Karimali) 'Prehistory and the Southern Euboea Exploration Project,' in N. Kennell (ed.), *Ancient Greece at the Turn of the Millennium: Recent Work and Future Perspectives* (Athens: Canadian Archaeological Institute at Athens, in press).

Jack L. Davis is the Carl W. Blegen Professor of Greek Archaeology at the University of Cincinnati. He has directed or codirected regional studies projects on the island of Keos (1983–84), in the Nemea Valley (1983–89), in the Pylos area (1991–95), and in the Durrës and Mallakastra districts of Albania (1998–2003). Recent publications include (with F. Zarinebaf and J. Bennet) *An Historical and Economic Geography of Ottoman Greece: The Southwestern Morea in the Eighteenth Century, Hesperia* supplement, in press; 'A foreign school of archaeology and the politics of archaeological practice: Anatolia, 1922' (*Journal of Mediterranean Archaeology* 16 [2003] 145–72); 'Are the landscapes of Greek prehistory hidden? A comparative approach,' in S. E. Alcock and J. F. Cherry (eds.), *Side-by-Side Survey: Comparative Regional Studies in the Mediterranean World*, 22–35 (Oxford: Oxbow Books, 2004); and (with S. R. Stocker) 'Animal sacrifice, archives, and feasting at the Palace of Nestor,' in J. C. Wright (ed.), *The Mycenaean Feast* (*Hesperia* 73.2) 59–75 (Princeton: American School of Classical Studies at Athens, 2004).

Michael Fotiadis is Assistant Professor in the Department of History and Archaeology at the University of Ioannina, Greece, where he teaches courses mainly in Stone Age archaeology. He has conducted excavations and surveys in Greece (Western Macedonia and Thrace) and has been involved in fieldwork elsewhere in Greece, Italy, and Ukraine. He also maintains a strong interest in the history and theory of archaeology (see, e.g., 'The historicism of post-processual archaeology and its pleasures,' in G. Most (ed.), *Historicization-Historisierung* [*Aporemata* 5, 2001], and 'Ruins into relics: classical archaeology, European identities and their refractions' [*Pharos* 11, in press]). With P. Darque and O. Polychronopoulou, he coorganized the 2002 conference *Mythos: La préhistoire égéenne du XIXe au XXIe siècle après J.-C.*, and is co-editor of the volume resulting from this conference (to appear as a Supplement to *Bulletin de correspondance hellénique*).

Evi Gorogianni, a doctoral candidate in the Department of Classics at the University of Cincinnati, is currently preparing a dissertation concerning finds from the excavations of the prehistoric site of Ayia Irini on the Greek island of Kea, in the Cyclades. She has also participated in many excavations and regional studies projects in Greece and Albania and has organized an ethnoarchaeological examination of changes in burial customs in Albania since the end of Communism. Her current research interests include the cultural history of the Cyclades, disciplinary history and practice, and social archaeology.

Yannis Hamilakis is Senior Lecturer in Archaeology at the University of Southampton, UK. His main research interests are the archaeology of the body and of the bodily senses, the sociopolitics of the past, Aegean prehistory, and social zooarchaeology. He studied at the University of Crete (BA) and the University of Sheffield (MSc and PhD), has taught at the University of Wales Lampeter (1996–2000), and has held research fellowships at the American School of Classical Studies in Athens, Princeton University, and the University of Cincinnati. He will be teaching a doctoral course on new approaches to the Minoan past at the Universitat Autònoma de Barcelona in 2005, and he will be the W. B. Stanford Lecturer at Trinity College Dublin in 2006. He is currently completing a book on archaeology and national imagination in Greece, is working on another one on the archaeology of the senses, and is also involved in a fieldwork project in West Crete, in collaboration with the Greek Archaeological Service. He sits on the editorial boards of the *Journal of the Royal Anthropological Institute* (including *Man*), *Journal of Mediterranean Archaeology*, *Aegean Archaeology*, and the Greek anthropology journal *Eterotites*.

Artemis Leontis is the author of *Topographies of Hellenism: Mapping a Homeland* (Ithaca, N.Y.: Cornell University Press, 1995), which has also appeared in Greek translation. She has published articles on Greek literature and culture and edited three books, including *Greece: A Traveler's Literary Companion* (San Francisco, Calif.: Whereabouts Press, 1997), a collection of 24 stories, organized geographically, by modern Greek writers. She was co-curator, with Lauren E. Talalay, of the exhibition 'Cavafy's World' at the Kelsey Museum of Archaeology. She teaches Modern Greek at the University of Michigan.

Despina Margomenou is a PhD candidate in the Department of Anthropology at the University of Michigan, and she is also completing a degree in the University's Museum Studies Program. Her dissertation focuses on storage practices in Northern Greece during the Late Bronze and Early Iron Ages. She has also studied Neolithic pottery from the Palace of Knossos and has participated in excavations and surveys in Northern Greece, Thrace, and Crete, as well as in Serbia and Bolivia. She is coauthor of the paper 'The Neolithic settlement of Knossos: new light on an old picture,' in *Knossos: Palace, City, State* (*BSA Studies* 12, 2004).

Colin Renfrew is now a Fellow (formerly Director) of the McDonald Institute for Archaeological Research, and Emeritus Disney Professor of Archaeology in the University of Cambridge. His book *The Emergence of Civilisation* (London, Methuen 1972) was based on his doctoral dissertation, and he has excavated in Greece at Saliagos near Antiparos, Sitagroi in the Plain of Drama, Phylakopi in Melos, Markiani on Amorgos, and directed fieldwork (with Lila Marangou and Christos Doumas) at Dhaskalio-Kavos on Keros. Final publications for Markiani and Phylakopi are in press with the British School at Athens, and the second volume of the Sitagroi excavation has been published as E. S. Elster and C. Renfrew (eds.), *Prehistoric Sitagroi: Excavations in Northeast Greece, 1968–1970. Volume 2: The Final Report* (*Monumenta Archaeologica* 20. Los Angeles: The Cotsen Institute of Archaeology, UCLA, 2003).

Lauren E. Talalay is Associate Director and Curator at the Kelsey Museum of Archaeology and Adjunct Associate Professor in the Department of Classical Studies at the University of Michigan. Her books and articles include *Deities, Dolls and Devices: Neolithic Figurines from Franchthi Cave, Greece* (Bloomington: Indiana University Press, 1993); 'A feminist boomerang: the Great Goddess of Greek prehistory' (*Gender & History* 6.2 [1994] 165–83); and 'The gendered sea: iconography, gender, and Mediterranean prehistory,' in E. Blake and A. B. Knapp (eds.), *Archaeology of Mediterranean Prehistory* (Blackwell Studies in Global Archaeology), 2005. She is also coeditor with A. Leontis and K. Taylor of a book on the modern Greek poet Constantine P. Cavafy ('...*What these Ithakas mean.' Readings in Cavafy*, Hellenic Literary and Historical Archive, Athens, 2002).

Authors' Addresses

Stelios Andreou

Department of Archaeology, University of Thessaloniki, 540 06 Thessaloniki, Greece
E-mail address: andrest@hist.auth.gr

Bryan E. Burns

Classics Department, Taper Hall of Humanities #224, University of Southern California, Los Angeles, CA 90089-0352, USA
E-mail address: bburns@usc.edu

John F. Cherry

Department of Classical Studies, University of Michigan, 2160 Angell Hall, 435 S. State St., Ann Arbor, MI 48109-1003, USA
and
Kelsey Museum of Archaeology, University of Michigan, 434 S. State St., Ann Arbor, MI 48109-1390, USA
E-mail address: jcherry@umich.edu

Tracey Cullen

American School of Classical Studies at Athens, 6–8 Charlton Street, Princeton, NJ 08540-5232, USA
E-mail address: tracey_cullen@ascsa.org

Jack L. Davis

Department of Classics, University of Cincinnati, Cincinnati, OH 45221-0226, USA
E-mail address: jack.davis@uc.edu

Michael Fotiadis

Department of History and Archaeology, University of Ioannina, Dourouti, Ioannina 451 10, Greece
E-mail address: mfotiadi@umich.edu

Evi Gorogianni

Department of Classics, University of Cincinnati, Cincinnati, OH 45221-0226, USA
E-mail address: gorogie@email.uc.edu

Yannis Hamilakis   Department of Archaeology, School of Humanities,
                              University of Southampton, Southampton SO17 1BF,
                              United Kingdom
                              E-mail address: Y.Hamilakis@soton.ac.uk

Artemis Leontis   Department of Classical Studies, University of Michigan,
                              2160 Angell Hall, 435 S. State St., Ann Arbor, MI
                              48109-1003, USA
                              E-mail address: aleontis@umich.edu

Despina Margomenou Museum of Anthropology, University of Michigan,
                              Natural Science Museum Building, 1109 Geddes Avenue,
                              Ann Arbor, Michigan 48109-1079, USA
                              E-mail address: margomen@umich.edu

Colin Renfrew   Department of Archaeology, University of Cambridge,
                              Cambridge CB2 3DZ, United Kingdom
                              and
                              The McDonald Institute for Archaeological Research,
                              Downing Street, Cambridge CB2 3ER, United Kingdom
                              E-mail address: dap38@cam.ac.uk

Lauren E. Talalay   Kelsey Museum of Archaeology, University of Michigan,
                              434 S. State St., Ann Arbor, MI 48109-1390, USA
                              and
                              Department of Classical Studies, University of Michigan,
                              2160 Angell Hall, 435 S. State St., Ann Arbor, MI
                              48109-1003, USA
                              E-mail address: talalay@umich.edu

Preface

And then said Socrates, I believe that the earth is extremely large and that we who live between the pillars of Herakles and Phasis inhabit some small part of it around the sea, just like ants or frogs around a pond. (Plato, *Phaedo* 109b.2)

This volume—the second in the new series Kelsey Museum Publications—emerged from a workshop organized by its coeditors at the University of Michigan during the weekend of March 14–16, 2003. As its title suggests, the principal aim of the workshop was to encourage discussion of the status and nature of Aegean prehistory, broadly defined as a discipline. We wished to initiate a frank dialogue about the 'identities' of our field, the sociopolitical agendas that both animate and constrain it, and the ways in which we might ascertain the relative state of its health soon after the beginning of a new century. Thus, the goal was not to solicit programmatic or prescriptive statements defining the field, nor papers exploring its history or biographies of its key practitioners; a certain amount of work in the latter directions has, in any case, already been attempted in recent years. Rather, we hoped that the small group of participants in the workshop might begin to resituate Aegean prehistory within a more self-conscious and self-critical context. We say 'begin' because—as Davis and Gorogianni rightly note (in ch. 5)—critical histories that examine the forces that have shaped the disciplinary pond in which we all swim are rare enough in classical archaeology as a whole, and virtually non-existent in Aegean prehistory.

The idea of organizing this workshop began in late summer 2002. At that time, Despina Margomenou (an Aegeanist and a doctoral candidate in the Museum of Anthropology at the University of Michigan) approached John Cherry and Laurie Talalay with the notion of convening a few Aegean prehistorians to discuss the status of the field in the terms just noted. She had good reasons for such a proposal since—from her particular vantage point, at least—Aegean prehistory looked to be in trouble: sidelined in the major theoretical debates within anthropological archaeology; both ignored by anthropologists and increasingly distant from the interests of classical colleagues; its general standing within archaeology and perhaps in the academy as a whole in decline; and professional positions decidedly scarce (especially for those not trained within the classical tradition). One might well reflect gloomily that—as Despina herself put it—Aegean prehistory seems to have 'won the battle, but lost its charm.'

These troubling thoughts generated some lively debate amongst us, and we retreated more than once to Ashley's (one of Ann Arbor's local watering holes), to chew over some challenging questions. Is the field's intellectual vitality truly ebbing away? What do we in fact intend by our use of the phrase 'Aegean Prehistory,' or for that matter the very word 'Aegean,' and when did that term become operational in the definition of Greek identity? How are Aegean studies portrayed in more popular venues such as the press, schools, and museums? How do we tease out nationalist traditions within the *topoi* we all share? And, above all, why has there never been a workshop on this topic, so far as we know—isn't self-reflection *de rigueur* these days? In the final analysis we all agreed that a gathering in which we defined the limits of our self-awareness and confronted our seeming complacency was long overdue and would be a worthwhile enterprise, irrespective of whether a subsequent published record of the event seemed justified.

Considerations of both money and space necessarily limited active involvement in the workshop to a dozen speakers and a comparable number of other participants. Almost all those we contacted accepted our invitation to attend: two from Europe, several from other American institutions, and the remainder from the University of Michigan itself. Inevitably, that made it an Anglophone group reflecting dominantly Anglo-American perspectives on the issues we wished to discuss. (This bias, incidentally, we sought to correct by establishing a chat room on the Internet in which other interested persons could register their opinions; but, in the event, this was not a success, perhaps due mainly to understandable reticence in committing personal viewpoints to public scrutiny.) For the present volume, however, we have attempted to widen the discussion by inviting three Aegean prehistorians *not* based in the United States to comment on the written papers and to offer their own ideas.

The meeting itself took place at the Kelsey Museum of Archaeology, a charming 19th-century building in the heart of the University's central campus. Since our initial invitation to participants had called for informal talks in response to our brief, followed by discussion, none of the papers was pre-circulated. Our introduction (ch. 1) sets out the larger intellectual and disciplinary context for the revised individual papers that follow. This was not an occasion from which we expected closure or clear-cut conclusions, and such was certainly the case; our hope is merely to have stimulated an appetite for further exploration of the issues that were raised.

∾

As with all academic gatherings and the publications that result from them, there are a number of people to thank. Our greatest debt goes to those who spoke at the workshop and the three commentators. We are particularly grateful to the workshop participants who agreed to rework their talks and ideas into formal papers once we decided to press ahead with a publication. Two of those who made interesting presentations at the workshop are not reflected in the pages that follow, and we thank them here for their stimulating contributions to the event itself: Johannes Foufopoulos (University of Michigan) and James Wright (Bryn Mawr College). Yannis Hamilakis offered a presentation at the workshop but has chosen to contribute in these pages as a commentator.

It is also our pleasure to extend our appreciation to those units of the University of Michigan that offered financial support, both for the workshop and for the present volume: Contexts for Classics, the Constantine A. Tsangadas Trust of the Rackham Graduate School, the Center for European Studies, the Kelsey Museum of Archaeology, and the Interdepartmental Program in Classical Art and Archaeology (IPCAA). We are especially indebted to the IPCAA Director's Research Account and to the Office of the Vice President for Research, which provided publication subventions. The Director of the Kelsey Museum of Archaeology, Sharon Herbert, enthusiastically supported the idea of hosting our event in the Museum, and we gladly acknowledge her support. Some of the necessary organizational tasks were undertaken by current and former graduate students at the University of Michigan; we are particularly grateful to Seth Button, Elissa Faro, Jennifer Gates, Catherine Lyon Crawford, Jessica Powers, and Amanda Sprochi. Peg Lourie, the production editor for Kelsey Museum publications, worked her usual wonders with layout and copyediting, and we are, as always, most appreciative of her talents and patience.

No gathering of Aegeanists would be complete without a *glendi* and celebration with food and beverages. Thano Masters of Thano's Lamplighter Restaurant provided the food that fueled our thoughts during the workshop itself, while John Roumanis, proprietor of the Mediterrano Restaurant, put on a spread fit for the gods and goddesses at the close of the weekend.

∾

Finally, a comment on this volume's main title (and that of the workshop, too). As many readers will recognize, it draws on the passage in Plato's *Phaedo* (109b.2) where Socrates likens those people who inhabit the Mediterranean to 'frogs around the pond.' That expression took on wider archaeological currency from its use in John Cherry's 1983 article 'Frogs round the pond: perspectives on current archaeological survey projects in the Mediterranean region.' More than 20 years later we again invoke the phrase in reference not only to the Mediterranean Aegean but more abstractly to Ann Arbor and its remarkable University. As it turned out, the pond analogy was particularly apt. Ponds are fine places to convene: they provide refuge, nourishment, good company, and inducements for reflection—in fact, precisely the kind of environment that emerged during our weekend of discussion.

John F. Cherry
Despina Margomenou
Lauren E. Talalay
Ann Arbor, August 2004

1 Reflections on the 'Aegean' and Its Prehistory: Present Routes and Future Destinations

Despina Margomenou, John F. Cherry, and Lauren E. Talalay

Introduction

Self-reflective discourse about an academic discipline is, one hopes, more than merely a fad of the postmodernist era. In Aegean prehistory, however, it certainly appears to have taken hold just recently. Indeed, it seems more a sign of the times than mere coincidence that, shortly after our own workshop conversations centered on being an Aegeanist within the contemporary academic establishment, comparable discussions have sprung up in various other venues—on *AegeaNet*, in the March 2003 issue of *Αρχαιολογία*, and in subsequent conferences held in Greece and elsewhere. Of course, syntheses and historiographies of Aegean prehistory are hardly new (e.g., Myres 1933). Yet as disciplinary self-evaluation has proliferated within classical archaeology in recent years, Aegean prehistorians too have started to consider their field within wider political, ideological, intellectual, and historical contexts.[1]

Thinking about one's discipline in this way is also ultimately a process of empowerment (cf. Wylie 1983: 120; Bourdieu 1988: 15–16). Our sense is that it may be time for Aegean prehistorians to engage in such a process, if we want the field to become more interdisciplinary, inclusive, and rigorous in the years to come. The past two or three decades have seen the gradual dissolution of a consensus concerning appropriate aims and procedures, as well as growing doubt and confusion about what it is that justifies the special status that Aegean prehistory has enjoyed as a field for well over a century. In North America, especially, these concerns appear to have been exacerbated by the fact that the niche generally occupied by Aegean prehistorians within the standard disciplinary divisions of the academy has led to a widespread sense of marginalization and the feeling that our core interests and those of colleagues in classics, anthropology, or history of art are now rather far apart. There is the danger, then, that an exercise in disciplinary self-reflection degenerates into little more than an arena for random expressions of indignation, frustration, and identity crises of all sorts, or—worse—just another transient 'sexy' topic. A useful conversation requires some clear objectives and the delineation of some expectations for the future.

In convening the 2003 workshop (and, now, in preparing this modest volume), our aim was not to be prescriptive but rather to open the door for future discussion of some of these themes. In particular, we thought it important to consider various objective ways of evaluating the current state of the field, as well as gaining a better feel for the ideas that some Aegeanists now have about the standing and likely future trajectory of this particular intellectual domain. In advance of the workshop, we raised a number of high-level questions with which to challenge its participants. Among them was the suggestion that, in many respects, their field does not stand alone but is implicated in discourses that lie not only outside the disciplinary boundaries of Aegean archaeology but also outside those of its 'surrogate parents' (in particular, classical archaeology and anthropology). How do things look, for example, to a scholar whose work, via literary critical theory, focuses on the aesthetic dimensions of the 'place' called the Aegean, proposing, amongst other things, that what has allowed all these disparate disciplinary voices to meet 'round this pond' and to bridge all sorts of 'Great Divides' has been a shared modernist aesthetic? And does this have anything to do with what the concept of 'the Aegean' might mean to, say, a biogeographer?

Determining the disciplinary boundaries of a field is surely more than merely classifying knowledge but constitutes a political act of interpreting the world. So it becomes both relevant and important to investigate the politics implicated in this Aegeanist endeavor. Whose politics in fact are these, and how are Aegean prehistorians involved in constructing and reproducing them? How do identities of all kinds become implicated in the narratives produced, from 'Aegeans' to 'Black Athenas'? Indeed, for us as editors, one of the most intriguing—and puzzling—issues is why the entirety of the prehistory of the Greek world has come to be co-opted under the term 'Aegean archaeology'. This is where we start in our introduction to the themes of the contributions that follow.

The 'Aegean' of 'Aegean Prehistory'

What exactly is the 'Aegean' that delimits the subject Aegean prehistorians claim to study, and what would be the best criteria for defining it? At first sight, the very question may seem fatuous. Yet it is hardly a trivial issue for the archaeologist whose work focuses primarily on Northern Greece, an area whose prehistory has recently been described as 'the Other of the Aegean' (Andreou *et al.* 1996; 2001). To be able to approach 'the Other,' it is necessary to understand the 'We' or the 'Self' (in this case, the 'Aegean') to which it stands in opposition—something that is neither self-evident nor fixed.

To those familiar with the field and its literature, what Aegean prehistory comprises is perhaps largely unproblematic: the prehistoric archaeology of the Greek mainland, the Aegean islands, and Crete. But then, of course, this definition shades off at the edges to include 'Aegean' interactions with coastal Anatolia (or from a Graeco-centric perspective, 'Aegean Turkey': Bean 1966), the Adriatic and the Ionian islands, peninsula Italy, Sicily, Sardinia, the Aeolian islands, Cyprus, the Levant, and Egypt—a region that is geographically far more encompassing and diverse than merely the Aegean Sea and the lands that border it. In actuality, very few general works in Aegean prehistory designate precisely what is meant by the word

'Aegean,' and fewer still engage in any investigation of the history of the usage of that term.[2] But it would be wrong to infer from this that 'Aegean' means the same thing to everyone or that it is a purely geographical description.

Books and university courses dealing with the prehistory of the region now occupied by the modern Greek nation-state have employed a wide variety of descriptive terminology. In an earlier age, one encountered titles such as 'Homeric archaeology,' 'Prehellenic archaeology,' and 'Preclassical archaeology'—words used to describe university classes in the archaeology of Bronze Age Greece, which now seem either to beg certain questions or (in the era since the decipherment of Linear B as Greek) to be downright anachronistic.[3] It is largely since World War II that 'Aegean prehistory' has taken hold as the predominant term to describe the archaeology of the Greek region in the period prior to ca. 1000 BC. The term, however, has experienced further extension. At many North American universities, courses are offered under the title 'Aegean archaeology'—meaning not, as might logically be supposed, 'the archaeology of the Aegean Sea and surrounding areas in all periods' but much more specifically 'Greek *prehistory*.' A purely geographical term, in other words, has been transmogrified into a chronological one.[4] This is a peculiarity that, we think, has not received much comment, and it is one for which it is hard to think of parallels in other archaeological subfields.

As regards the etymology of the word 'Aegean,' it has been suggested recently (Giatromanolakes 1995: 434; Doumas *et al.* 1999: 11) that the word is derived from the Homeric verb Ἀῖσσω (= to leap, cf. Αἴξ = goat) and therefore is '. . . a *metaphorical* synonym of the wave. So the Aegean Sea means the restless, wavy, stormy, sea' (Doumas *et al.* 1999: 11; our emphasis). If the term 'Aegean' was conceived as a metaphor, then there is in this word an inherent absence of literal, 'factual,' meaning; rather, it allows for multiple, alternative, and culturally relative conceptualizations (cf. Tilley 1999: 3–35). It is hardly surprising, thus, that among Aegeanists even geographically based definitions are mutually inconsistent. A few examples serve as illustration.

The recent *Archaeological Atlas of the Aegean*, published in 1999 by the Ministry of the Aegean and the University of Athens under the aegis of a distinguished Scientific Committee, describes the Aegean as follows:

> Of the three geographical zones in the Aegean region—the island, the coastal and the inland zone of the surrounding lands—the first two participated actively in forming its single civilization. The area extending from the coast of Macedonia and Thrace in the North to Crete in the South, and from the coastal zone of Asia Minor in the East to the shores of the Greek Mainland in the West was an internally cohesive geographical unit that hosted the economic, social and political evolution of the peoples inhabiting it. [. . .] The flow of waters on land—rivers and torrents—towards the sea also provides a route of communication between the inland and the island world. So the term Aegean for a cultural region

1

encompasses not only the islands and the coastal zones, but also those
sites in the hinterland that are directly linked with these along river val-
leys and whose culture exhibits a strong Aegean orientation. (Doumas *et
al.* 1999: 11)

A 'result of man's responses to the pressing challenges of the environment,'
this 'Aegean culture' is at the same time unifying and common to those who communicate via sea routes; but it also has 'local peculiarities' due to the variability of Aegean
ecosystems (Doumas *et al.* 1999: 12). The *Atlas* includes a total of 61 Map Sheets for
the North, Central, and Southern Aegean, with the Greek and Asia Minor coastlines.
Sites farther inland are not included. Thus, in accordance with geography, but despite
the cultural dimensions of the definition provided in the introduction to the *Atlas*,
the 'Aegean culture' as mapped includes (for instance) Nemea but not Pylos.

Nikos Svoronos, an historian attempting an overview of the prehistory and
history of the Aegean, brings Pylos back into the picture with his more comprehensive definition:

> The region bordering the southern part of the Balkan Peninsula (Epirus,
> Southern Macedonia and Thrace) on the north, the Ionian Sea on the
> west, the coastline of western Asia Minor on the east, and Crete and Cy-
> prus on the south constitutes one geographic unit with the Aegean as its
> center. Indeed, the entire mainland of this region that penetrates deeply
> into the Mediterranean, and functions as a boundary between its eastern
> and southern parts, faces the Aegean and the East. The main rivers of this
> mainland flow towards the Thracian and Aegean Seas. (Svoronos 1995:
> 34; our translation)

According to Dickinson, whose main goal in his book *The Aegean Bronze
Age* is 'to emphasize the element of continuity':

> I shall also be limiting coverage effectively to the region of the Minoan,
> Cycladic, and Helladic cultures in the southern part of the Aegean; the
> northernmost parts of modern Greece, the north Aegean islands, and
> most of the Turkish coastal areas are culturally separate and, although of-
> ten demonstrably in contact with the Aegean cultures, have an essentially
> different history. (Dickinson 1994: xviii)

One might argue that, for the Bronze Age, it is possible to limit the definition of the 'Aegean' to the area suggested by Dickinson. Yet another archaeologist,
also focusing on the Bronze Age, gives a succinct, but quite different, geographic
definition:

> The region with which we are concerned coincides closely with modern
> Greece and the western coast of Turkey. (Warren 1989, vii)

It is obviously futile to seek to impose disciplinary boundaries over a sea, particularly when (as demonstrated by the definitions just cited) the question is not a purely geographical one: cultural, historical, and political criteria and perspectives inevitably intervene. So in determining what is and what is not 'Aegean,' there is a constant negotiation and fluidity, consistent with the relativism inherent in the very term itself.

In Search of Disciplinary Identity: Aegean Prehistory as an Academic Field
The same kind of fluidity is present when it comes to defining the disciplinary boundaries of Aegean archaeology within the neatly organized universe of the academy. In Europe (including Greece), and unlike the United States, departments of archaeology are generally independent of classics (although some of them began their existence within classics) and certainly independent of anthropology (the latter being conceived more narrowly as cultural or social anthropology). Aegean archaeology is in most cases a specialization within archaeology departments; in the case of Greek universities, prehistoric archaeology primarily features courses in Aegean prehistory and constitutes one of the three main divisions of an archaeology department, together with classical and Byzantine archaeology. In the United States, on the other hand, Aegean archaeology is most usually taught in departments of classics, although also to some extent in history of art or Near Eastern studies, and in some cases (as, for instance, at the University of Michigan) within interdisciplinary programs nested between classical studies and history of art. Interestingly, what is *common* to both Europe and the US is the implicit equation of 'Aegean archaeology' with the prehistoric archaeology of Greece, thus (as noted above) temporally restricting the purely geographical term 'Aegean' to the pre-Classical periods.

The Department of Classics at the University of Cincinnati, one of the best-known centers for the study of Aegean prehistory in the United States, is a revealing example of how perceptions of Aegean archaeology have altered over the years. Davis and Gorogianni (ch. 5, this volume) mention the various designations for graduate courses and degrees in Aegean offered at Cincinnati: the successive terms used since 1927 range from 'Homeric' and 'Preclassical' (until the 1960s), to 'Aegean archaeology' (in the 1970s), and now 'Bronze Age.' The choice of terms reflects changing views of the role and scope of archaeology in general, as well as the significance of Aegean prehistory archaeology *vis-à-vis* classical studies. Thus, from an original emphasis on complementing ancient texts and providing evidence for the origins of Classical Greece and the continuity of Hellenism (cf. Andreou, ch. 4, this volume), study of the prehistoric archaeology of Greece at Cincinnati has become increasingly 'emancipated,' as it were; and, in its current incarnation as 'Bronze Age' studies, it is expected not only to embrace a wider research area than the Aegean alone but also to encompass a more ambitious diachronic perspective that includes the Neolithic, and even the Palaeolithic. This is entirely consistent with

1

the directions followed by Cincinnati's archaeological field research, which in recent years has moved beyond excavations in Greece to include large-scale, intensive surveys and projects in Turkey, Cyprus, and Albania (Davis 2004).

Not surprisingly, if we probe a bit deeper, we find that complicated theoretical histories, not simply geographic, chronological, or text-based distinctions, have structured the disciplinary divisions amongst Aegean prehistory, classics, and classical archaeology. Morris (1994) has argued that, with the rejection of Hellenism by many academics, classical studies faced its own epistemic challenges. The issue has been further discussed (e.g., Morris 2000; Dyson 1981; 1985; 1989a; 1989b; 1993; 1998) in what Davis and Gorogianni (ch. 5, this volume) call 'crisis literature.' Within that context, classical archaeology is criticized for having remained isolated, both methodologically and theoretically, from other fields of archaeology. Aegean archaeology, the 'bridge' over Renfrew's 'Great Divide' (1980) between classical and anthropological archaeology, is thus seen as diverging significantly from classical archaeology (Morris 1994: 14–15; 2000: 74–75). Emerging from a perspective that favors connections to anthropology, Davis and Gorogianni note that in the case of UC, and despite the status of Aegean archaeology within the Department of Classics (the result of an 80-year tradition that significantly influenced the institutional policies of the American School of Classical Studies at Athens), its relevance to the field of classics is becoming increasingly tentative.

The effects of this 'gap' are not merely epistemological. Aegeanists are still employed within classics departments, yet as Cullen has noted elsewhere (2001b: 14), financial support for Aegean archaeology projects is difficult to obtain: the National Endowment for the Humanities largely eliminated its independent archaeology program in 1996, and the National Science Foundation rarely awards funding to Aegeanists, who are viewed as more closely aligned with the humanities. UC is probably a unique case in this respect, shaped by the particular historical coincidence of an endowment and the intellectual interests of its faculty.

More recently, however, the notion that classical archaeology remains isolated from theoretical and methodological developments in other fields has been challenged (Morris 2004; Burns, ch. 6, this volume). Within the last generation a significant shift has occurred: classical archaeologists are now considered part of the 'theoretical noise,' having joined a broader movement within historical archaeology (Snodgrass 1985; 1987; 1991; Morris 2004: 256). In fact, Morris (2004) argues that classical archaeology is actually very well equipped to address questions of power and individual agency, as formulated within the post-processualist school of archaeology.

What, then, is the role of Aegean prehistorians within this new 'enlightened' classical archaeology or, to quote Morris (2004: 265), 'a classical archaeology without the classical'? Like Morris, Burns suggests that archaeologists can grapple most effectively with the formation and organization of complexity or, for example, the subject of power and agency in the mature Greek city-state, by deploying the additional evidence provided by the documentary and literary texts examined and analyzed by classicists. The 'Great Tradition' can, according to Burns, also complement the diachronic perspectives of archaeological survey, informing answers to questions of identity, ethnicity, and memory.

In the past, Aegeanists had been perceived as the 'intermediaries' spanning the disciplinary divide between classics and the social sciences. While perhaps no longer a disciplinary intermediary in this sense, Aegean archaeology still bridges the chronological divide that separates the prehistoric from the historical (i.e., Classical) periods. Burns, again, suggests that comparisons with the prehistoric past can be used not to find origins or to show continuity but to demonstrate what is particular and unique to each culture. In addition, he proposes that the prehistoric past can provide a venue for teaching such topics as the use of material culture in isolation or in conjunction with textual material within classics. Classical studies, in this view, is seen as a remarkably flexible field, one capable of accommodating the increasing specialization of subfields and the inclusion of cultures and topics once considered geographically, chronologically, or intellectually marginal. Although Aegean prehistorians may have wandered off into anthropology, they still remain 'with at least one foot planted in the field of classics' (Burns, ch. 6, this volume). Their contribution to the 'tradition' is that their research clearly expands the chronological range of the field and focuses on the complexity and diversity of the ancient Mediterranean.

In 2000, Morris wrote that 'Archaeologists of Greece must overcome formidable obstacles if they are to transcend their appointed role as an inferior kind of classicist' (2000: 75). Indeed, this seems to be the motivation behind some of the papers in this volume, although not every author proposes to cope with or transcend their classicist identities in the same way.

If Aegeanists do have at least one foot planted firmly in the field of classics, their other foot seems at least partially set in the fertile grounds of anthropology. Given that stance, it is useful to ask how best to define Aegean prehistory's relation to anthropology and to anthropological archaeology, fields that style themselves as both more scientific and more thoroughly theorized than classical archaeology or classics (and, by extension, than Aegean prehistory).

Interestingly, only one of the participants in this workshop belongs to an anthropology department. There are, of course, some Aegeanists employed within anthropology departments in the USA, yet no literature concerning their disciplinary identities and status seems to be produced from that 'side of the fence.' One might argue that their designation as 'anthropologists' takes precedence over the specific area of research. The comparative and generalizing nature of anthropological archaeology permits unusually wide scope for the investigative interests and teaching curricula of archaeologists; the 'Aegeanist' identity within anthropological archaeology is thus subsumed under that of 'anthropologist' (after all, they would claim that 'archaeology is anthropology or it is nothing'). Even so, area specialists are abundant within anthropological archaeology, at least as much so as within classics, and some of them (such as 'Mesoamericanists' or 'Southwestern' archaeologists) have a long tradition within the discipline. Aegeanists, however, are not singled out: at best they tend to be lumped together with other 'Old World' archaeologists whose interests include the Near East, Egypt, and other parts of the Mediterranean, as well as, in some cases, the Balkans and Central Europe. It may be possible to 'read' this lack of fine distinctions, where the Old World is concerned, as an indication that anthropological archaeology has historically been a New World endeavor—an alternative to what in the Old World tends to be called 'national archaeology.' The primary spheres of focus have included areas that have come under the 'imperialist' interests of the New World at one time or other (Mesoamerica, South America, and to a certain extent the Far East). Taking this line of argument one step further, we might reinscribe the 'Great Divide,' so that much of the 'Old World' is seen as primarily the territory of 'traditional' classical archaeology, the Balkans and Central Europe being an exception, since these areas did not attract the interests of classicists, at least initially. One may wonder, then, whether the focus of Aegean prehistorians on the material culture of an area that was 'tainted' by the long presence of classicists and classical archaeology renders these area specialists 'an inferior kind of anthropologist.' Exploring the validity and implications of this statement would require the active involvement of Aegeanists from 'the other side of the fence' in public discourse on the status and future of Aegean archaeology. But so far this has not been the case and, as was evident at this workshop, self-reflective discourse on Aegean archaeology has involved only Aegeanists of 'classicist descent.'

'Aegean' Identities and Narratives: Scholarly Visions, Nationalist Aspirations, and Modernist Aesthetics

The fluidity of the term 'Aegean' is perhaps best seen when the term is used as a modifier of the equally polysemic term 'culture' or the trendier notion of 'identity.' Since the spectacular discoveries of Schliemann, Tsountas, Evans, Blegen, Wace, and others that gave a physical presence to a remote literary past previously known only through Homer, the Aegean has become an arena of quests for all sorts of origins: of the Greek language, of Hellenism, even of European civilization itself (Andreou, ch. 4, this volume). In one respect, this is what Morris meant when he characterized Aegean prehistory as 'the soft underbelly of Hellenism' (1994: 15).

In this context, arguments ascribing cultural developments in the region to influences from the East continue to be prominent in scholarly discourse and can have considerable impact, as demonstrated by the relatively recent incarnation of the *ex oriente lux* paradigm in Martin Bernal's *Black Athena* (1987). Despite its shaky grasp of classical literature and historical methodology, noted elsewhere (Lefkowitz and Rogers 1996; Marchand and Grafton 1997; Morris 2004: 265), the book demonstrates the extent and scope of claims to the 'Hellenic' identity. As the watery medium connecting the various peoples who have claims to this identity, the 'Aegean' is implicated in such quests.[5] Thus, while contemporary nations vie over its airspace and coastlines, the 'Aegean' is contested and negotiated as well by scholars deeply invested in their interpretations of its remote (or not so remote) past.

Despite a multitude of claims, the appropriation of the term 'Aegean' occurred primarily within Greece, and by Greeks, sometime after the 1920s and through the 1970s, with Elytis's Nobel Prize–winning 1959 poem 'To Axion Esti,' about 'this small world the Great,' signaling the culmination of this process. Leontis (ch. 7, this volume) traces the invention of the term through images of the Aegean as they appeared in Greek writing and art from the 1930s to the 1970s. During this period, she argues, a group of Greece's modernists 'discovered' the Aegean, forging an alternative Greek identity, one that stressed historical depth, continuity, human scale, and the indigenous aesthetic, and one untainted by the demise of the expansionist 'Great Idea' in 1922.

The Aegean-centered vision of Greece is in many ways different from visions engendered after the Greek War of Independence (1821–30). Several scholars have discussed the formation of national identity in modern Greece (e.g., Herzfeld 1987; Friedman 1992; Kitromilidis 1997; Koliopoulos 1997), as well as the role of Greek archaeology in sanctioning the antiquity and continuity of Greek national identity (Kotsakis 1991; 1998; Andreou, ch. 4, this volume). Within a Europe that was seeking a return to an idealized classical past (Morris 1994: 15–23; 2000: 41–48), viewing contemporary Greeks as living ancestors of European civilization (Herzfeld 1987: 19), Greeks themselves were instead seeking to be included in the European present (Herzfeld 1987: 50). Thus, contemporary Greece found itself in a rather peculiar position, 'being both Europe's oldest state and its younger nation' (Morris 2000: 47), as well as being both the object of study by Hellenists and what these Hellenists claimed was their identity (at the same time, as it were, both 'the other' and 'us'). These ambiguities were internalized in somewhat different ways by Greek intellectuals (Morris 1994: 23; 2000: 47–48). The prevalent tendency, however, was that Greeks perceived themselves as both superior and inferior to Western culture and ultimately as unique (Kotsakis 1991; Gourgouris 1996); at the same time, however, they relied on Western approval of whether or not they were living up to their esteemed heritage.

The visions of Greece engendered within this context were in a sense 'extrovert'; they sought to prove the relevancy of contemporary Greece to the quests of European Hellenism. The monuments of Athens, as well as other great discoveries in Southern Greece such as Mycenae, Olympia, Delphi, and Delos, provided ample signifiers of the 'Greek spirit' to fulfill European expectations and Greek aspirations. Yet, as both Kotsakis and Leontis have noted, from about 1844 to 1922 an alternative narrative of Greece was operative *within* Greece—one that centered on Constantinople as the emblem of the greatness that Greek civilization had once achieved and of the power and territorial limits it aspired to reach once more. Within this

1   narrative, Byzantium was assumed to be 'a purely Greek civilization which secured continuity with the Greek past albeit indirectly' (Kotsakis 1998: 49).

It is this particular *internal* narrative, with its expansionist overtones, that provided ideological support for the foreign policy known as the 'Great Idea.' Surprisingly, the failure of that enterprise did not render the Constantinople-centered narrative totally obsolete, but it did open a 'space' for an alternative vision of Greece to emerge. The new internal national image forged after 1922 centered on the Aegean. In this case, temporal and historical depth redeemed what the country had lost in geographical breadth; and this, as Leontis points out, was when prehistory entered the history of Greece. Andreou, in ch. 4, discusses the process by which Aegean prehistory eventually came to denote Greek prehistory not only for Greek academics but also within national discourse and national consciousness. *Continuity* is closely related to the discovery of prehistory and adds to the effectiveness of this alternative national narrative: linking the millennia, the Aegean holds the origins of a timeless 'Greek spirit.'[6] This new Aegean-centered vision of Greece is also an *intimate* one—a *topos*, which, as Leontis explains here, is a place of return, a place where the Greek feels at home, a place that recalls the depths of Greek history, a place where humble contemporary artists continue traditions that started millennia ago (cf. also Leontis 1995). Most significantly, though, this new conception of Greece was part of the modernist narratives that emerged in Greece as an influential group of artists, architects, poets, and intellectuals were seeking alternative routes of expression after the disillusionment of 1922.

Leontis's paper in this volume focuses on the internal dialogue within which the Aegean-centered vision of Greece operated and concludes by wondering whether the archaeological focus on the Aegean is somehow related to the Greek 'discovery' of its antiquity (primarily, its prehistory) within more or less the same period. Although the timing coincides, there seems at first glance to be no other direct link between this *internal* vision of Greece and *external* European quests. Yet on closer inspection, it emerges that this narrative was extended outward, finally to address the quests of a very specific Western audience of artists, intellectuals, and archaeologists, whose aspirations were situated beyond Hellenism and the classicist tradition of Winckelmann. What they shared with their Greek counterparts was a modernist aesthetic.

In the course of the 20th century, and especially since 1945, European sculptors and painters sought their inspiration not only in non-Western but also in prehistoric and ancient art, whose primitivism attracted them to the alterity of the spatially and temporally distant. Aegean artifacts came to play a significant part in this aesthetic appropriation of the past. Schnapp *et al.* (2004: 6–7) and Tourni-kiotes (2003: 70–74) describe how, beginning in 1926, Christian Zervos used his journal *Cahier d'art: Revue d'actualité artistique* to showcase the avant-garde of the time (figures such as Braque, Gris, Léger, and his favorite, Picasso), while at the same time featuring articles on Cycladic figurines, Cretan faience, Etruscan murals, and Mesopotamian pottery. Indeed, in 1927 and later in 1932, Zervos advocated the radical gesture of using objects out of context in the pages of this journal 'in order to show the unity of the human spirit under its surface complexity and the modernity of the great works of the past' (Schnapp *et al.* 2004: 6). The journal *Minotaure*, published by E. Tériade (1933), and the journal *Le Voyage en Grèce* (1934), published by Herakles Ioannides in collaboration with Tériade, also promoted 'an archaeology that was not classical but archaic; not European but world-wide; not museified but site-specific' (Schnapp *et al.* 2004: 6; cf. Tournikiotes 2003: 70).

Returning to the Aegean, it is impossible not to conjure up Arthur Evans's reconstructions of the palace of Knossos and his modernist visions of Minoan society (see MacGillivray 2000; Treuil 2003; Farnoux 1993; 2003); or the long and twisted story of the Cycladic figurines as narrated by Gill and Chippindale (1993). In his introduction to Christos Doumas's catalogue for the exhibition of the N. P. Goulandris Collection at the British Museum, Colin Renfrew (1983: 11) quoted Thomas Carlyle's surprisingly pertinent words:

> Transport yourselves into the early childhood of nations, the first beautiful morning light of Europe, when all yet lay in fresh young radiance as of a great sunrise and our Europe was first beginning to think, to be! Wonder, hope, infinite radiance of hope and wonder, as of a young child's thoughts, in the hearts of these strong men!

With this single passage, Renfrew manages not only to deliver the essential elements of the Aegean-centered identity prevalent in Greece by 1983 but also to make it relevant to his British (Western) readership, attaching it to their Hellenist quests. At the same time, the aesthetics of the catalogue (as in most such exhibitions and books about Cycladic figurines, most notably Renfrew's *The Cycladic Spirit* [1991]) draw a direct line connecting these prehistoric objects to works of art by Picasso or Brancusi.

The modernist aesthetic inherent in the new vision of Greece was equally attractive to archaeologists coming to the Aegean from an anthropological point of view. After all, as Julian Thomas (2004a; 2004b) has demonstrated, archaeology in general is a modernist undertaking and is inconceivable within any other historical conditions. Colin Renfrew's seminal work *The Emergence of Civilization: The Cyclades and the Aegean in the Third Millennium B.C.* (1972) advocated an anthropological and processual approach, with a particular interest in applying systems theory to Aegean prehistory. From the outset, a very strong connection was posited between Aegean civilization and Europe—a connection that (notwithstanding the considerable paradigmatic differences) actually brings him very close to Doumas's European vision. In the preface to the book, Renfrew explained how the diffusionist view, whereby 'Aegean civilization was something borrowed by *Europe* from the Orient,' was inadequate to explain developments in the area (Renfrew 1972: xxv; our emphasis). He regarded the emergence of civilization in the Aegean as a

1 largely local process. The Cycladic and Minoan-Mycenaean civilizations were not the result of the diffusion of ideas or objects but rather an indigenous phenomenon, as Aegean societies were adapting to an external environment (both natural and social), while at the same time innovations in some aspects of human life ('subsystems') favored developments in others (the 'multiplier effect'). One is tempted to draw connecting lines between Renfrew's systemic-functional narrative of prehistoric societies in the Aegean and the quests of figures such as Yannopoulos, Pikionis, or Konstandinides for the indigenous aesthetic in architecture (the 'indigenous spirit'; see Tournikiotes 2003: 74), as well as the set of timeless principles they 'discovered' in Aegean architecture—namely, human scale, response to climate and lifestyle, correspondence of function, building requirements and form, integration of building materials and landscape (Leontis, ch. 7, this volume). In a way, Renfrew found in archaeology what the Greeks of the modernist circle were seeking in art, literature, and architecture and what Elytis (1993) so succinctly described with his 'small world the Great.'

It is perhaps possible to argue, therefore, that the two archaeological paradigms—the art-historical or traditionalist and the anthropological—met in the Aegean, as it was envisioned by the Greek modernists. In many respects, the divide between them is huge; yet they share a common modernist aesthetic, one that, in the case of the Aegean, is also responsible for inventing the object and focus of their study. Although Tournikiotes (2003: 76) is writing about architecture when he says 'This Aegean is the joyful Aegean of our time; an ideal construction of the 20th century,' his words could apply equally to archaeology.

The implication of this line of thought is rather surprising. Although there can be no doubt that foreign excavations in the Aegean during the 1920s and 1930s were essentially 'colonial' enterprises, the scenario sketched above ascribes an active role to Greeks in the process of appropriating their prehistoric past after the 1930s. In this narrative, appropriating the Aegean within an alternative Greek identity came to be crucial to the practice of archaeology in the area during the 1960s and 1970s—and by Greeks and non-Greeks alike.

Tracing Routes and Projecting Future Destinations for Aegean Archaeology
'Aegean archaeology' or 'Aegean prehistory'—whatever those terms mean—certainly has a presence in some form within many academic institutions in the USA, in Europe, and elsewhere, providing opportunities for teaching and research. Does it offer a sufficiently promising future, however, for fresh generations of students who choose to engage with this specialization, in hopes of participating in fieldwork or even aspiring to academic employment? The question, certainly, formed a subtext for the workshop, the original proposal for which was entitled 'Has Aegean prehistory won the war, but lost its charm?' It does seem that assessing the strengths and weaknesses of the field is a timely endeavor and one also necessary for its future. A series of very useful papers taking stock of where we stand in terms of research has

recently been published (Cullen 2001a). One of the chief goals of our workshop, however, was to consider ways in which to evaluate Aegean prehistory's state and status in *disciplinary* terms, and several of the papers approach this issue, employing a number of different indices and criteria.

One such measure (extensively discussed by Cullen, in ch. 3) is the number of Aegeanists in any given institution. Size itself, nonetheless, does not provide any real indication of the field's robustness (or marginalization), unless taken in conjunction with other relevant considerations. Those upon which Cherry and Talalay (ch. 2) have chosen to focus include, for instance, the number of achievement awards given to Aegean prehistorians (as opposed to other breeds of archaeologist), the relative representation of articles on Aegean prehistory in mainstream journals, the percentage of Aegean prehistorians among those presenting papers at the annual AIA meetings, as well as the numbers of doctoral dissertations being produced in this field. The data analyzed pertain primarily to North America and Britain (although the information on journal articles and conferences certainly includes non-American and non-British Aegeanists); they should be treated as only a partial analysis, bearing in mind the obvious fact that programs of academic teaching and scholarship also exist in many places outside the USA and UK. Greece, of course, is a rather special case. In fact, if Andreou's paper (ch. 4) is any indication, then Aegean prehistory in Greece is as vigorous and active as is classical archaeology there, and not only in the realm of academe but also in the public arena. A more comprehensive examination of relevant journals and professional meetings, consequently, may provide an even better picture of the field, given its 'interdisciplinariness' (or, perhaps, 'disciplinary ambiguity').

The availability of adequate funding sources can be another telling indicator of the health of the field, something discussed by Cullen (2001b) and mentioned by Cherry and Talalay (ch. 2). Despite swingeing cuts in the USA in the levels of financial support for archaeological research from federal agencies such as the National Endowment for the Humanities, Aegean prehistorians everywhere— happily, and uniquely—have come to depend on the reliable and generous support of the Institute for Aegean Prehistory (INSTAP), which has become by far the most significant patron of both fieldwork and publication in this field. Only a few institutions (e.g., the University of Cincinnati) command the resources to provide significant research funding for their own projects. Oddly (and very unfairly), American-based projects seeking funding for Aegean-related projects, no matter how rigorous their methodology or how anthropological in orientation, fail to attract support from the National Science Foundation—at least, if the proposal emanates from a humanities rather than a social science department. This is a doubly unkind cut, both because a scholar with Aegean interests and based in an anthropology department would receive preferential consideration and because, of all subfields in classical and Mediterranean archaeology, Aegean prehistory is the one that most effectively straddles the humanities–social sciences divide—to its considerable intellectual benefit. In

1

Europe, matters are quite varied from one country to another (although INSTAP serves as an important source of funding for Aegean scholars there as well); state funding and support from foundations and private institutions are also available in some cases. Assessing the financial potentials of the field requires a more detailed consideration of all sources for the countries where Aegean prehistory is practiced. However, funding should not be considered only in terms of research; Aegean prehistory as an academic field has an educational component, with undergraduate and graduate programs in need of support. The situation in the US seems to rely on the financial capabilities of each institution and department; yet there are no independent foundations or institutions that specifically address educational needs.

Beyond academic education, however, Aegean archaeology has a 'public' component (or at least it should have one), which includes museum exhibitions, presentation of Aegean-related topics in the media, and other venues that serve the needs of the general public. Cherry and Talalay (ch. 2, this volume) cite Aegean-focused conferences in the US and the UK as well as *Nestor*, the long-running bibliographic newsletter now produced by the University of Cincinnati, and *AegeaNet*, the web list linking Aegeanists worldwide. Although such efforts are clear indications of a vigorous field, all these activities are directed to the more academic circle of Aegeanists, not to the general public. Andreou's paper in this volume (ch. 4) examines the situation in Greece, where Aegeanists actively participate in public discourse through newspapers as well as other media. Greece, however, is a special case since Aegean archaeology is there embraced as a national endeavor. Yet the issue of the 'public' component of Aegean archaeology is a serious one, and it is perhaps no coincidence that it emerged during discussions here at Michigan; it also dominated the very few comments we received on the workshop's web site. Cherry and Talalay critically assess a paper by Terrenato (2002), who, among other things, argues that since the 1970s Aegeanists, following their classicist colleagues, have retreated into their 'ivory towers.' Whether or not this is an aphorism, the 'public' component of Aegean prehistory is something that requires further consideration and in the long run might provide venues for the employment of future generations of Aegean prehistorians.

The issue of research opportunities for the future arose as another theme during the discussions at Michigan, and Davis and Gorogianni's paper in this volume voices some of the concerns. For most non-Greek archaeologists, as well as for many Greeks who practice Aegean prehistory through foreign institutions, permits and access to the material remain a profound source of frustration. The existence and operation of foreign schools of archaeology in Greece (and Anatolia) have been extensively discussed, especially in recent years, by both Greeks and non-Greeks and not merely within the academic community (Zoes 1990; Morris 1994; Davis 2003; *Καθημερινή* 05/21/00). We will not repeat those discussions here; besides, Davis and Gorogianni's paper draws a vivid picture of the development of the institutional politics and objectives of the American School of Classical Studies at

Athens in the 1920s and 1930s. Suffice it to say, despite changes in institutional politics and the appointment of Greeks in powerful positions within these schools, many Greek archaeologists (*ephors* as well as academics) still view the operation of such schools with distrust and suspicion: the schools were founded upon, and to some extent still retain, colonialist interests. In many ways, the decision to reduce the number of permits available to foreign schools is a consequence of this attitude and a systematic effort to render Greek archaeology more strictly a Greek affair. Although this is perhaps an isolationist movement on the part of the Greeks, the situation is currently more complex; it is within this complexity that it might be possible for Greeks and non-Greeks alike to redefine the *synergasia* and render it a more inclusive and democratic undertaking.

Nine months after the workshop at Michigan, Greek prehistorians assembled in Rethymno, Crete (December 5–7, 2003) to discuss and assess the state of prehistory in Greece. The organizer of the conference, Katerina Kopaka, in a subsequent e-mail message to us, provided some interesting reflections. She voiced the concerns of many contemporary Greek prehistorians who have spent a good deal of 'self-reflective' time assessing the nationalist tendencies inherent in the quests of Greek archaeology and Greek prehistory, as well as the role of Westerners in shaping some of those preoccupations. This new generation of archaeologists aspires to redefine the practice of prehistoric archaeology in Greece. They are mandating better communication among universities, museums, and regional archaeological authorities (*ephories*) within Greece; a retreat from the isolationist tendencies of many Greek researchers; and the use of broader theoretical models in the archaeological practice of their country. In addition, they propose more systematic communication and vigorous dialogue with their colleagues in other Mediterranean countries (including Turkey, Anatolia, and North Africa) and in the Balkans (N. Efstratiou, pers. comm.). To that list, of course, one might add all other places where Aegean archaeology is taught and practiced. Until the proceedings of the Rethymno meeting are published, the nuances and implications of these propositions generated by Greek prehistorians cannot be further processed: but they certainly constitute a challenge, perhaps signifying a new 'turn' for Aegean archaeology.

Our objectives at the 2003 workshop were also, we hope, a new 'turn.' We began our 'self-reflective' endeavor with an effort to evaluate the state of the field today, suggesting criteria that might help do so—very much aware that the choice of criteria is itself a matter that ought to be part of a wider discussion within the community of Aegeanist prehistorians. Even so, the picture of Aegean prehistory depicted in the pages that follow is far from pessimistic. Despite fundamental ambiguities, the field remains a healthy and vibrant one that can certainly look confidently to the future. But what is the future we envision? The gathering at Rethymno proposed that Aegean archaeology should overcome old distinctions between 'centers' that actively practice archaeology and generate theoretical discourse and 'peripheries' that passively accept or attempt to imitate such 'foreign' models of

1 archaeological practice. We instead proposed another sort of transgression: the future of Aegean prehistory, perhaps, can also be sought in the disciplinary ambiguity so extensively discussed by our workshop participants. There we tried to engage several disciplinary voices and implicate others. In the end, our ability to engage in such a multidisciplinary discourse proved as empowering as our 'self-reflective' efforts; it stands, we feel, as further proof of the rigor and intellectual breadth of the field, despite the modest geographical definition of its subject matter.

Notes

1. For recent reflections on the disciplinary status of classical archaeology, see, e.g., Renfrew 1980; Snodgrass 1987; Dyson 1981; 1985; 1989a; 1989b; 1993; 1998; Morris 1994; 2000; 2004. For examples of Aegean prehistorians' attempts to contextualize their field, see Kotsakis 1991; 1998; Fotiadis 1993; 1995; 2001; Kardulias 1994; Hamilakis and Yalouri 1996; Cullen 2001a; 2001b; Davis 2001; 2003; Brown and Hamilakis 2003; Darcque *et al.* in press.

2. There is, however, a brief overview of the term in literary sources by Giorges Giatromanolakes (1995: 434–47).

3. University courses bearing these titles nonetheless continue to be taught at various universities in the United Kingdom.

4. Conversely, in many departments of classics the course title 'Bronze Age archaeology' has the very particular connotation of 'Greek/Aegean Bronze Age archaeology' (without any possibility of confusion with, say, the Bronze Age archaeology of Italy or Anatolia).

5. As an example of the kinds of discourses within which 'Aegean' is often found, see the following posting on *AegeaNet* (K. Theodorides, November 12, 2003): 'Now coming to the Bronze Age . . . Since there was no 'Hellenic identity' how do we call these people? By calling them Aegeans we indicate a geographical term that is nonetheless distinct from Greek. This scheme presupposes that there was at that time such a thing as a Greek identity distinct and often antithetical to Aegean. The rest follows: peaceful civilizations vs. invaders, invaders civilizing vulgar locals etc.'

6. A particularly clear example was to be seen in the pageant of the opening ceremonies of the 2004 Olympic Games in Athens. The show began with the gradual emergence, from beneath the waters of the flooded stadium, of a five-story-high replica of the head of an Early Cycladic marble figure, which then broke apart to reveal Classical-era sculpture; this, in turn, prefaced 'Klepsydra: a parade of Greek history with characters brought to life

from Greece's mythology, art, and science'—a processional tableau taking the viewer on a steady journey from the Minoan snake-goddess through to the first Olympiad of the modern era (albeit with some notable elisions, such as the Roman and Ottoman empires). The intended message was clear: unbroken continuity and steady evolution over the millennia, linking the contemporary Greek spirit with its origins in the depths of prehistory, *in the Aegean.*

References

Andreou, S., M. Fotiadis, and K. Kotsakis
    1996   Review of Aegean prehistory V: The Neolithic and Bronze Age of Northern Greece. *American Journal of Archaeology* 100: 537–97.

Bean, G .E.
    1966   *Aegean Turkey: An Archaeological Guide.* New York: Praeger.

Bernal, M.
    1987   *Black Athena* I: *The Fabrication of Ancient Greece 1785–1985.* New Brunswick, NJ: Rutgers University Press.

Bourdieu, P.
    1988   *Homo Academicus.* Stanford: Stanford University Press.

Brown, K. S., and Y. Hamilakis (eds.)
    2003   *The Usable Past: Greek Metahistories.* Lanham, MD: Lexington Books.

Cullen, T. (ed.)
    2001a   *Aegean Prehistory: A Review. American Journal of Archaeology* supplement 1. Boston: Archaeological Institute of America.
    2001b   Introduction: voices and visions of Aegean prehistory. In T. Cullen (ed.), *Aegean Prehistory: A Review. American Journal of Archaeology* supplement 1: 1–18. Boston: Archaeological Institute of America.

Darcque, P., M. Fotiadis, and O. Polychronopoulou (eds.)
    in press *Mythos: La préhistoire égéenne du XIXe au XXIe siècle après J.C.* Paris: De Boccard.

Davis, J. L.
    2001   Classical archaeology and anthropological archaeology in North America: a meeting of minds at the millennium? In G. M. Feinman and T .D. Price (eds.), *Archaeology at the Millennium: A Sourcebook,* 415–37. New York: Kluwer Academic/Plenum Publishers.
    2003   A foreign school of archaeology and the politics of archaeological practice: Anatolia, 1922. *Journal of Mediterranean Archaeology* 16: 145–72.
    2004   *Mediterranean Expeditions: Archaeological Field Research by the Department of Classics. A Brief Overview Compiled on the Eightieth Anniversary of the First Departmental Excavations at Nemea in 1924.* Cincinnati: Department of Classics, University of Cincinnati.

1   Dickinson, O. T. P. K.

1994   *The Aegean Bronze Age*. Cambridge: Cambridge University Press.

Doumas, Ch.

1983   *Cycladic Art: Ancient Sculpture and Pottery from the N. P. Goulandris Collection*. London: British Museum Press.

Doumas, Ch., V. Lambrinoudakis, L.G. Mendoni, and E. Simantoni-Bournia (Scientific Editorial Committee)

1999   *Archaeological Atlas of the Aegean: From Prehistoric Times to Late Antiquity*. Athens: Ministry of the Aegean and The University of Athens.

Dyson, S. L.

1981   A Classical Archaeologist's response to the 'New Archaeology'. *Bulletin of the American Schools of Oriental Research* 242: 15–29.

1985   Two paths to the past: a comparative study of the last fifty years of *American Antiquity* and *American Journal of Archaeology*. *American Antiquity* 50: 452–63.

1989a   The role of ideology and institutions in shaping classical archaeology in the nineteenth and twentieth centuries. In A. L. Christenson (ed.), *Tracing Archaeology's Past: The Historiography of Archaeology*, 127–35. Carbondale: University of Southern Illinois Press.

1989b   Complacency and crisis in late twentieth century Classical archaeology. In P. Culham and L. Edmunds (eds.), *Classics: A Discipline and Profession in Crisis?*, 211–20. Lanham, MD: University Press of America.

1993   From New to New Age Archaeology: archaeological theory and classical archaeology—a 1990's perspective. *American Journal of Archaeology* 97: 195–206.

1998   *Ancient Marbles to American Shores: Classical Archaeology in the United States*. Philadelphia: University of Pennsylvania Press.

Elytis, O.

1993 (1959)   *Τὸ Ἄξιον Ἐστί* [*To Axion Esti*]. 19th ed. Athens: Ikaros.

Farnoux, A.

1993   *Cnossos, l'archéologie d'un rêve*. Paris: Gallimard.

2003   Μινωίτες και Μυκηναίοι στον 20ο αιώνα [Minoans and Mycenaeans in the twentieth century]. *Αρχαιολογία και Τέχνες* (special issue: *Ιστοριογραφία της Αρχαιολογίας: Προϊστορικό Αιγαίο* [*Historiography of Archaeology: Prehistoric Aegean*]) 86 (March 2003): 36–41.

Fotiadis, M.

1993   Regions of the imagination: archaeologists, local people, and the archaeological record in fieldwork, Greece. *Journal of European Archaeology* 1(2): 149–66.

1995   Modernity and the past-still-present: politics of time in the birth of regional archaeological projects in Greece. *American Journal of Archaeology* 99: 59–78.

2001   Imagining Macedonia in prehistory, ca. 1900–1930. *Journal of Mediterranean Archaeology* 14: 115–35.

Friedman, J.
1992   The past in the future: history and the politics of identity. *American Anthropologist* 4: 837–59.

Giatromanolakes, G.
1995   Το Αιγαίο και η Ελληνική Λογοτεχνία [The Aegean and Greek literature]. In *Το Αιγαίο: Επίκεντρο Ελληνικού Πολιτισμού* [*The Aegean: Epicenter of Hellenic Culture*], 433–47. Athens: Melissa.

Gill D. W. J., and C. Chippindale
1993   Material and intellectual consequences of esteem for Cycladic figures. *American Journal of Archaeology* 97: 601–59.

Gourgouris, St.
1996   *Dream Nation: Enlightenment, Colonization, and the Institution of Modern Greece*. Stanford: Stanford University Press.

Hamilakis, Y., and E. Yalouri
1996   Antiquities as symbolic capital in modern Greek society. *Antiquity* 70: 117–29.

Herzfeld, M.
1983   *Anthropology through the Looking Glass*. Cambridge: Cambridge University Press.

Kardulias, P. N.
1994   Archaeology in modern Greece: bureaucracy, politics and science. In P. N. Kardulias (ed.), *Beyond the Site: Regional Studies in the Aegean Area*, 373–87. Lanham, MD: University Press of America.

Καθημερινή
2000   Οι ξένες αρχαιολογικές σχολές στην Ελλάδα [Foreign archaeological schools in Greece]. *Εφημερίδα Καθημερινή, Επτά Ημέρες*, 21 May 2000.

Kitromilidis, P.
1996   «Νοερές κοινότητες» και οι απαρχές του Εθνικού Ζητήματος στα Βαλκάνια ['Imagined communities' and the origins of the national cause in the Balkans]. In Th. Veremis (ed), *Εθνική Ταυτότητα και Εθνικισμός στη Νεότερη Ελλάδα* [*National Identity and Nationalism in Modern Greece*], 53–131. Athens: Morphotiko Idryma tes Ethnikes Trapezes.

Koliopoulos, J. S.
1996   The war over the identity and numbers of Greece's Slav Macedonians. In P. Mackridge and E. Yannakakis (eds.), *Ourselves and Others: The Development of a Greek Macedonian Cultural Identity since 1912*, 39–58. Oxford: Berg.

Kotsakis, K.
1991   The powerful past: theoretical trends in Greek archaeology. In I. Hodder (ed.), *Archaeological Theory in Europe*, 65–90. London: Routledge.

1

1

    1998   The past is ours: images of Greek Macedonia. In L. Meskell (ed.), *Archaeology under Fire: Nationalism, Politics and Heritage in the Eastern Mediterranean and Middle East*, 44–67. London: Routledge.

Lefkowitz, M., and G. Rogers (eds.)

    1996   *Black Athena Revisited*. Durham, NC: University of North Carolina Press.

Leontis, A.

    1995   *Topographies of Hellenism: Mapping the Homeland*. Ithaca, NY: Cornell University Press.

MacGillivray, J. A.

    2000   *Minotaur: Sir Arthur Evans and the Archaeology of the Minoan Myth*. London: Jonathan Cape.

Marchand, S., and A. Grafton

    1997   Martin Bernal and his critics. *Arion* (3rd series) 5: 1–35.

Morris, I.

    1994   Archaeologies of Greece. In I. Morris (ed.), *Classical Greece: Ancient Histories and Modern Archaeologies*, 8–47. Cambridge: Cambridge University Press.

    2000   *Archaeology as Cultural History: Words and Things in Iron Age Greece*. Oxford: Blackwell.

    2004   Classical Archaeology. In J. Bintliff (ed.), *A Companion to Archaeology*, 253–71. Oxford: Blackwell.

Myres, J. L.

    1939   The Cretan Labyrinth: a retrospect of Aegean research. (Huxley Memorial Lecture for 1933.) *Journal of the Royal Anthropological Institute of Great Britain and Ireland* 63: 269–312.

Renfrew, C.

    1972   *The Emergence of Civilization: The Cyclades and the Aegean in the Third Millennium B.C.* London: Methuen.

    1980   The Great Tradition versus the Great Divide: archaeology as anthropology? *American Journal of Archaeology* 84: 287–98.

    1983   Introduction. In Ch. Doumas, *Cycladic Art: Ancient Sculpture and Pottery from the N. P. Goulandris Collection*, 9–26. London: British Museum Press.

    1991   *The Cycladic Spirit: Masterpieces from the Nicholas P. Goulandris Collection*. London: Thames and Hudson.

Schnapp, J. T., M. Shanks and M. Tiews

    2004   Archaeology, modernism, modernity. *Modernism/ modernity* 11(1) (special issue: *Archaeologies of the Modern*, January 2004): 1–16.

Snodgrass, A.

1985   The New Archaeology and the Classical archaeologist. *American Journal of Archaeology* 89: 31–37.

1987   *An Archaeology of Greece: The Present State and the Future Scope of a Discipline*. Berkeley: University of California Press.

1991   Structural history and Classical archaeology. In J. L. Bintliff (ed.), *The Annales School and Archaeology*, 57–72. Leicester: Leicester University Press.

Svoronos, N.

1995   Μια αναδρομή στην ιστορία του Αιγαιακού χώρου (A review of the history of the Aegean). In *Το Αιγαίο: Επίκεντρο Ελληνικού Πολιτισμού* [*The Aegean: Epicenter of Hellenic Culture*], 33–80. Athens: Melissa.

Thomas, S. J.

2004a *Archaeology and Modernity*. London: Routledge.

2004b Archaeology's place in Modernity. *Modernism/ modernity* 11(1) (special issue: *Archaeologies of the Modern*, January 2004): 17–34.

Tilley, C.

1999   *Metaphor and Material Culture*. Oxford: Blackwell.

Treuil, R.

2003   Μινωική Κρήτη: Ένας χαμένος παράδεισος; [Minoan Crete: a Paradise Lost?]. *Αρχαιολογία και Τέχνες* (special issue: *Ιστοριογραφία της Αρχαιολογίας: Προϊστορικό Αιγαίο* [*Historiography of Archaeology: Prehistoric Aegean*]) 86 (March 2003) 31–35.

Tournikiotes, P.

2003   Το Αιγαίο είναι Μοντέρνο [The Aegean is modern]. In D. Philippides (ed.), *Νησιά του Αιγαίου: Αρχιτεκτονική*, 68–77. Athens: Melissa.

Warren, P.

1988   *The Aegean Civilizations*. New York: Peter Bedrick Books.

Wylie, M. A.

1983   Comments on the 'socio-politics of archaeology': the de-mystification of the profession. In J. M. Gero, D. M. Lacy, and M. L. Blakey (eds.), *The Socio-politics of Archaeology*. Research Report 23: 119–30. Amherst, MA: Department of Anthropology, University of Massachusetts.

Zoes, A. A.

1990   *Η αρχαιολογία στην Ελλάδα: Πραγματικότητες και προοπτικές* [Archaeology in Greece: Realities and Perspectives]. Αθήνα: Πολύτυπο.

1

2 'Just the Facts, Ma'am': Surveying Aegean Prehistory's State of Health

John F. Cherry and Lauren E. Talalay

Abstract

This paper investigates the 'rumor' that Aegean prehistory, which held some measure of disciplinary prominence in the late 19th century, has become increasingly marginalized, particularly over the last few decades. In order to explore whether there indeed exists concrete evidence for the field's decline, we provide quantitative information on: (a) the number and proportion of published articles on Aegean prehistory in a dozen prominent academic journals; (b) the quantity (and, to a lesser extent, the range) of papers delivered at the annual meetings of the Archaeological Institute of America; and (c) the number of completed doctoral dissertations from the United Kingdom and North America during the last 30 and 20 years respectively. Our results strongly suggest that Aegean prehistory continues to maintain a robust academic presence and that reports of its decline are premature.

Introduction

We begin by explaining both our title and the aims of our paper. This volume (as mentioned in the preface) has its origins in a proposal from our coeditor Despina Margomenou for a workshop, playfully entitled 'Has Aegean prehistory won the war but lost its charm?' Her basic premise, more or less, was that Aegean prehistory had an exciting beginning and achieved some real measure of disciplinary prominence in the later 19th and early 20th centuries, with another surge of widespread interest following the decipherment of Linear B in the early 1950s. But it has subsequently somehow 'lost its charm' and become an increasingly peripheral subfield, one marginalized and receiving scant respect within every discipline (classics, classical archaeology, history of art, anthropology) that assisted in its birth or with which it now seeks to make common cause.

These are fighting words. Understandably, as scholars who have defined ourselves largely as Aegean prehistorians throughout our careers, we felt challenged, and even a little threatened, by the suggestion that Aegean prehistory may have drifted into disciplinary insignificance. To be sure, most professional Aegean archaeologists (in the English-speaking world, at least) find employment as a subspecies of classical archaeologist, and most classical archaeologists sit as a minority group within classics departments. The obvious mismatch here is revealed by the following characterization of 'traditional' classical archaeology (i.e., as it has been for most of its existence as a discipline): '. . . the study of ancient Greek and Roman

2

artefacts with the aim of showing how Graeco-Roman culture was expressed in material terms, focusing on the connections between Greek and Roman works of art and Greek and Latin literary culture' (Morris 2004: 257). The Aegean prehistorian who finds employment in an archaeology department, however, may feel a greater community of purpose, questions, and methods with his or her colleagues—more so, certainly, than with classical philologists or art historians. Very few departments indeed, whether classical or archaeological, enjoy the luxury of employing more than one or at most two Aegean prehistorians, and there exist virtually no specialized degree courses in this field. As for anthropology, there has been plentiful discussion elsewhere of the historical reasons for the 'Great Divide' (Renfrew 1980) that separates anthropological from classical archaeology (including Aegean prehistory), to the continuing detriment of both sides (Morris 1984; Snodgrass 1985; Galaty and Parkinson 1999: 1–3). If many Aegean prehistorians have a pervasive sense of being beleaguered, it is doubtless both because their numbers in any one place are so few (we leave it to Cullen [ch. 3, this volume] to describe the size and nature of the current body of practitioners) and because the field itself has failed to find for itself a disciplinary home that is entirely comfortable.

Yet to note that the field is not very large and that its interests awkwardly straddle a number of disciplines is not to say that it has been deliberately marginalized or that interest in it is on the wane. Intuition, indeed, suggests otherwise: for a subject so circumscribed in temporal and spatial terms, it appeared to us to have a disciplinary prominence out of all proportion to its actual size and (by some accounts) importance. Our coeditor's challenge, nonetheless, forced us to think in a more focused way about the current health and wider reputation of Aegean prehistory. As we reflected on the matter, we could not bring to mind obvious signs of a discipline in decline or one receiving little attention—in fact, rather the opposite. Let us cite some examples.

At the 2003 Archaeological Institute of America (AIA) meetings that had taken place a couple of months prior to the Ann Arbor workshop, for instance, both the Institute's annual James R. Wiseman Prize in recognition of the best recent book and its Gold Medal for Distinguished Archaeological Achievement went to Aegean prehistorians (Cyprian Broodbank and Philip Betancourt respectively); indeed, over the past 37 years of awarding AIA Gold Medals, almost one quarter of them has been conferred on Aegean prehistorians, notwithstanding the enormously wider remit of the Institute's interests.[1] Similarly, despite permit problems that have become increasingly frustrating, Aegean prehistorians continue to conduct fieldwork on a regular basis, and—what is more—they can still rely on the unique, generous, and much-envied funding available through INSTAP (the New York-based Institute for Aegean Prehistory). It is noteworthy that the biennial *Aegaeum* conferences have continued since 1986 with undiminished vigor, as does the annual Aegean Round Table at Sheffield, the monthly Mycenaean seminar in London, the New York Aegean Bronze Age Colloquium, the occasional international conferences of the Swedish Institute, and other such venues. The long-running bibliographic newsletter for our field—*Nestor: The Monthly Bibliography of Aegean Prehistory and Related Areas* (how many other subfields of archaeology in the classical lands have such a thing?)—continues to thrive at the University of Cincinnati, now with a searchable on-line database spanning almost half a century. Vigorous, if sometimes bizarre, discussion continues daily among the 750 subscribers to the *AegeaNet* e-mail list. *IDAP*, the *International Directory of Aegean Prehistorians*, a professional worldwide registry of more than 400 scholars is now too available online (Cherry *et al.* 1995–), letting us all know who's who and what they are doing. Other examples in the same vein could be cited. None of this gives the impression of a moribund field of study or one that has simply been overtaken by broader developments in archaeology.

The instances just cited, however, are largely anecdotal. We began to wonder how it might be possible to explore whether or not there exists any quantifiable evidence from recent years of its decline and increasing marginality (or, perhaps, of the opposite). This chapter, therefore, reports some preliminary and limited efforts to lay down a baseline of information toward that end: or, as our title says, in the famous words of the TV show *Dragnet*, 'Just the facts, ma'am.' We present these data simply as a neutral springboard for further consideration of changes in the state and status of the field of Aegean prehistory. (This chapter is deliberately intended to dovetail with Cullen's [ch. 3, this volume], which explores some of the same issues from a somewhat different perspective.)

First, we look at what has been published during the past generation in a number of academic journals, in order to get a sense of the proportion of articles on subjects relating to Aegean prehistory (an analysis of changes in the types of subjects treated in those articles, however, lies beyond our current scope). Next, we examine the quantity and variety of papers in this field delivered at the annual meetings of the Archaeological Institute of America. The third category of evidence relates to the production of higher degrees, in North America and in the United Kingdom, on topics related to Aegean prehistory. We close with a few thoughts on what this information may indicate.

The Representation of Aegean Prehistory in Journal Articles

We began by tracking the contents of a dozen journals that provide a representative sample of the sorts of places where Aegean prehistorians tend to publish, as well as some where their work appears with less regularity. They include the flagships of various Athens-based foreign schools and institutes: for the UK (*Annual of the British School at Athens* [*BSA*]), the USA (*Hesperia*), France (*Bulletin de correspondance hellénique* [*BCH*]), Germany (*Athenischer Mitteilungen* [*AthMitt*] and *Archäologischer Anzeiger* [*AA*]), Italy (*Annuario della Scuola archeologica di Atene e delle missioni italiane in Oriente* [*Annuario*]), and Australia and New Zealand (*Mediterranean Archaeology* [*MeditArch*]). We have also consulted other periodicals with a

2

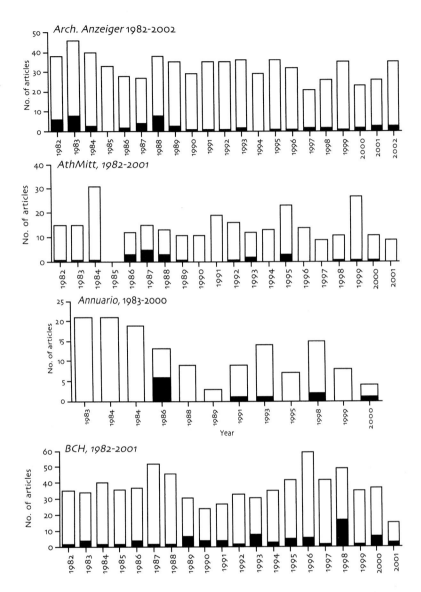

Figure 2.1. The relative representation of Aegean prehistory among all articles published during the past two decades in various archaeological journals affiliated with foreign schools and institutes in Athens.

considerably wider remit, such as the *Journal of Mediterranean Archaeology* [*JMA*], *Oxford Journal of Archaeology* [*OJA*], and *Cambridge Archaeological Journal* [*CAJ*]; the premier American outlet for classical archaeology, *American Journal of Archaeology* [*AJA*]; and, lastly, a journal with worldwide coverage, *Antiquity*. Our straightforward purpose was to track, on a year-by-year basis, the number of published articles on Aegean prehistoric themes, compared with all other articles. In general,

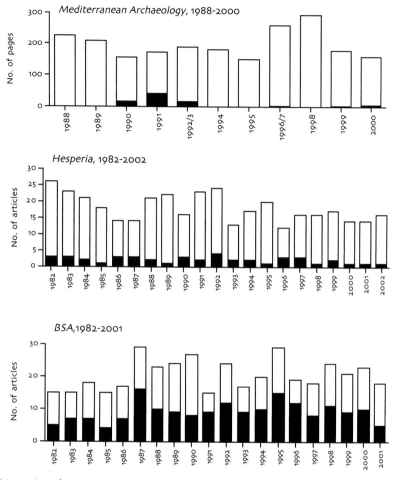

Figure 2.1 continued.

the figures cover the past two decades, with a shorter span for three more recently established journals and in the case of *AJA* more than half a century.[2]

Not surprisingly, the publications of the various foreign schools generally reflect their fieldwork endeavors rather than the degree of enthusiasm for Aegean prehistory itself: these are, after all, primarily 'journals of record'. Thus, the Australian *MeditArch* has devoted only 5% of its pages to Aegean prehistory in the dozen years since its inception—understandably so since the Australian Institute has not been active at any dominantly prehistoric site in Greece during this period (figure 2.1). Likewise, there is relatively feeble representation (8.4%) in the German *AthMitt*, many volumes including just one paper or even none at all; and *AA*, while showing a more consistent record from year to year, has a virtually identical percentage. The *Annuario* is, if anything, even patchier, with not much more than occasional articles on aspects of the Italian School's work at Poliochni on Lemnos

2

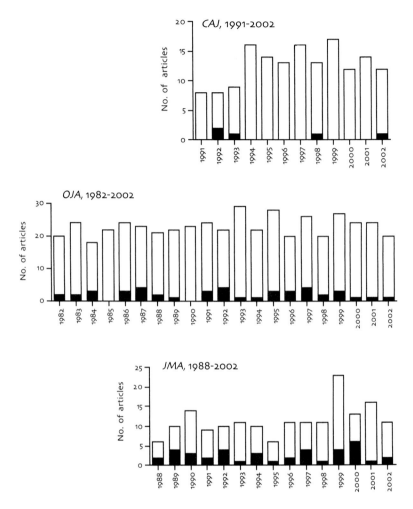

Figure 2.2. The relative representation of Aegean prehistory among all articles published in *CAJ*, *JMA*, and (since 1982) *OJA*.

or at Ayia Triada on Crete. Only the British, American, and French Schools break double digits in the percentage of Aegean prehistory articles in their respective journals: in all three cases, indeed, there has been no volume of *BCH*, *Hesperia*, or *BSA* over the past two decades without papers in this field (figure 2.1). Most striking are the statistics for *BSA*. Of course, it is well known that the British School has been heavily invested in prehistory, ever since its excavation projects at Phylakopi on Melos and at Knossos began more than a century ago, and that a number of its past directors have been prominent prehistorians. Yet we had not appreciated that almost half (44%) of the contents of the School's *Annual*, at least over the past 20 years, has been devoted to Aegean prehistory.

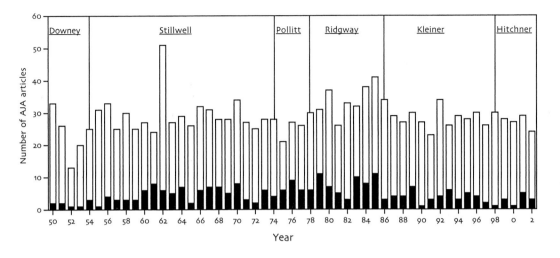

Figure 2.3. Number of articles in the field of Aegean prehistory, compared with all other articles, published in *AJA* between 1950 and 2002. (The tenures of the various editors-in-chief are shown above the graph.)

Turning next to other journals *not* closely affiliated with a foreign school in Greece, the picture is both varied and, in some respects, counterintuitive (figure 2.2). *CAJ*, for example, is published in a noted center of Aegean research (the University of Cambridge) and by the McDonald Institute of Archaeology, whose only director thus far is a rather well-known Aegean prehistorian (Colin Renfrew). Yet its first two dozen issues have contained a total of just five papers in this field, and only two in the past decade—a reflection, doubtless, of its far broader mission to 'cover all areas and periods of archaeology, with a particular focus on the role of human intellectual abilities as reflected for example in the art, religion and symbolism of early societies.' *OJA*, on the other hand, has shown a regular interest in publishing anywhere from one to four relevant articles in almost every volume, amounting to just under 10% of all the papers accepted over the past 20 years. There is a much stronger representation of Aegean prehistory in *JMA* during its 16 years of publication—in fact, close to one-quarter of all material that has appeared in its pages and more than any of the other journals except *BSA*. This is of some interest since *JMA*'s remit covers *all* periods of Mediterranean prehistory and history, from the Palaeolithic to the Early Modern, and geographically embraces the entire circum-Mediterranean world in the broadest sense. Aegean and Cypriot prehistorians, nonetheless, have flocked to this journal, perhaps partly in the knowledge that its two coeditors are prehistorians, of the Aegean and Cyprus respectively. If they say that people come to resemble their dogs, perhaps a journal too may gradually come to look like its editors, whatever its expressed editorial policy and despite pleas for a more catholic range of submissions (Cherry and Knapp 1996: 4–5; 1999: 5; on Mediterranean journals more generally, see Alcock, in press).

2

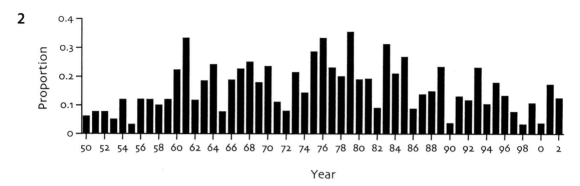

Figure 2.4. Aegean prehistory articles as a proportion of all articles published in *AJA*, 1950–2002.

This point about editors, in fact, is something also worth examining in the case of *AJA*, the journal that enjoys the largest circulation of any professional periodical in archaeology and that provides the chief venue in North America for publication in Old World archaeology. *AJA*'s status and extensive publishing history suggested that it might prove instructive in this case to expand our tabulation back to 1950, so that figures 2.3 and 2.4 summarize more than a half-century of publication. Astonishingly, each and every volume published over this time span has included at least one Aegean prehistory article (and more often several). It needs to be borne in mind that, as its own guidelines state, '*AJA* is devoted to the art and archaeology of ancient Europe and the Mediterranean world, including the Near East and Egypt, from prehistoric to late antique times'—a truly vast extent of time and place. Even so, roughly 16% of all the articles represented in figure 2.3 fall within the field of Aegean archaeology, thus constituting a quite remarkable emphasis on the prehistory of just one quite modestly sized part of *AJA*'s overall mandate.

Aegean prehistory's level of representation in *AJA* over many decades, incidentally, seems not to have been much affected by the proclivities of its various editors-in-chief (displayed across the top of the graph in figure 2.3), none of whom were or are prehistorians of any sort; so this case seems to differ from that of journals such as *JMA* (see above). Somewhat more Aegean papers appear to have been accepted under the editorships of the Greek art historians Jerome Pollitt and Brunilde Ridgway in the mid-1970s to mid-1980s than has been the case more recently, when we *can* see some decline in this field's share of *AJA*'s space (figure 2.4) and in the proportion of women contributing articles (table 2.1). Yet is also worth remembering that between 1992 and 1998, under Fred Kleiner's editorship, there appeared 'Reviews of Aegean Prehistory,' the lengthy and authoritative series of syntheses of developments over the past few decades, subsequently reprinted with updates as *Aegean Prehistory: A Review* (Cullen 2001)—a volume of great value to the field.

An analysis of articles in *Antiquity*, the one journal of truly global scope in our sample, can be taken back to its foundation in the 1920s. In the December 2002

Table 2.1. Gender of authors of Aegean prehistory articles appearing in *AJA* 1950–99

Years	Male authors	Female authors	Female authors as percentage of total
1950–54	10	1	9.1
1955–59	11	1	8.3
1960–64	33	6	15.4
1965–69	26	6	18.8
1970–74	18	8	30.8
1975–79	33	11	25.0
1980–84	24	12	33.3
1985–89	24	11	31.4
1990–94	16	4	20.0
1995–99	15	4	21.1

issue of *Antiquity*, celebrating its 75th year, Nicola Terrenato published a provocative short paper on the history of publication in the field of classical archaeology within that journal.[3] Figure 2.5 is a reworked version of Terrenato's chart (2002: fig. 1) in which he tracked the number of *Antiquity* articles dealing with classical archaeology between 1927 and 2000, divided into three 25-year spans (in each of which, incidentally, the journal published a total of about 600 papers). Helpfully for present purposes, Terrenato distinguished amongst several subfields of classical archaeology, of which 'Aegean' (sc. prehistory) is one. His contention is that, until

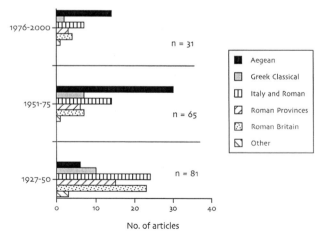

Figure 2.5. The number of *Antiquity* articles dealing with different subfields of classical archaeology, divided into three 25-year spans between 1927 and 2000 (data from Terrenato 2002: fig. 1).

Table 2.2. Numbers of articles in different subfields of classical archaeology published in *Antiquity* (data courtesy of Nicola Terrenato)

Subfield	1927–50	1951–75	1976–2000	Total no. of articles
Aegean Prehistory	6	30	14	**50**
Greek Classical	10	7	2	**19**
Italy and Roman	24	14	7	45
Roman Provinces	15	6	3	24
Roman Britain	23	7	4	34
Other	3	1	1	5
Totals:	**81**	**65**	**31**	177

about 1970, classical archaeology was regarded as an important and valued field, comprising about 15% of the journal's content overall; but that with the loss of innocence and the rise of processual and post-processual paradigms, it simply failed to keep up. Turning away from mainstream periodicals like *Antiquity*, mainstream classical archaeology now 'entrenches itself instead in a handful of specialist journals' (Terrenato 2002: 1107)—and intentionally so, to set itself apart from other archaeological scholarship, as a self-perpetuating, privileged field.

Irrespective of the merits of that conclusion, the evidence certainly seems to show that—in the pages of *Antiquity*, at least—the classical scene was stolen in the 1950s and 1960s by the 'exciting epic of the decipherment of Linear B' (Terrenato 2002: 1106), in which this journal did indeed play an important role. There has been a progressive decline in the absolute quantity and proportion of classical archaeology publication in *Antiquity* over these 75 years, falling from 81 articles (ca. 14%) in 1927–50 to 31 articles (ca. 5%) in 1976–2000 (figure 2.5). On the other hand, Aegean prehistory, only feebly represented in the years before midcentury, actually experienced a boom in 1951–75: in fact almost as many Aegean articles were published then as in all the other subfields put together (table 2.2). In the most recent quarter-century, Aegean has continued to dominate all other subcategories of classical archaeology in *Antiquity*—additional evidence, seemingly, of its continued vitality as a discipline, as well as of its steadily growing distinctiveness and separation from the classical traditions that gave it birth. The reality is a little less encouraging, as may be seen in figure 2.6, which, by breaking down the data in 5-year periods, reveals perceptible overall decline since midcentury in the percentage of all *Antiquity* articles represented by Aegean prehistory. In recent years, as Terrenato wrote, 'the Aegean contributions continued to trickle in, with remarkable papers by excellent scholars . . . but the rest of the discipline was no longer represented' (2002: 1107).

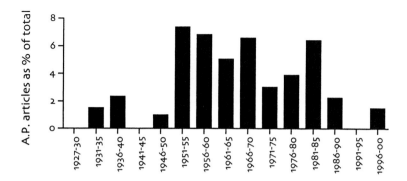

Figure 2.6. Articles in Aegean prehistory, as a percentage of all articles published in *Antiquity*, 1927–2000, broken down by 5-year periods (data courtesy of Nicola Terrenato).

Aegean Prehistory at the AIA Meetings

A second quantifiable body of information that might usefully inform us about changes in the state and status of the field concerns papers delivered at the annual meetings of the Archaeological Institute of America (AIA). Admittedly, and as already noted, the AIA's mandate, like that of its official journal *AJA*, encompasses a vastly larger purview than Aegean prehistory alone; but, for better or for worse, these meetings do represent the largest and most influential annual conference for our field. (Aegean prehistory has never established any presence at the meetings of the Society for American Archaeology or of the American Anthropological Association, while those of the European Association of Archaeologists—in which Aegeanists *have* been participating in some numbers recently—are too freshly established to provide useful data here.)

Our survey of the information available to us revealed that some 3,210 papers (not including poster sessions) were presented at the AIA meetings between 1982 and 2001; of these, 445 (14%) are broadly classifiable as lying in the field of Aegean prehistory, and 46% of them were by women (figure 2.7).[4] It would help here, obviously, to have comparative data, particularly on the relative percentage of papers in other subfields (such as Roman architecture or Greek sculpture and vase-painting) that are regularly represented at these meetings. Even without it, however, it seems to us that, in a discipline characterized by a significant number of fragmented and regional interests, 14% is a very respectable and even a surprising figure. We also don't know (since the AIA does not regularly maintain these kinds of statistics) what this percentage means in terms of the overall number of academics of either sex who are members of AIA and who also identify themselves as Aegean prehistorians. Likewise, while roughly 20% of all paper abstracts are rejected, we do not have any information on how many of these each year relate to Aegean topics.

2

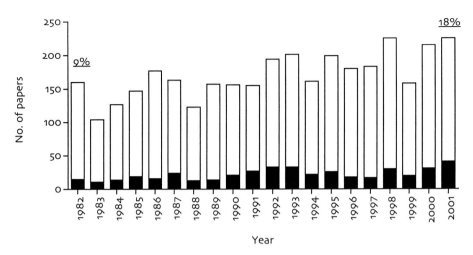

Figure 2.7. Number of papers on topics in Aegean prehistory delivered at the annual meetings of the Archaeological Institute of America, compared with the total number of papers, 1982–2001.

Nonetheless, figure 2.7 at least gives us some sense of Aegean prehistory's relative presence at these meetings since 1982. What is most striking is the consistency from year to year during these two decades; the annual percentage has ranged from 9% (in 1982) to 18% (in 2001) but without any marked overall increase or decline during the intervening years. This stability is especially interesting since the AIA Program Committee, which is charged with accepting or rejecting anonymously submitted abstracts, does not operate with any kind of quotas (i.e., limits on the number of papers or sessions devoted to particular sorts of topics).

What it has not been possible to tease from this survey is any quantitative classification of the *nature* of these papers, the possible categories being inevitably fuzzy and very subjective. Nonetheless, we offer here a few impressionistic comments. Many of the papers tend to be corralled by the Program Committee under dull but serviceable titles such as 'Aegean Prehistory,' 'Minoan Crete,' or 'Aegean and Eastern Mediterranean Prehistory.' Particularly in the last 10 years, however, there has been a fairly consistent effort to design sessions that are more focused, thematic, and even problem-oriented events. Thus, some recent AIA colloquium titles include: 'The Production of Power: Economy and Ideology in the Mycenaean World,' 'Minoan and Mycenaean Ritual Vessels: Their Function and Relationship to Specific Deities,' 'The Mycenaean Feast,' or 'Values of Identity, Values of Exchange: Art, Commerce, and Ideology in the Aegean Bronze Age.'

It is hardly surprising that most of the papers presented over the past two decades have focused on Minoan or Mycenaean topics, with a sprinkling of talks on the Early Bronze Age, particularly in the Cyclades; the Neolithic has a meager showing, represented by a small band of stalwarts, while the number of talks on Palaeolithic or Mesolithic studies may be counted on one hand. Interestingly, although there have been occasional sessions (such as the 2001 AIA Gold Medal Colloquium honoring Emmett Bennett), very few AIA papers seem to reflect current scholarship on Aegean scripts: as they have done ever since the decipherment in the 1950s, Linear B specialists still tend to meet in private conclave, by invitation only. A modest number of papers do grapple with overarching methodological and theoretical issues, such as the rise of the state in the Bronze Age, sociopolitical complexity, ideology, identity, value, the economic landscape, and so on. Sometimes, topics 'hot' in other fields cross over into Aegean prehistory—most recently, for instance, gender, feasting, and archaeoastronomy. Far more often, however, the papers focus on chronology, excavation and survey reports, iconography, pottery analysis, technology, or material studies—all of which *could* contribute to wider discourses, of course, but they are rarely framed in a way that does so. By and large, these AIA talks are neither particularly self-reflexive nor highly theorized: they reflect the more traditional aspects of the discipline, emphasizing reports on recent discoveries from the field and only occasionally tackling complex social, political, and ideological aspects of Aegean prehistory. Whether this is due to the nature of our field, to the character of the AIA meetings, to the brevity of the talks themselves, or perhaps all of the foregoing, is not easy to say. Certainly, one looks to other venues, such as the *Aegaeum* conferences, or the Sheffield Round Tables, or other such occasional gatherings, for more exciting discussion.

In short, it seems that Aegean prehistory is far from marginalized at these annual meetings. Quite to the contrary, it has maintained a strong and consistent presence there: indeed, in the most recent year for which we have data (2001), nearly one-fifth of all the papers presented were in this field. This of course says nothing about quality. Nonetheless, the extent to which Aegean archaeology has become a dominant field of specialization at the AIA meetings is remarkable and has not, we think, been remarked upon before.

Aegean Prehistory as a Topic for Doctoral Research

The final category we wish to discuss here concerns doctoral-level research in the field of Aegean prehistory. This, surely, ought to provide one of the clearest indices of the relative state of the field since it is, after all, the cutting edge of regeneration and change for the whole discipline, as well as an investment in its own future. So far, we have only been able to consider quantified data from the United Kingdom and North America, although for a more thorough and representative evaluation it would be important also to consider what is happening in Europe, including Greece itself (cf. Andreou, ch. 4, this volume).

In the UK there exists a useful and reasonably reliable source of data, reaching back as far as the mid-1950s—namely, the annual report, published in the *Bulletin of the Institute of Classical Studies* [*BICS*], of dissertations in classics, classical archaeology, and archaeology completed in the UK during the previous year. The main patterns are clear (figure 2.8). There have been very few years over the

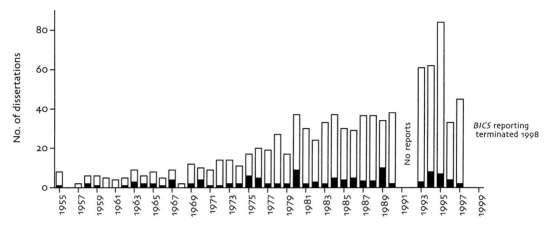

Figure 2.8. Dissertations completed in the UK, 1955–97, showing (in black) those on topics in Aegean prehistory compared with all other dissertations in classics, classical archaeology, and archaeology (data from annual reports appearing in *BICS*).

more than four decades of reporting this information in which there has not been a handful of Aegean prehistory dissertations successfully completed (and occasionally as many as 10 in a single year). Equally obvious is the growth of archaeology as a subject area in UK universities, beginning in the 1970s but really taking off in the 1980s and reflected in PhD degrees approved in the early 1990s—to such an extent, indeed, that *BICS* seems in 1998 to have abandoned its attempts to track and publish the titles of all completed dissertations. As for Aegean prehistory, figure 2.8 shows that the quantity of UK dissertations in this field has not expanded *pari passu* with the field of archaeology as a whole; but, by the same token, there has been no obvious long-term decline in absolute numbers.

Doctoral dissertations in North America are in general easier to locate and access than in Europe, as a consequence of the availability of *Dissertation Abstracts* and now its on-line version *Digital Dissertations*. In practice, however, both the huge numbers of dissertation titles listed and the cross-cutting and overlapping systems of classification by discipline rather than subject (necessitating keyword searches in Old World archaeology, archaeology, anthropology, classical archaeology, classics, Near Eastern studies, etc.) make it far from straightforward to pluck out relevant titles in Aegean prehistory and to set them against an appropriate comparative sample of dissertations in closely cognate fields. Our inspection of data from *Digital Dissertations* for the period 1992–2002 has produced results in whose details we do not have great confidence, but the overall picture seems fairly clear: each year has produced anywhere between 2–3 and 9–10 Aegean prehistory dissertations, without marked fluctuations from one year to another in terms of what percentage these represent of all PhDs in classical archaeology. We have compared our results with those compiled independently, for the period 1981–93, by the Old World Archaeology

Committee of the Archaeological Institute of America.[5] While there are differences in the particulars, these two sources of information are in agreement that the production of doctoral degrees in Aegean prehistory has remained quite steady over the past 20 years, even though this field remains a minor contributor to the level of dissertation research in Old World archaeology as a whole.

Conclusions

The preceding three sections have simply presented some bald figures, about journal articles, AIA papers, and doctoral dissertations, as a crude means of taking the pulse of Aegean prehistory as a discipline at the outset of the 21st century. It will be quite obvious that there exist some other measures that would also be worthwhile exploring in this regard. One is the extent of Aegean prehistory's representation in undergraduate and graduate teaching curricula and the ways in which the subject has been, and is now being, taught. Another is the number of Aegean prehistorians holding established university- or museum-based positions.[6] Above all, we are very aware that the picture we have painted in the preceding sections requires modification and nuance by incorporating comparative data from a number of other European countries, each with its own distinctive scholarly tradition.

Our general conclusions are summarized in table 2.3 and figure 2.9, from which we draw three main observations. First, in none of the indices we have examined do we see any obvious signs of decline in the *level of activity* in Aegean prehistory in recent years. Second, while table 2.3 compares quite different things and reveals a good deal of variability, Aegean prehistory's 'showing' is generally a very respectable 10 to 15%. And lastly, these figures make quite apparent the fact that this field enjoys a standing that is far in excess of what one might expect if we were dealing with nothing more than a few millennia of prehistory in just one Mediterranean basin. Of course, the Aegean has benefited from a status that derives from the *longue durée* of its own scholarship, from its pivotal position geographically, from the importance of the larger sociopolitical issues to which its prehistory has relevance, but above all from the significance of the narrative it purports to provide concerning the roots of Greek civilization, and therefore of European civilization as a whole (Morris 1994; 2004).

We end, however, with some questions. Terrenato's paper, discussed earlier, reveals an interesting tension, in that he cannot decide whether Aegean prehistory is like classical archaeology and part of it (thus sharing in what he sees as its sorry story of decline and increasing isolation from trends in world archaeology)—or not. He seems to imply the former when he asserts that since the 1970s 'the Aegeanists have largely followed their colleagues in their retreat to the ivory towers' (2002: 1108). On the other hand, he seems to want to segregate Aegean prehistory from the rest of classical archaeology whenever it bucks the trend. In effect, he is reflecting something of the Janus-like quality of this field—looking inward at its roots, practices, and quests, all entrenched in the classical lands and in classical archaeology;

2

Table 2.3. Summary of the relative prominence of Aegean prehistory, as reflected in the various data sources discussed in this paper

Type of information	Dates	% of total related to Aegean prehistory
Articles published in journals:		
Antiquity	1927–2000	2.8
CAJ	1991–2002	3.3
MeditArch	1988–2000	5.8
Annuario	1983–2000	7.6
AthMitt	1982–2001	8.4
AA	1982–2002	8.6
OJA	1982–2002	9.4
Hesperia	1982–2002	12.1
BCH	1992–2001	14.5
AJA	1950–2002	15.7
JMA	1988–2002	23.3
BSA	1982–2002	43.8
Archaeological Institute of America:		
Papers delivered at annual meetings	1982–2001	13.9
Gold Medals awarded	1965–2003	22.5
PhD Dissertations:		
UK dissertations in archaeology	1969–97	13.3
UK dissertations in classics and archaeology	1969–97	1.1
US dissertations in classical archaeology	1982–2002	23.0

but also looking outward to the interests it shares with a number of cognate disciplines (anthropology, non-classical archaeologies, history of art, Near Eastern studies, classics, and so on).

Observations about these kinds of tensions within Aegean prehistory have been raised before, mostly in passing; but it is only recently that a few archaeologists have offered any reflective discussion of the topic. It is, moreover, not just Aegean prehistorians who are trying to disentangle the long and complex skeins that bind Aegean prehistory and classical archaeology. Scholars such as Ian Morris, for example, have approached the problem from the other side by attempting 'to explain what Classical Archaeology is' (2004: 253) and how recent changes in that discipline may ultimately impact fields like Aegean prehistory. This is no simple task, given that classical archaeology (like classics) has lately been experiencing its own identity crisis. Some classical archaeologists are moving away from their

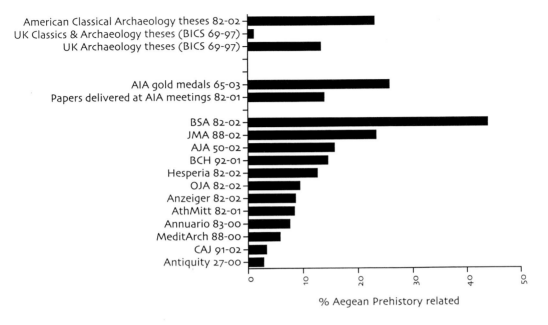

Figure 2.9. The relative prominence of work in Aegean prehistory, as measured in the various sources of data discussed in this chapter (data in table 2.3).

traditional and rather confined intellectual frameworks and are beginning to contemplate broad social, economic, and historical questions first posed by new archaeologists, postprocessualists, and modern historians (Morris 2004: 266). It may well be that in the future classical archaeology and Aegean prehistory will once again converge, after a long period of mutual isolation and misunderstanding.

Attempts to reconstruct and contextualize the histories of these intertwined disciplines inevitably raise a number of important issues of real relevance. Exactly who are we Aegean prehistorians, and what intellectual worlds do we straddle? Can a regionally defined archaeology that does not consort seriously with larger intellectual issues expect to survive in a landscape that is becoming increasingly more globalized? What kinds of intellectual hazards do globalized structures pose for our discipline? Should we be content to continue to define Aegean prehistory in terms of classical culture, 'the only one whose very name is a value judgement,' as Terrenato (2002: 1109) acidly puts it? The continued robust health of Aegean prehistory will depend to some extent on our abilities to pose and effectively answer such questions.

Notes

1.   The nine Aegean prehistorians to have received the AIA's Gold Medal for Distinguished Archaeological Achievement, 40 of which have been awarded since 1965, are: Carl W. Blegen (1965), Hetty Goldman (1966), George

2

E. Mylonas (1970), John L. Caskey (1980), William A. McDonald (1981), Saul S. Weinberg (1985), George R. Bass (1986), Emmett L. Bennett, Jr (2001), and Philip Betancourt (2003). Other recipients too, such as Oscar Broneer and Rhys Carpenter (both 1969) or Machteld J. Mellink (1991), have also made substantial contributions to this field.

2. The tables and graphs that follow may seem to imply statistical rigor, but the truth is that many of the numbers are, necessarily, somewhat impressionistic, because judgment calls are required. We are very grateful to Seth Button, Catherine Lyon Crawford, and Jennifer Gates (graduate students in the Interdepartmental Program in Classical Art and Archaeology at the University of Michigan) for their assistance in compiling some of this information.

3. We thank Nicola Terrenato for kindly providing to us the raw data on which the figures in his article (Terrenato 2002) are based, but broken down in more detail by 5-year periods.

4. Tracey Cullen provided welcome assistance in acquiring this information.

5. Jack L. Davis, Chair of the AIA Committee on the Future of Old World Archaeology, kindly made available to us both his committee's final report and the database of American dissertations in the field of Old World archaeology, compiled by the committee as part of the preparation of its report.

6. This would be an especially difficult type of information to acquire. Our sense is that there are many university instructors with doctorates in Aegean prehistory who have been appointed to positions in which the opportunity to teach their specialty is very limited.

References

Alcock, S. E.

　　in press　Alphabet soup in the Mediterranean basin: the emergence of the Mediterranean serial. In W. V. Harris (ed.), *Practical Mediterraneanism: Ancient and Modern Conceptions of the Mediterranean*. New York: Oxford University Press.

Cherry, J. F., and A. B. Knapp

　　1996　Editorial. *Journal of Mediterranean Archaeology* 9: 3–6.

　　1999　Editorial. *Journal of Mediterranean Archaeology* 12: 3–6.

Cherry, J. F., J. L. Davis, and E. H. Cline (eds.)
  1995– *International Directory of Aegean Prehistorians.* 3rd revised Internet edition. Available at http://classics.uc.edu/nestor/nsearch.lasso.
Cullen, T. (ed.)
  2001 *Aegean Prehistory: A Review. American Journal of Archaeology* supplement 1. Boston: Archaeological Institute of America.
Davis, J. L.
  1996 Old World Archaeology Teaching Survey. Report of the AIA Committee on the Future of Old World Archaeology, December 8, 1996.
Galaty, M. L., and W. A. Parkinson
  1999 Putting Mycenaean palaces in their place. In M .L. Galaty and W. A. Parkinson (eds.), *Rethinking Mycenaean Palaces: New Interpretations of an Old Idea.* Cotsen Institute of Archaeology Monograph 41: 1–8. Los Angeles: Cotsen Institute of Archaeology, University of California, Los Angeles.
Morris, I.
  1994 Archaeologies of Greece. In I. Morris (ed.), *Classical Greece: Ancient Histories and Modern Archaeologies,* 8–47. Cambridge: Cambridge University Press.
  2004 Classical archaeology. In J. Bintliff (ed.), *A Companion to Archaeology,* 253–71. Oxford: Blackwell.
Renfrew, C.
  1980 The great tradition versus the great divide: archaeology as anthropology? *American Journal of Archaeology* 84: 287–98.
Snodgrass, A. M.
  1985 The new archaeology and the classical archaeologist. *American Journal of Archaeology* 89: 31–37.
Terrenato, N.
  2002 The innocents and the sceptics: *Antiquity* and classical archaeology. *Antiquity* 76: 1104–11.

2

3 A Profile of Aegean Prehistorians, 1984–2003

Tracey Cullen

Abstract

It is commonly assumed that Aegean prehistory holds a marginal position within the wider discipline of classical archaeology, the focus and funding of which pertain primarily to the historical era. Little is known, however, about the sociopolitics of the field of Aegean prehistory. In an effort to contribute to our understanding of the current status of the discipline, I present a profile of those who identify themselves as Aegean prehistorians, drawing on directories and questionnaires spanning the past 20 years. Variables considered include age, gender, residence, citizenship, employment, areas of research, fieldwork, publication record, and participation in conferences. The trends that emerge indicate that Aegean prehistory is an evolving, thriving field of inquiry with growing international participation, but they also reveal considerable gender inequity in key measures of professional success and advancement.

Introduction

The discipline of Aegean prehistory traces its formal origins to the late 19th century, to Heinrich Schliemann's excavations in Greece and Turkey. From Schliemann's early efforts to illuminate ancient texts, the field has evolved in several directions over the 20th century and into the 21st. A consuming interest in cultural origins gave way to a fascination with the details of individual cultures, questions of environmental adaptation, social interaction, political evolution, symbol and ritual, but only recently to an examination of disciplinary practice. Historical accounts situate Aegean prehistory within the wider traditions of Hellenism and classical studies in the West, and scholars have explored the relation and indebtedness of the discipline to anthropological archaeology (e.g., Renfrew 1980; Davis 2001). Biographers of pioneering prehistorians offer intriguing glimpses of the field over the past century but rarely examine their subjects within the particular intellectual and historical context of their time (e.g., McDonald and Thomas 1990; Allsebrook 1992; but see now McEnroe 1995; 2002; MacGillivray 2000). Intellectual histories of archaeology (Trigger 1989; Schnapp 1996), classical archaeology (Morris 1994; 2004; Dyson 1998), and even prehistory (Daniel and Renfrew 1988) devote only a few pages to the practice of Aegean prehistory, contributing to the impression that the field holds a marginal position within the wider discipline.

But does it? Marginality can be defined in terms of intellectual vitality or professional standing, and the position of Aegeanist studies shifts according to the

3 yardstick chosen. While the focus and funding of classical archaeology still pertain overwhelmingly to the historical era, Aegean prehistorians have been credited with far-reaching innovations in theory and practice, blazing a trail followed only later (and sometimes reluctantly) by classical archaeologists (see, e.g., Snodgrass 2002: 191; Morris 2004: 262–63). The disciplinary coherence of Aegean prehistory is undeniable, evident not only in shared research problems within a common geographic and temporal sphere but also by virtue of a wide range of publications, conferences, and research tools devoted solely to the dissemination of the work of Aegean prehistorians. One need cite only a few vehicles—*Nestor*, the *Aegaeum* series, the Institute for Aegean Prehistory, AegeaNet, the New York Aegean Bronze Age Colloquia, the Sheffield Round Table Workshops—to support the view that Aegean prehistory has distinct disciplinary boundaries. But to assess the relative contribution and status of the field within the larger discipline—be that classical archaeology or world prehistory—we need to know more about Aegean prehistorians themselves. How large a subfield do Aegeanists represent, and how and where are they employed? What is the makeup of the field in terms of nationality, age, and gender? What are the primary research questions occupying Aegean prehistorians, and to what extent have these changed over the past 20 years? How productive are Aegean prehistorians as a group in publishing, giving papers at conferences, and carrying out field projects? And finally, how do Aegean prehistorians compare to classical archaeologists and others in these respects? The search for answers to these questions defines the scope of the present paper. By building on similar earlier efforts (Cherry and Davis 1994; Nixon 1994; Webb and Frankel 1995; Cullen 1996: 412–13; 1999; 2001: 14–15; 2002; Cullen and Keller 1999), I hope to shed light on the structure and workings of Aegean prehistory and its relation to the wider discipline.

In this aspect of disciplinary introspection, Aegean prehistorians—and classical archaeologists in general—have lagged behind classicists and anthropologists, who have routinely sent out questionnaires to their membership and published their findings (see, e.g., Nelson *et al.* 1994; Zeder 1997). Although we have fewer such studies to draw on, a profile of Aegean prehistorians over the past 20 years can nevertheless be compiled in several ways. Elsewhere in this volume (ch. 2), Cherry and Talalay document the relative prominence of Aegean prehistory in terms of the proportion of journal articles published, papers given at the meetings of the Archaeological Institute of America (AIA), and doctoral dissertations; and Andreou (ch. 4) explores trends in academic employment, publishing, and research priorities among Greek prehistorians. To complement their work, I consider here the ways in which Aegean prehistorians describe themselves in directory listings and survey questionnaires. I draw on the following sources:

(1)   three editions of the *International Directory of Aegean Prehistorians (IDAP)*: the 1984 and 1995 paper editions (Petruso and Talalay 1984; Cherry and

Davis 1995), with 216 and 298 entries, respectively, and the current (2003) on-line edition, listing 405 individuals;

(2)   the results of the *IDAP* survey (Cherry and Davis 1994), a questionnaire mailed to subscribers of *Nestor* and subsequently filled out by 295 prehistorians;

(3)   the 1995 *AIA Directory of Professionals in Archaeology*, including 928 entries from which I separated 139 individuals who checked 'prehistory' as their major research interest; and

(4)   a four-page questionnaire sent out by AIA in 1996 to its 10,000 members. Designed by the AIA Subcommittee on Women in Archaeology, the survey was AIA's first attempt to collect census data about its professional membership. Questions were also intended to elicit the potentially different experiences of men and women in archaeology (Cullen 1998). Of the 1,508 surveys returned, 998 were filled out by professionals or students in archaeology or a related discipline. From that sample, I isolated a subgroup of 157 individuals who hold a doctorate and are active in Aegean prehistory (through teaching, publishing, fieldwork, or studying materials).[1]

The Sample

Size of the Discipline. It is critical to establish the size and makeup of the discipline to serve as a baseline in evaluating the relative productivity of men and women within it. We can best estimate the size of the field over the past two decades from *IDAP* listings (table 3.1). The most recent directory lists 405 individuals—nearly double the 216 entries collected in 1984 and substantially higher than the 298 listed in the 1995 *IDAP*. This increase surely reflects the growth of the discipline, but it is also undoubtedly the result of the extended reach of the on-line directory. While 65% of the entries in the 1995 *IDAP* represent new listings, only 27% of the 2003 listings are new, most of the names in the on-line *IDAP* having also appeared in the 1995 *IDAP*. One problem in interpreting the expanded size of the on-line directory is that entries are not systematically culled: the 1995 directory was presumably digitized to serve as the basis for the on-line version, which by 2003 had accumulated 108 new listings. Some individuals listed are no longer active in the field, while others have moved or undertaken new research without updating their entries. The majority, however, are well-known names in Aegean prehistory. Even acknowledging that a small portion of *IDAP* 2003 is out of date, the 108 new listings surely reflect a growing field.

It is impossible to know the proportion of active Aegean prehistorians represented in the current *IDAP*. In evaluating the representativeness of the 1994 *IDAP* survey, Cherry and Davis (1994: 2) observed that the number of questionnaires

Table 3.1. Sample of Aegean prehistorians in *IDAP* 1984, 1995, and 2003

	IDAP 1984		IDAP 1995		IDAP 2003	
Number of entries	216		298		405	
Sex						
Male	134	(64%)	159	(53%)	214	(54%)
Female	77	(36%)	139	(47%)	185	(46%)
Total	**211**		**298**		**399**	
Primary residence						
US	94	(43%)	114	(38%)	138	(34%)
Greece	19	(9%)	55	(19%)	86	(21%)
UK	41	(19%)	33	(11%)	48	(12%)
Other	62	(29%)	96	(32%)	133	(33%)
Total	**216**		**298**		**405**	

returned corresponded closely to the number of *Nestor* individual subscribers at the time, an indication that a substantial proportion of Aegean prehistorians were represented in the survey. Though we do not know the percentage of prehistorians who subscribe to *Nestor*, the 405 names in the 2003 *IDAP* considerably exceed the current number of individual subscribers (268).[2] Another measure, however, might suggest that only a small proportion of prehistorians appear in *IDAP*: of the 1,029 individual authors of articles, books, and reviews listed in the 2003 volume of *Nestor*, the names of only 174 (17%) are found in *IDAP* for the same year. *Nestor*'s bibliography covers a wide span of Aegean prehistory and related areas, and certainly not all authors cited there are Aegean prehistorians. Nevertheless, it seems reasonable to assume that at least half would consider themselves Aegeanists, yet far fewer than that appear among the 405 names in *IDAP*. On the basis of this measure, one could infer that the number of practicing Aegean prehistorians is considerably larger than the number recorded in the 2003 *IDAP*.

Primary Residence and Citizenship. The *IDAP* and AIA surveys and directories all provide significant information about the primary residence and, in some cases, nationality of Aegean prehistorians (tables 3.1, 3.2). The individuals listed in the most recent edition of *IDAP* work in 25 countries, up from 18 countries listed in 1984 (table 3.3). If representative, the figures indicate that the field is dominated by scholars working in the United States, Greece, and the United Kingdom, with far fewer from France, Sweden, Germany, and Turkey and only a handful from elsewhere. Large parts of the world (e.g., Africa, South America, the Far East) are barely represented, if at all. Today, just over a third of the prehistorians in *IDAP* list

Table 3.2. Sample of Aegean prehistorians in the *IDAP* and AIA surveys and the *AIA Directory of Professionals in Archaeology*

	IDAP Survey (1994)		AIA Directory (1995)		AIA Survey (1996)	
Number of entries	295		139		157	
Sex						
Male	155	(53%)	77	(57%)	91	(58%)
Female	140	(47%)	59	(43%)	66	(42%)
Total	**295**		**136**		**157**	
Primary residence						
US	—		107	(77%)	130	(84%)
Greece	—		5	(4%)	2	(1%)
UK	—		7	(5%)	6	(4%)
Other	—		20	(14%)	17	(11%)
Total			**139**		**155**	
Citizenship						
US	112	(39%)	—		130	(84%)
Greece	50	(17%)	—		2	(1%)
UK	33	(12%)	—		7	(5%)
Other	92	(32%)	—		15	(10%)
Total	**287**				**154**	

the United States as their primary residence, down from 43% in 1984 (table 3.1). Twelve percent work in the United Kingdom, down from 19% in 1984, while the number listing Greece as their primary residence has risen from 9% to 21%. The change in relative proportions is a result not of fewer prehistorians working in the United States or Britain but of the dramatic increase of directory listings for scholars residing in Greece (cf. Andreou, ch. 4, this volume, who also documents the rapidly growing number of Greek prehistorians). Citizenship was polled in the two surveys only (table 3.2), with results very similar to those seen in the residence categories. In contrast to the more international *IDAP* samples, the AIA samples are dominated by prehistorians who work in the United States and are also American citizens, an expected result given the North American focus of the AIA.

Aegean Prehistory as a Subset of Classical Archaeology. How large a subset of classical archaeologists do Aegean prehistorians comprise? This is not easy to determine without good census data for classical archaeology worldwide, but rough measures

3   Table 3.3. Primary residence for Aegean prehistorians

Residence	*IDAP 1984*		*IDAP 1995*		*IDAP 2003*	
	n	*%*	*n*	*%*	*n*	*%*
Australia	3	1.4	6	2.0	7	1.7
Austria	2	0.9	5	1.7	7	1.7
Belgium	3	1.4	8	2.7	8	2.0
Brazil	—	—	—	—	1	0.3
Canada	7	3.2	11	3.7	14	3.5
Cyprus	4	1.9	2	0.7	4	1.0
Czech Republic	—	—	1	0.3	1	0.3
Denmark	1	0.5	—	—	—	—
France	7	3.2	17	5.7	18	4.4
Germany	9	4.2	7	2.3	13	3.2
Greece	19	8.8	55	18.5	86	21.2
Hungary	3	1.4	1	0.3	1	0.3
Ireland	3	1.4	2	0.7	3	0.7
Israel	1	0.5	1	0.3	3	0.7
Italy	9	4.2	4	1.3	7	1.7
Netherlands	—	—	5	1.7	6	1.5
Norway	—	—	1	0.3	2	0.5
Poland	2	0.9	6	2.0	7	1.7
Russia	—	—	2	0.7	2	0.5
Spain	—	—	1	0.3	3	0.7
Sweden	7	3.2	13	4.4	16	4.0
Switzerland	1	0.5	—	—	1	0.3
Turkey	—	—	3	1.0	8	2.0
United Kingdom	41	19.0	33	11.1	48	11.9
United States	94	43.5	114	38.3	138	34.1
Yugoslavia (former)	—	—	—	—	1	0.3
Total	**216**		**298**		**405**	

using AIA data do exist. In 2003, roughly 2,100 individuals subscribed to the *American Journal of Archaeology (AJA),* most of whom can presumably be considered professionals in classical archaeology or a related field.[3] Not all classical archaeologists subscribe to *AJA,* however, so the figure represents a minimum estimate more relevant to AIA's professional membership than to the size of classical archaeology overall. While the *AJA* subscription figures may indicate the minimum number of active classical archaeologists, the relative percentage of Aegean prehistorians can be better approximated by other measures: 15% of the *AIA Directory* entries (139 out of 928) and 16% of the AIA surveys returned (157 of 998) were submitted by Aegean prehistorians. These figures tally closely with the percentages reported by Cherry and Talalay (ch. 2, this volume) for several indices relating to publications and conference presentations. The North American bias of the AIA samples must be considered, however, as well as the fact that the subset of prehistorians isolated within the AIA survey includes only those with a doctorate, and excludes undergraduate and graduate students.

I suspect, therefore, that Aegean prehistorians make up more than 15–16% of the larger field of classical archaeology, which would correspond more closely with Cherry and Talalay's finding (this volume) that 23% of American classical archaeology doctorates pertain to Aegean prehistory. Among the 572 PhDs who returned the AIA questionnaire, Aegean prehistorians make up a full 27%. If half of the authors recorded in *Nestor* for 2003 can be considered prehistorians in the broadest sense, and these are added to the *IDAP* entries (removing duplicates) for the same year, we arrive at a sample of about 700, conceivably about 20% of the wider field of classical archaeology.[4]

Gender. Although the size of the field of Aegean prehistory can be debated, its makeup in terms of gender is clear: there are more men than women in the discipline (tables 3.1, 3.2). Cherry and Davis (1994: 3) found that 53% of the respondents to the *IDAP* survey were male, and 47% female (though, if only those from North America were considered, the ratio was 50:50). The ratio in the most recent *IDAP* is comparable—54% male, 46% female—and significantly different from that of the 1984 *IDAP,* in which nearly two-thirds of the entries are by men. On a whim, I tallied the gender of the 126 contributing authors to a large, three-volume festschrift in honor of Malcolm Wiener (Betancourt *et al.* 1999), a sample that might be viewed as a representative cross-section of Aegean prehistorians: the result—54% male, 46% female—matches the ratio in the current *IDAP* exactly.

In the *AIA Directory*, a higher proportion (57%) of Aegean prehistorians are male, while 43% are female—a division similar to that in the AIA survey but a more skewed ratio than in the contemporary *IDAP* survey (table 3.2). The discrepancy between the *IDAP* and AIA samples is presumably not explained by the North American bias of the latter, given the 50:50 ratio among the *IDAP* survey entries for North America. It may be partly explained by the exclusion of archaeology students (the majority of whom are female) from the AIA samples. If students had been included in the sample, the ratio of male to female would have more closely approximated that in *IDAP*.[5]

Subscribers to *Nestor* in 2003 provide another measure of the relative number of men and women in the field: of the 258 subscribers for whom gender could be determined, 62% are men, and 38% women. Compare the breakdown of the

3

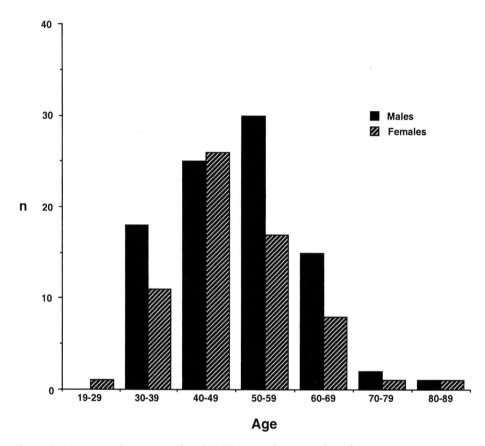

Figure 3.1. Aegean prehistorians in the 1996 AIA survey, by age and gender.

1996 *AJA* roster (the only year for which gender has been determined): 56% of the 2,600 individual subscribers were men (Cullen 2002: 435). Assuming that the majority of *AJA* subscribers are classical archaeologists and that the majority of *Nestor* subscribers are prehistorians, the field of Aegean prehistory would seem to include a higher proportion of men than is the case for classical archaeology. This finding is consistent with the AIA survey data: 58% of the sample of Aegean prehistorians are men, while 49% of the classical archaeologists are men (n = 635). Most Aegean prehistorians in the AIA sample are married (70% of the men, 67% of the women), but while nearly two-thirds of the men have children, only half of the female respondents do.[6] One might wonder whether this disparity is explained by the difference in ages among the male and female respondents. As shown in figure 3.1, women in Aegean prehistory—at least those in the AIA survey—are as a group somewhat younger than their male counterparts: 59% of the female respondents are less than 50 years of age, while only 47% of the men fall within that range, but the average age of male and female respondents overall is similar (for men, 50, and for women, 48.5). It seems more likely that in Aegean prehistory, as in many other academic disciplines, combining a career with raising a family is more difficult for women than for men.

The index of authors for the 2003 volume of *Nestor* presents a male/female ratio similar to that seen in the AIA samples: of the 844 authors for whom gender could be determined, 59% are men and 41% are women. The *Nestor* index provides a measure of *publishing* Aegean prehistorians, however, and not of the makeup of the field *per se*. The dominance of men in this sample is not unexpected, given the higher rate at which men publish in archaeology (see below). The greater representation of male Aegean prehistorians in all of these samples should perhaps not surprise us, given the bonds between Aegean prehistory and anthropology, a field traditionally dominated by men, at least in the senior ranks (Zeder 1997: 9–12). Classical archaeology, on the other hand, is more closely allied with ancient art, an area of research traditionally of interest to women, and therefore could reasonably be expected to include more women in its ranks.

Employment

Most Aegean prehistorians work in academic settings: 63% of those who responded to the *IDAP* survey and 82% of those in the AIA survey (table 3.4). Among academics, the majority teach at universities with graduate programs but affiliated with many different departments: in Europe, primarily archaeology, prehistory, and history; in North America, primarily classics and art history but also in classical archaeology, ancient history, anthropology, and history. A prehistorian teaching in a European university is more likely to have archaeological colleagues within his or her department than is a prehistorian teaching at an American institution. Aegean prehistorians also fill a wide array of non-academic positions in museums, research libraries, contract firms, non-profit organizations, and so on: roughly a third of these positions are filled by individuals working in museums. The ratio of academic to non-academic positions is considerably more balanced in Europe than in North America: subtracting the *IDAP* North American sample from the worldwide sample listed in table 3.4 produces a ratio of 57% academic to 43% non-academic (cf. 71% academic to 29% non-academic in North America). This finding may represent the effect of greater government sponsorship of archaeological activity in Europe than in North America and, in Greece, the influential role of the state Archaeological Service and of the Archaeological Society of Athens (see Andreou, ch. 4, this volume). A wide variety of positions—not all relating to archaeology—are subsumed under the categories of 'other' in the *IDAP* survey; examples include posts in ministries of culture and foreign archaeological schools, editors of scholarly journals, librarians, civil service employees, and journalists (for a full list, see Cherry and Davis 1994: 5). Nearly half of the 109 respondents in the *IDAP* survey who held positions outside academia reported that they would have preferred an academic position.

3   Table 3.4. Employment among Aegean prehistorians in the *IDAP* and AIA surveys

Position	IDAP Survey				AIA Survey	
	Worldwide		North America			
Academic						
University	167	(88%)	79	(83%)	98	(75%)
4-year college	15	(8%)	13	(14%)	24	(19%)
Junior college	1	(0.5%)	1	(1%)	3	(2%)
Secondary school	6	(3%)	2	(2%)	5	(4%)
Total	**189**		**95**		**130**	
Non-academic						
Museum	33	(30%)	11	(29%)	10	(36%)
Conservation	1	(1%)	1	(3%)	—	
Contract firm	12	(11%)	4	(11%)	—	
Research center/library	—		—		4	(14%)
Non-profit organization	—		—		5	(18%)
Consulting firm	—		—		2	(7%)
Government agency	—		—		3	(11%)
Business	—		—		1	(4%)
Other (archaeological)	39	(36%)	11	(29%)	3	(11%)
Other (non-archaeological)	24	(22%)	11	(29%)	—	
Total	**109**		**38**		**28**	
Academic / Non-academic						
Held by men (n=91)	—		—		90% /	10%
Held by women (n=67)	—		—		75% /	25%
Total	**63% /**	**37%**	**71% /**	**29%**	**82% /**	**18%**
Full-time / Part-time & temp.						
Held by men (n=87)	—		—		90% /	10%
Held by women (n=61)	—		—		61% /	39%
Total	—		—		**78% /**	**22%**
% M/F in full-time positions	—		—		68% /	32%
% M/F in part-time & temp.	—		—		27% /	73%
Tenured or tenure-track						
Held by men	—		46	(75%)	61	(75%)
Held by women	—		15	(25%)	20	(25%)
Total	—		**61**		**81**	

Note: The dashes in the table indicate that data were not available for these categories.

Breaking the AIA employment data down by gender reveals striking patterns: 90% of male prehistorians hold academic rather than non-academic positions compared with 75% of women (table 3.4). Women also fill nearly three-quarters (73%) of the temporary and part-time positions in the field. Only a quarter (25%) of the 81 tenured or tenure-track positions held by Aegean prehistorians in the survey are held by women, despite the fact that women make up nearly half of the field. This figure describing tenure corresponds precisely to that found for North America in the *IDAP* survey (Cherry and Davis 1994: 8). Since more women than men are working in non-academic positions, a somewhat lower percentage of tenured women might be expected, but why then are the rates of tenure between males and females so different? In the AIA survey, 79% of the (76) men teaching at a university or college hold tenured positions, while only 37% of the (46) women are in such lines. That female respondents to the survey are slightly younger than the males can hardly explain this discrepancy, which is mirrored in the sample of classical archaeologists and is clearly not a problem unique to Aegean prehistory nor indeed to archaeology in general.

As in so many areas of academic and other employment, men's salaries in Aegean prehistory are considerably higher than those of women. Of the 140 prehistorians who answered this question in the AIA survey, nearly three-quarters (71%) of the men earned over $40,000 a year in 1996, while only 40% of the women made as much. The higher salary ranks are filled almost exclusively by men: within the small sample of 35 individuals who indicated that they earned more than $60,000 a year, 30 are men. Given the greater numbers of women in part-time and non-academic positions and the indication that, within academe, men advance to tenured positions more rapidly than women, these differences in salary are not unexpected. The men in the sample are on average slightly older than the women and thus can be expected to have accrued a bit more earning power, but, as in the case of tenure rates, the difference in age is not substantial enough to explain the disparities in salary.

Despite such numbers, job satisfaction is relatively high among prehistorians recorded in the AIA survey, though men are apparently more content than women. When asked 'Is your present situation consistent with your preferred or projected career path?' 79% of men said it was, compared with 62% of women. When asked to rate their general level of satisfaction with their current situation, nearly half (45%) of the men said they were 'very satisfied,' while only a quarter (26%) of the women were that enthusiastic. On the basis of this admittedly superficial measure, prehistorians seem to be a happier lot than classical archaeologists: only about a third (35%) of male classical archaeologists in the survey said they were 'very satisfied' (vs. 45% of the prehistorians), while again a quarter of the women declared themselves very content with their job.

Research Interests

We can detect clear trends in research interests among prehistorians by looking at entries in the successive editions of *IDAP*. Table 3.5 records the number of times each of

3   Table 3.5. Research interests recorded in *IDAP* 1984, 1995, and 2003

| Topic | IDAP 1984 | | IDAP 1995 | | IDAP 2003 | | Change in rank |
	n	*rank*	*n*	*rank*	*n*	*rank*	*1984–2003*
Economy, trade, & foreign contacts	117	1	193	1	266	1	—
Ceramics	88	2	163	3	209	3	−1
Aegean art	70	4	159	4	207	4	—
Field excavation	70	4	167	2	224	2	+2
Settlement/demography	70	4	121	6	165	6	−2
Religion	54	6	92	7	128	7	−1
Linear B	40	7	50	11.5	74	11	−4
Homer	39	8	59	10	80	10	−2
Field survey	38	9	133	5	176	5	+4
Metallurgy	34	10	68	8	94	8.5	+1.5
Linguistics (general)	25	11	24	17	32	18	−7
Linear A	24	12.5	28	16	42	16	−3.5
Ethnoarchaeology	24	12.5	66	9	94	8.5	+4
Quantitative methods	22	14	43	13	71	12	+2
Palaeoenvironment	21	15	50	11.5	69	13	+2
Oral poetry, folklore	14	17	22	19	27	19	−2
Floral/faunal analyses	14	17	32	14	43	15	+2
Lithic technology	14	17	30	15	37	17	—
Physical/chemical analyses of artifacts	9	19	23	18	48	14	+5
Physical anthropology	3	20	12	20	18	20	—

n = number of times research area is chosen.

20 research areas was checked in the three directories. The 1984 version allowed up to five boxes to be checked, while no limit was set in the 1995 and 2003 editions, and individuals were allowed to write in other interests. (While one productive prehistorian listed 20 areas of research, most listed fewer than eight.) To permit comparison of all three directories, table 3.5 presents only the 20 categories selected for the 1984 edition of *IDAP*. The subject areas are ranked by frequency of choice and then compared over the years in terms of increased or decreased rankings. The order of topics is determined by the frequency with which they were chosen in 1984, with economy, trade, and foreign contacts chosen most often and physical anthropology chosen least.

The most notable changes in research interests between 1984 and 2003 are the dramatic increases in field survey, ethnoarchaeology, and physical/chemical studies. Just as dramatic, though the absolute numbers are much smaller, is the relative decrease of apparent interest in Linear A and B and linguistic studies in general. While the rank of linguistic studies has fallen in relation to that of other areas, the number of individuals claiming expertise in this area has risen over the years (e.g., from 40 entries for Linear B studies to 74 entries in 2003). Judging from the number of recent conferences and publications in this area of research (see Palaima 2003), the *IDAP* survey may reflect not the decline of interest in textual studies but quite the opposite, the greater autonomy and increasing segregation of the subfield of Mycenology from other areas of Aegean prehistory. Notwithstanding notable successes in integrating textual and archaeological evidence (e.g., Bennet 1990; Driessen 2000; Shelmerdine 2001), Palaima (2003: 70) has aptly observed that 'the hyper-technicality of the field and the proliferation of specialist publications devoted to problems in sub-areas of research within the field of Mycenology often make the tracking of scholarship problematical for archaeologists and general prehistorians.' Nevertheless, he firmly identifies Mycenology as a subdiscipline not only of linguistics and epigraphy but of Aegean prehistory as well (Palaima 2003: 45).

The relative increase of entries within research areas recorded in *IDAP* over the years varies widely. Physical anthropology, although consistently ranking last in absolute numbers, boasts the greatest change, from 3 entries in 1984 to 18 entries in 2003, an increase of 500%. The steep rise in the relative number of entries for field survey (38 vs. 176) and physical/chemical studies (9 vs. 48) also corresponds to the increased ranking for these areas of interest. More modest increases can be seen in studies of economy and trade, ceramics, settlement and demography, and religion.

Most of these trends were already clear by the 1995 *IDAP*. The frequency of categories chosen in the 2003 *IDAP* broadly defines the mainstream of current Aegean research: 65% of the selections fall in the categories of economy, trade, and foreign contacts; field excavation; ceramics; Aegean art; field survey (archaeological reconnaissance); settlement and demography; and religion. What is particularly interesting about the current *IDAP* is the range of new subject areas introduced. More than a third of the respondents (150 of 405) felt constricted by the standard categories and wrote in 'other' interests. Grouping their answers yielded more than a dozen new areas: architectural studies (with 20 entries), mortuary archaeology (16), underwater archaeology (16), chronology (9), social archaeology (7), history of the discipline (7), sociopolitics of archaeology (6), gender studies (6), archaeological theory (6), education and museums (5), island archaeology and colonization (4), music (4), and ethnicity (3). Single entries for warfare and ancient medicine were also recorded. Some of these areas could be consolidated, but few of the entries fit easily into the original 20 categories.

Many of these subjects were also of interest in 1984, although the approach to them has often widened or shifted over the intervening years (cf. Andreou, ch. 4, this volume, who tracks a similar expansion of research topics in Greek scholarship). Archaeological reconnaissance, for example, is transformed in the 1995 *IDAP* into

3

field survey, and in the 2003 *IDAP* incorporates 'palaeosurface reconstruction,' 'GIS applications,' and 'remote sensing.' The rapid escalation of survey projects undertaken in the Aegean (see Cherry 2003: 138–40, figs. 9.1–9.3) finds ample confirmation in the *IDAP* figures. Other terms that appear in the 2003 *IDAP* are revealing: 'epistemology' and 'historiography' now occur for the first time, together with 'politics of value' and 'world-systems theory' and phrases such as 'the theory and history of archaeological practice' and 'the ideological use of the past in modern Greece.' Complementing these entries, however, are many more that pertain to specific materials, places, or periods (e.g., 'Aegean animal style (lions),' 'beads and pendants,' 'small finds from Pylos,' 'LBA Cyprus'), reflecting the discipline's enduring focus on classificatory systems, chronology, and specific descriptive studies.

The geographical and chronological limits of Aegeanists' research in 2003 can be tracked impressionistically through the *IDAP* category of 'works in progress.' The geographical range encompasses not only mainland Greece, Crete, and the islands but also the Balkans, Egypt, Anatolia, the Levant, Cyprus, and Mesopotamia, though rarely in a comparative framework. Italy and western Europe are cited only three times, curious in view of the rich opportunities for research into the relations between western Europe and the prehistoric Aegean and ongoing fieldwork by Aegean prehistorians in Italy (see below).[7] The chronological range spanned by the entries reflects the continuing emphasis in Aegean prehistory on the Bronze Age, in particular the Late Bronze Age. Explicit references to the Early and Middle Bronze Age are surprisingly few (11), though a tabulation of sites, topics, and regional surveys mentioned would surely yield more research into these periods. Fifty prehistorians record Neolithic interests, testament to the recent upsurge of research into the Greek Neolithic (see, e.g., Halstead 1999; Andreou, ch. 4, this volume), while far fewer explicitly refer to the Palaeolithic (6), Mesolithic (3), Dark Ages (13), and Iron Age (16)—the periods that bracket the traditional arena of Aegean research.

The entries in *IDAP* provide only a crude gauge of the breadth of research undertaken by Aegean prehistorians over the past two decades. It is difficult to convey the nuances of research strategies when asked to check one or more boxes and summarize current projects in a brief phrase or two. Prehistorians increasingly pose questions of social and political import, place their inquiries within a regional context, and adopt a more self-reflexive perspective on the constraints that influence their interpretations. Nevertheless, the impression that emerges from *IDAP* of a relatively conservative discipline is sobering. Notwithstanding sophisticated contributions to issues of archaeological theory and practice, Aegean prehistory as a whole remains a strongly empiricist enterprise, firmly rooted in an approach to material culture that has wavered little over the past century.

Fieldwork

Most Aegean prehistorians participate actively in fieldwork in the Mediterranean at some point in their career. The *IDAP* survey indicates that three-quarters (76%)

Table 3.6. Fieldwork experience of Aegean prehistorians in the *IDAP* and AIA surveys

	IDAP Survey			
	Worldwide		*North America*	*AIA Survey*
Excavations				
Greece	220	(76%)	—	—
Italy	43	(15%)	—	—
Turkey	31	(11%)	—	—
Cyprus	59	(20%)	—	—
Surveys				
Greece	129	(44%)	—	—
Italy	14	(5%)	—	—
Turkey	15	(5%)	—	—
Cyprus	29	(10%)	—	—
Projects directed				
Greece	153	(53%)	42 (33%)	—
Italy	11	(4%)	10 (8%)	—
Turkey	16	(6%)	11 (9%)	—
Cyprus	32	(11%)	18 (14%)	—
Other	54	(19%)	—	—
Positions held				
Director	—		—	23M 9F
Museum staff	—		—	4M 8F
Independent scholar	—		—	8M 15F
Supervisor	—		—	18M 12F
Specialist	—		—	13M 17F
Field crew	—		—	7M 8F
Support staff	—		—	4M 1F
Other	—		—	5M 4F

Note: The dashes in the table indicate that data were not available for these categories. Sample sizes: *IDAP* survey: n = 291 respondents (worldwide) and 127 respondents (North America); AIA survey: n = 88 male (M) respondents and 64 female (F) respondents.

of the 291 respondents had excavated in Greece, while nearly half (44%) had taken part in a survey project there (table 3.6). Cyprus follows in popularity, with a fifth of prehistorians excavating there and a tenth involved in survey. Italy and Turkey are also chosen frequently for fieldwork, and a wide range of other countries are mentioned as well (e.g., Albania, France, Hungary, Israel, and Portugal). A large

3

number of prehistorians have also directed fieldwork in these countries: for example, over half of the respondents worldwide indicated that they had at one time directed an excavation or survey in Greece.

Just over half (54%) of the prehistorians in the AIA survey, when asked if they had participated in fieldwork over the previous five years, answered in the affirmative. Positions held include director (21% of the sample), supervisor (19.7%), specialist such as ceramicist or geologist (19.7%), independent scholar (15.1%), crew member (9.9%), museum or laboratory staff (7.9%), and support staff (3.3%). Men are more likely to assume directorships than women (26.1% vs. 14.1% of the respective samples), while the reverse holds true for museum staff and independent scholars (raw counts are given in table 3.6). This finding for Aegean prehistory, although based on a small sample, is in keeping with Gero's assertion (1985: 344) that, in anthropological archaeology, men ('the cowboys of science') tend to hold the higher positions on excavations and surveys while women more often sort and catalogue finds ('archaeological housework').

The situation is similar in Greek archaeology overall, at least among projects initiated by the foreign archaeological schools. For example, 27% of the field projects (including prehistoric) sponsored by the American School of Classical Studies at Athens between 1982 and 1994 were directed or codirected by women, an improvement over the number earlier in the century but still a considerably lower figure than might be expected on the basis of women's proportional representation (ca. 45%) in the discipline (Cullen 1996: 413; cf. Nixon 1994: 15, table 1.1). From 1995 to 2001, the American School sponsored 18 excavations and surveys, four (22%) of which had a female director or codirector; expressed proportionally (using fractions to count codirectors), women make up only 16% of the total number of directors of these projects.[8] Ten ongoing excavation or survey projects are currently listed on the American School's Web site, six with substantial prehistoric components. Three of these prehistoric projects are codirected by women; proportionally, however, women represent a fifth (20%) of the directors and codirectors.

One might object that these rather dismal statistics apply only to fieldwork carried out by Americans in Greece, but the pattern appears to have wider relevance. In an informal survey of all the foreign archaeological schools in Athens in the early 1990s, Nixon (1994: 15) found that only 15 women (from Australia, the United States, the United Kingdom, and Sweden) had ever obtained the necessary funding and permit to direct their own field project in Greece. 'To put these numbers in perspective,' Nixon writes (1994: 15), 'we have only to recall that six of the foreign schools have existed for over a century, during which time they each had three excavation permits.'[9] Archaeological fieldwork in Cyprus also conforms to this pattern. Webb and Frankel (1995: 98, 100, fig. 6) found that, prior to 1989, women consistently represented fewer than a fifth of the total number of directors and codirectors of excavation and survey projects, and only about a tenth (11%) of all projects were directed or codirected by women. Subsequently, the picture has improved, with as many as 40% of projects in 1992 boasting female participation at the top levels and women holding nearly a third of the directorships (31.5%) for that year. As in Greece, however, the proportional representation of female directors on Cypriot projects remains well below that of women in the discipline.

Publications and Conference Papers

The final part of this profile of Aegean prehistorians concerns their relative productivity in publishing and giving conference papers, areas that can be linked directly to the figures presented by Cherry and Talalay and by Andreou (in chs. 2 and 4, this volume). The AIA survey presents an opportunity to examine prehistorians' publication record over a five-year period (1991–95) in some detail and to compare the publishing rates of prehistorians against those of non-prehistorians (mostly classical archaeologists but also a few classicists and historians). Respondents were asked how many publications relating to archaeology they had produced (as author or coauthor) over this period; categories included books, journal articles, articles in collected works, technical reports, newspaper or magazine articles, and book reviews. (Articles were divided into two categories because journal articles are more often refereed than articles that appear in collections or published proceedings.) Figure 3.2 shows the

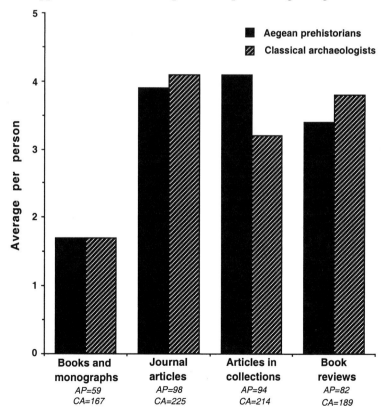

Figure 3.2. Average number of publications per person for Aegean prehistorians (AP) and classical archaeologists (CA) who published between 1991 and 1995. The total number of doctorates who had written one or more items in each category is also given (source: 1996 AIA survey).

3

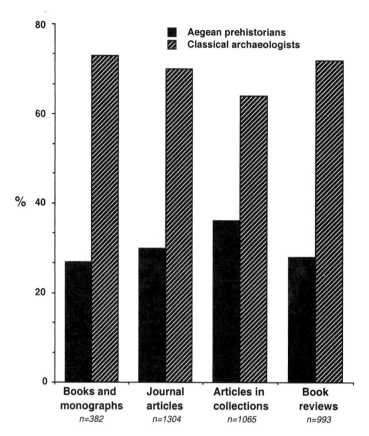

Figure 3.3. Relative percentages of books, journal articles, articles in collected works, and book reviews by Aegean prehistorians and classical archaeologists publishing between 1991 and 1995. The total number of works in each category is also given (source: 1996 AIA survey).

average number of books, articles, and book reviews per person produced by both groups between 1991 and 1995. The numbers are generally very close: individuals in the two groups averaged the same number of books, and prehistorians produced slightly fewer journal articles per person than did classical archaeologists. The largest disparity is seen in articles written for edited collections, with prehistorians in the sample averaging 4.1 per person, and classical archaeologists 3.2, perhaps a reflection of the ready outlets provided for prehistorians by series such as *Aegaeum* and the Sheffield Round Table volumes. Individuals in both groups write approximately the same number of book reviews per person.

Another way to describe this pattern is to look at the authorship of the total collection of books, articles, and reviews produced by the doctorates in the AIA survey (figure 3.3). Prehistorians make up 27% of that sample, so the relative numbers of publications should be evaluated against that baseline. Indeed, of the 382 books written by these individuals, 27% were written by prehistorians, and 73% by non-prehistorians, a ratio that corresponds precisely to their proportional

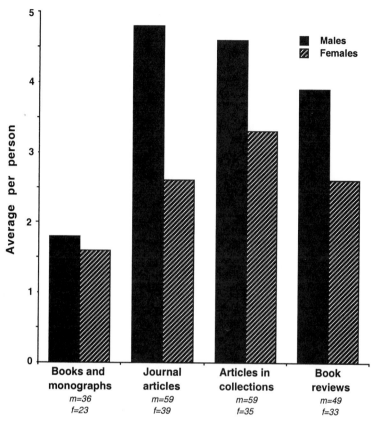

Figure 3.4. Average number of publications for male and female Aegean prehistorians publishing between 1991 and 1995. The total number of doctorates who had written one or more items in each category is also given (source: 1996 AIA survey).

representation. On the other hand, more than a third (36%) of the articles written for edited collections are by Aegean prehistorians, a substantially higher number than we might expect. In general, then, Aegean prehistorians more than hold their own in publishing, at least in this small, and largely North American, sample.

Virtually identical proportions of male and female prehistorians in the AIA survey wrote at least one article or book over the five-year period: 79% of the women and 80% of the men. Women, however, publish less often than men in every category (figure 3.4), a finding reported for other areas of archaeology as well (see, e.g., Victor and Beaudry 1992: 14; Webb and Frankel 1995: 98; Zeder 1997: 145–48). Male prehistorians in the survey published on average 1.8 books, 4.6 articles in collections, and 3.9 book reviews (cf. 1.6, 3.3, and 2.6 per publishing female prehistorian for the same categories). The divergence is particularly striking in journal articles: men in the sample published on average five (4.8) articles over the five-year period preceding the survey, while women averaged only three (2.6). Another way to summarize this pattern is to say that women contributed only slightly more than

3   a quarter (26%) of the (385) journal articles written by prehistorians in the sample—a showing well below their proportional representation in the field. A similar pattern is thus seen for refereed publications (books and journal articles) as well as publications not usually refereed (proceedings and book reviews).

The figure of 26% from the AIA survey corresponds roughly to that reported by Cherry and Talalay (ch. 2, this volume) for the proportion of female authors writing prehistory articles in *AJA* during the 1990s. For *Hesperia* over the same decade, the proportional representation of women is considerably higher: 38% of the authors of the 24 articles published on Aegean prehistory are women. Extending the survey to cover 1982–2003 indicates that this figure is not atypical for the journal: women represent 34% of the total number of authors of the 49 articles pertaining to Aegean prehistory.[10] The difference in gender ratios at the two journals is curious. *Hesperia* has long been viewed as the journal of record for the American School of Classical Studies at Athens, where, as we have seen above, fieldwork is primarily controlled by men. Publishing the finds from School excavations is at the core of *Hesperia*'s mission, while *AJA* has traditionally maintained a wider purview. In an earlier article (Cullen 1996: 412), I noted that 38% of all *AJA* authors (excluding book reviewers) for 1986–95 were women, a considerably higher figure than the 27% reported by Cherry and Talalay for prehistorians publishing in *AJA* over roughly the same span (1985–94). The higher figure can perhaps be attributed to the sizable number of classical archaeologists, many of whom are women, writing in *AJA* on ancient art, though this remains to be documented. *Hesperia,* on the other hand, while featuring relatively few articles on ancient art, publishes many studies of artifacts, and the proportion of female authors is relatively high, in recent years approaching women's representation in the wider field (see below). Studies of other archaeological journals in terms of the gender of contributing authors confirm that, while nearly half the field of classical archaeology (including Aegean prehistory) is composed of women, only about a third of the archaeological literature is published by women (see Cullen 2002: 435 for brief reference to the *Journal of Mediterranean Archaeology, Report of the Department of Antiquities, Cyprus,* and *American Antiquity*). As a result, the work of women in the field is presumably cited less often, which is correlated with intellectual standing in the field and rates of advancement.

The higher publishing rates of men than of women in archaeological journals appear to indicate a difference in scholarly productivity rather than, for example, the influence of editorial decision-making. Comparison of submission and acceptance rates for male versus female authors at *AJA* between 1986 and 1995 (Cullen 2002: 435) and at *Hesperia* from 1999 through 2003 reveals no evidence for bias in the editorial process; at *AJA*, 38% of all manuscripts submitted were by women, as were 38% of the manuscripts published; at *Hesperia*, 39% of the articles submitted were by women, but because the acceptance rate for women is higher than that for men, 43% of the articles published over the past five years were by women. The more important point, however, is that the percentage of articles submitted by women to these journals is lower than one might expect strictly on the basis of women's proportional representation in the field. While no doubt a reflection of some women's choice to focus their professional energy elsewhere, the recurring pattern of lower submission rates for women than for men suggests that different social and academic constraints affect performance in the two groups (see below).

In contrast to trends in archaeological publishing, similar proportions of male and female prehistorians polled by the AIA survey gave papers at conferences (78% and 76%, respectively), with women averaging 4.6 and men 5.2 over the five-year period—not a large difference. Cherry and Talalay (ch. 2, this volume) have tabulated the number of papers given at the annual meetings of the AIA from 1982 to 2001 and found that, overall, 14% of the papers (and as many as 18% in 2001) pertain to Aegean prehistory, nearly half (46%) of which were given by women. The increasing participation by women in archaeological conferences is presumably related to the increasing number of women entering the field as students over recent years (see note 5), a pattern also observed in Cypriot archaeology (Webb and Frankel 1995: 96–97, fig. 4).

There thus appears to be a discrepancy between women's higher visibility in giving papers at archaeological conferences and their lower publication rate. This pattern is not confined to prehistorians but is also seen among classical archaeologists (Cullen and Keller 1999: 7), Cypriot archaeologists (Webb and Frankel 1995: 103–4), and anthropological archaeologists (Zeder 1997: 144–48). For many women, giving oral presentations appears to be more feasible than publishing books and articles and a preferred venue of interaction with colleagues in the field.

Conclusion

In a recent collection of essays on theory and practice in Mediterranean archaeology, Renfrew (2003: 311) remarks that archaeologists now enjoy a much greater awareness of the social context in which they work than was previously the case, a sentiment echoed by several other contributors. These scholars are primarily addressing issues of heritage management, asking 'whose archaeology' we are practicing, exposing the devastating consequences of accelerating development and of the antiquities market, and stressing the need to communicate the results of fieldwork to a wider public. While this aspect of the social context of archaeology, and of Aegean prehistory in particular, has received considerable attention in recent years (see, e.g., Chippindale and Gill 2000; and, more broadly, Zimmerman *et al.* 2003), another dimension of equal importance has been comparatively neglected—the disciplinary structure of the field and the identity of its practitioners.

In the above pages, I have presented a profile of Aegean prehistorians, based primarily on recent directory listings and questionnaires. Some of the most positive and encouraging conclusions that can be derived pertain to the growing cultural diversity of Aegean prehistorians themselves and of their widening research interests. As shown in table 3.3, the number of nationalities (inferred from countries of residence) participating in the field has risen substantially over the last 20 years. Although residents of the United States still comprise the largest category, the proportional representation of residents of Greece and several other countries has increased. This trend will ultimately enrich the field with a more powerful arsenal of theoretical and methodological approaches and also ensure that the results of Aegean research are made accessible to a wider international audience.

Similarly, the increasing variety of research priorities documented, broadening to include a wide range of sociocultural and political topics, theoretical orientations, and analytical techniques, can only enhance the depth and quality of our perspectives on the past. There is cause for optimism in the expansion of the geographic and chronological limits of the field and in the radically transforming effect of regional projects on the goals and methods of the discipline. It is encouraging that a large number of prehistorians listed in the 2003 edition of *IDAP* felt constricted by the categories of research formulated in 1984, choosing instead to write in many other topics—a further indication that the field is expanding and evolving in new directions.

At the same time, there is cause for concern in the results outlined above. Classical archaeology has long been criticized for its excessively particularizing tendency, the goal of research often being the detailed description of classes of objects divorced from questions of function, social context, or wider relevance (e.g., Snodgrass 1985; Dyson 1993). Despite groundbreaking research by prehistorians over the past few decades, influenced strongly by processual and post-processual schools of thought, Aegean prehistory as a whole would also appear to suffer from this tendency. The terms chosen (or not) by *IDAP* contributors and survey respondents confirm a dearth of comparative studies and a continued privileging of the Bronze Age over earlier and later periods. The isolation of prehistorians within classics and art history departments in North America and the pigeonholing of scholars by narrow specialties have worked against the interdisciplinary collaboration and cross-cultural aspirations underlying recent survey archaeology (e.g., Alcock and Cherry 2004). While the traditional scope of Aegeanist studies has expanded, research straddling the Greek Bronze Age and Iron Age is still rare (Renfrew 2003: 317–18). The integration of textual and archaeological evidence is also problematical, particularly when comparative studies across time are attempted; see, for example, Morris's reflections (2003: 82) on the critical response to her essay on Theran frescoes and later Greek poetry.

Even more sobering are the patterns that emerge when we stratify the questionnaire data by gender. Despite the rising numerical and proportional representation of women among Aegean prehistorians, substantial gender inequities exist in the awarding of tenure, academic versus non-academic employment, levels of compensation, directorship of field projects, and rates of publication. The disjunction in publishing rates—the primary measure of professional success within the field—is perhaps most jarring: while women make up nearly half the ranks of Aegeanists, they contribute only about a quarter of the journal articles written on prehistory. A number of interlocking factors are likely to contribute to this pattern. Women hold nearly three-quarters of the part-time, temporary, and adjunct positions in Aegean prehistory—and these positions do not generally provide adequate resources or incentives for frequent publishing. Women in academic positions have a much lower tenure rate than men; tenure, though itself a reflection of productivity in publishing, is also critical in providing employment stability and financial security. Women may spend a disproportionate amount of time mentoring students and serving on committees, and familial responsibilities are likely to interfere more frequently with women's ability to publish than with men's. Issues of self-confidence and motivation may also play a role. Finally, as discussed above, most field projects in the Aegean are organized and directed by men, offering a ready focus for grant applications and a rich source of material to publish.

Few of these factors are unique to Aegean prehistory or archaeology in general. Studies in science and engineering in the 1990s reveal that women publish roughly half as many papers as their male colleagues, and significant gendered differences exist in promotion and tenure rates, salary levels, and several measures of professional recognition (Zuckerman 1991). Attributing these patterns solely to sex discrimination is not wholly convincing. Among Aegean prehistorians in the AIA survey, for example, few women offer anecdotes of deliberate discrimination. One cannot assume that men and women in our field necessarily hold the same goals; a substantial number of women may choose to frame their careers differently than men. They may prefer part-time to full-time work and choose to present the results of their research in conference papers rather than in refereed publications in order to reserve time for other aspects of their lives.[11] Nevertheless, the notion of 'an accumulation of disadvantage' for women, whereby small differences in conditions and individuals' responses combine cumulatively over the course of a career to produce major differences in productivity (Cole and Singer 1991; Zuckerman 1998), is surely relevant in Aegean prehistory as in many other contexts (for Cypriot archaeology, see Webb and Frankel 1995: 102–4; cf. also the papers in Nelson *et al.* 1994).

I would like to close with a few comments on one of the issues framing discussion at the workshop 'Prehistorians Round the Pond'—the presumed marginal status of Aegean prehistory within the wider discipline of classical archaeology. Although prehistorians may make up as much as a fifth of the field (see above), indications of a marginalized status can certainly be found. Andreou (ch. 4, this volume) points to the single question on prehistory in the recent entrance examination for the Greek Archaeological Service. A comparable situation can be seen in the entrance examination given in 2003 to prospective members of the American School of Classical Studies at Athens. Though a larger number of essay questions pertain to prehistory (4 out of 16), they reveal a closely circumscribed view of the

3

discipline. One question concerns Mycenaean fortifications, and the others pertain to the 'coming of the Greeks,' the origins and antecedents of temple architecture, and the value of Homer as a historical source. The value of Greek prehistory is thus defined largely in terms of its contribution to classical culture. Moreover, all students must also demonstrate proficiency in ancient Greek, a requirement that effectively sidelines prehistory students coming from any background other than classics.

On the other hand, it is clear from the statistics marshaled above that Aegean prehistorians compare favorably with classical scholars in terms of professional productivity (figures 3.2 and 3.3). Exciting developments are taking place in classical archaeology (Morris 2004: 262–65), but the discipline as a whole remains encumbered by the weighty ideological baggage of its historical mission to uncover the roots of Western civilization (and help maintain the cultural superiority of that tradition). Aegean prehistory, because of its marginal position in respect to the classical tradition, has been freer to forge interdisciplinary bonds, explore a range of theoretical currents, and develop new ways of working. In terms of intellectual vitality, therefore, Aegean prehistorians can hardly be considered marginal within classical archaeology. Indeed, Terrenato (2002: 1109) refers to 'a crack team of Aegeanists . . . on the loose,' and Morris (2004: 253) writes of the 'ferment' that has taken place in prehistoric studies, going on to claim that 'the major archaeological debates since the 1960s were among prehistorians, and historical archaeologists have been marginalized, plowing ahead with agendas no one else cares about' (2004: 264). While the polemic of the last statement seems extreme, it makes clear that the assignment of marginality depends very much on the criteria chosen and on one's point of view.

The shape of Aegean prehistory is influenced by a complex set of academic, social, and historical constraints that encompass the traditions of our training and the ways in which we make a living, carry out fieldwork, and disseminate the results of research. The profile that I have drawn above is based largely on Aegeanists' own descriptions of their professional status, accomplishments, and interests and in no way can be expected to summarize the full scope and complexity of the field over the past 20 years. The directories and survey questionnaires provide, at best, roughly painted signposts to recent developments in Aegean prehistory. They nevertheless generate a tremendous amount of information relevant to the sociopolitics of our field. The data we deem relevant to collect in the future may change, particularly if we wish to compare the structure and contributions of Aegean studies with those of other disciplines. I hope that monitoring the background and professional experience of Aegean prehistorians will become standard practice in our field, as in so many others, and thereby contribute to greater disciplinary self-knowledge.

Acknowledgments

I am grateful to John Cherry, Lauren Talalay, and Despina Margomenou for inviting me to participate in the workshop 'Prehistorians Round the Pond: Reflections on Aegean Prehistory as a Discipline,' held in March 2003 at the Kelsey Museum of Archaeology in Ann Arbor, Michigan. I would also like to thank Jack Davis, Priscilla Keswani, Jeremy Rutter, and Lauren Talalay for their thoughtful comments on an earlier version of this article.

Notes

1. In a preliminary examination of the AIA survey (Cullen 2001: 15), I identified 135 respondents as Aegean prehistorians; a more detailed look at the survey data, however, with particular attention to the research interests entered, yielded the larger, more accurate sample referred to here.

2. I am grateful to Kalliopi Efkleidou at the University of Cincinnati for providing current subscription figures for *Nestor* and also calculating a breakdown of individual subscribers by gender, discussed below.

3. I thank Marni Blake Walter, the former Associate Editor of *AJA*, for supplying recent subscription figures. The majority of individual subscribers (1,900, or 90% of the total) reside in the United States and Canada.

4. A figure of 700 coincides roughly with the number of subscribers (730 to 750) to the AegeaNet discussion list. While all who subscribe to AegeaNet are presumably interested in Aegean prehistory, it is apparent from the discussion that not all members are professional Aegean prehistorians.

5. Although students in Aegean prehistory were not specifically identified in the AIA survey, the 202 students within the entire sample (in archaeology or a related field, and for whom gender was determined) include 69 men (34%) and 133 women, in sharp contrast to the more equal representation of men and women in the non-student sample: 405 men (51%), 387 women. Whether these figures indicate ever-increasing numbers of women turning to archaeology for a career or a number of women dropping out of the field after graduate school—or both—is unclear. Within the AIA sample, more women than men have been awarded PhD degrees in the past two decades (Cullen 1999: 7, fig. 3), a reversal from earlier trends, but more than half (55%) of those who have a doctorate and are currently active in the field are men.

6. This finding for the small sample of 157 prehistorians is borne out in the larger survey sample of 998 professionals in archaeology or a related field: 61% of men have children, while only 42% of women do (Cullen 1999: 7). Within the larger sample, marriage rates are also significantly lower among women (53%) than men (67%), a pattern not nearly so pronounced in the small sample of prehistorians (cf. Cullen 1999: 7, fig. 2).

3

7. One measure of this area's increasing prominence in Aegean studies is that a review of the subject was commissioned (though not carried out) as part of the series of 'Reviews of Aegean Prehistory' published in *AJA* in the 1990s (collected and updated in Cullen [ed.] 2001). Other subjects that the organizing committee for this series felt warranted a review were prehistoric western Anatolia and the rise of intensive survey in the Aegean (Cullen 2001: 2–3). In contrast to research on western Europe, these areas of interest, especially the latter, are reflected in the *IDAP* survey entries.

8. To allow comparison with the figures gathered for earlier years, the 18 projects referred to here do not include joint Greek-American projects (*synergasias*) or projects only in study seasons. If *synergasias* are included in the tally, the number of field projects sponsored by the American School for 1995–2001 rises to 22, seven (32%) of which have female directors or codirectors. Proportionally, women make up 22% of the total number of directors or codirectors of these projects. I compiled information for this period from the American School of Classical Studies at Athens' *Annual Reports* (nos. 116–20) and from reports filed by the School's Excavation and Survey Committee.

9. Nixon's figure of 15 female directors of foreign projects in Greece does not include women who have codirected projects with men, nor is it clear precisely which years are covered by her survey. Neither of these points, however, detracts seriously from her clear demonstration that men organize and direct field projects in Greece much more frequently than do women.

10. I thank Seth Button of the Interdepartmental Program in Classical Art and Archaeology at the University of Michigan for sharing with me his breakdown of Aegean prehistory articles in *Hesperia*. I extended his survey slightly and calculated the proportions of male and female authors.

11. I am grateful to both Jack Davis and Jeremy Rutter for reading an earlier draft of this article and reminding me of this possibility.

References

Alcock, S. E., and J. F. Cherry (eds.)
  2004   *Side-by-Side Survey: Comparative Regional Studies in the Mediterranean World*. Oxford: Oxbow Books.
Allsebrook, M.
  1992   *Born to Rebel: The Life of Harriet Boyd Hawes*. Oxford: Oxbow Books.
Archaeological Institute of America
  1995   *AIA Directory of Professionals in Archaeology: A Preliminary Survey*. Boston: Archaeological Institute of America.

1996   *Archaeology in 1996: An AIA Survey.* Boston: Archaeological Institute   **3**
        of America.

Bennet, J.
1990   Knossos in context: comparative perspectives on the Linear B admin-
        istration of LM II–III Crete. *American Journal of Archaeology* 94: 193–
        211.

Betancourt, P. P., V. Karageorghis, R. Laffineur, and W.-D. Niemeier (eds.)
1999   *Meletemata: Studies in Aegean Archaeology Presented to Malcolm H.
        Wiener as He Enters His 65th Year. Aegaeum* 20. Liège: Université de
        Liège.

Cherry, J. F.
2003   Archaeology beyond the site: regional survey and its future. In J. K.
        Papadopoulos and R. M. Leventhal (eds.), *Theory and Practice in Medi-
        terranean Archaeology: Old World and New World Perspectives.* Cotsen
        Advanced Seminars 1: 137–59. Los Angeles: Cotsen Institute of Ar-
        chaeology, University of California, Los Angeles.

Cherry, J. F., and J. L. Davis
1994   Aegean prehistory in 1994: results of the *IDAP* survey questionnaire.
        Distributed with *Nestor* 21(8).

Cherry, J. F., and J. L. Davis (eds.)
1995   *International Directory of Aegean Prehistorians.* 2nd ed. Ann Arbor
        and Cincinnati.

Chippindale, C., and D. W. J. Gill
2000   Material consequences of contemporary classical collecting. *American
        Journal of Archaeology* 104: 463–511.

Cole, J. R., and B. Singer
1991   A theory of limited differences: explaining the productivity puzzle in
        science. In H. Zuckerman, J. R. Cole, and J. T. Bruer (eds.), *The Outer
        Circle: Women in the Scientific Community,* 277–310. New York: Nor-
        ton.

Cullen, T.
1996   Contributions to feminism in archaeology. *American Journal of Ar-
        chaeology* 100: 409–14.
1998   Archaeology in 1996: AIA survey update. *AIA Newsletter* 13(2): 3.
1999   Report on the AIA survey of professionals in archaeology. *AIA News-
        letter* 14(2): 6–7.
2001   Introduction: voices and visions of Aegean prehistory. In T. Cullen
        (ed.), *Aegean Prehistory: A Review. American Journal of Archaeology*
        supplement 1: 1–18. Boston: Archaeological Institute of America.
2002   Research and publication in classical archaeology in the United States.
        In D. Bolger and N. Serwint (eds.), *Engendering Aphrodite: Women
        and Society in Ancient Cyprus.* CAARI Monograph 3: 434–38. Boston:
        American Schools of Oriental Research.

3   Cullen, T. (ed.)
         2001   *Aegean Prehistory: A Review. American Journal of Archaeology* supplement 1. Boston: Archaeological Institute of America.

Cullen, T., and D. Keller
         1999   Productivity in archaeology: report on the AIA survey. *AIA Newsletter* 15(1): 6–7, 10.

Daniel, G., and C. Renfrew
         1988   *The Idea of Prehistory.* 2nd ed. Edinburgh: Edinburgh University Press.

Davis, J. L.
         2001   Classical archaeology and anthropological archaeology in North America: a meeting of minds at the millennium? In G. M. Feinman and T. D. Price (eds.), *Archaeology at the Millennium: A Sourcebook,* 415–37. New York: Kluwer Academic Press.

Driessen, J.
         2000   *The Scribes of the Room of the Chariot Tablet at Knosses: Interdisciplinary Approach to the Study of a Linear B Deposit. Minos* 15, supplement 16. Salamanca: Ediciones Universidad de Salamanca.

Dyson, S. L.
         1993   From new to new age archaeology: archaeological theory and classical archaeology—a 1990s perspective. *American Journal of Archaeology* 97: 195–206.

         1998   *Ancient Marbles to American Shores: Classical Archaeology in the United States.* Philadelphia: University of Pennsylvania Press.

Gero, J. M.
         1985   Socio-politics and the woman-at-home ideology. *American Antiquity* 50: 342–50.

Halstead, P. (ed.)
         1999   *Neolithic Society in Greece.* Sheffield Studies in Aegean Archaeology 2. Sheffield: Sheffield Academic Press.

MacGillivray, J. A.
         2000   *Minotaur: Sir Arthur Evans and the Archaeology of the Minoan Myth.* New York: Hill and Wang.

McDonald, W. A., and C. G. Thomas
         1990   *Progress into the Past: The Rediscovery of Mycenaean Civilization.* 2nd ed. Bloomington: Indiana University Press.

McEnroe, J. C.
         1995   Sir Arthur Evans and Edwardian archaeology. *Classical Bulletin* 71: 3–18.

         2002   Cretan questions: politics and archaeology 1898–1913. In Y. Hamilakis (ed.), *Labyrinth Revisited: Rethinking 'Minoan' Archaeology,* 59–72. Oxford: Oxbow Books.

Morris, I.

    1994   Archaeologies of Greece. In I. Morris (ed.), *Classical Greece: Ancient Histories and Modern Archaeologies,* 8–47. Cambridge: Cambridge University Press.

    2004   Classical archaeology. In J. Bintliff (ed.), *A Companion to Archaeology,* 253–71. Oxford: Blackwell.

Morris, S. P.

    2003   New worlds, ancient texts: perspectives on epigraphy and archaeology. In J. K. Papadopoulos and R. M. Leventhal (eds.), *Theory and Practice in Mediterranean Archaeology: Old World and New World Perspectives.* Cotsen Advanced Seminars 1: 81–85. Los Angeles: Cotsen Institute of Archaeology, University of California, Los Angeles.

Nelson, M. C., S. M. Nelson, and A. Wylie (eds.)

    1994   *Equity Issues for Women in Archeology.* Archeological Papers of the American Anthropological Association 5. Arlington: American Anthropological Association.

Nixon, L.

    1994   Gender bias in archaeology. In L. J. Archer, S. Fischler, and M. Wyke (eds.), *Women in Ancient Societies: An Illusion of the Night,* 1–23. New York: Routledge.

Palaima, T. G.

    2003   Archaeology and text: decipherment, translation, and interpretation. In J. K. Papadopoulos and R. M. Leventhal (eds.), *Theory and Practice in Mediterranean Archaeology: Old World and New World Perspectives.* Cotsen Advanced Seminars 1: 45–73. Los Angeles: Cotsen Institute of Archaeology, University of California, Los Angeles.

Petruso, K. M., and L. E. Talalay (eds.)

    1984   *International Directory of Aegean Prehistorians.* 1st ed. Boston and Ann Arbor.

Renfrew, C.

    1980   The great tradition versus the great divide: archaeology as anthropology? *American Journal of Archaeology* 84: 287–98.

    2003   Retrospect and prospect: Mediterranean archaeology in a new millennium. In J. K. Papadopoulos and R. M. Leventhal (eds.), *Theory and Practice in Mediterranean Archaeology: Old World and New World Perspectives.* Cotsen Advanced Seminars 1: 311–18. Los Angeles: Cotsen Institute of Archaeology, University of California, Los Angeles.

Schnapp, A.

    1996   *The Discovery of the Past: The Origins of Archaeology.* London: British Museum Press.

3

3   Shelmerdine, C. W.

2001   Review of Aegean prehistory VI: the palatial Bronze Age of the southern and central Greek mainland, with addendum: 1997–1999. In T. Cullen (ed.), *Aegean Prehistory: A Review. American Journal of Archaeology* supplement 1: 329–81. Boston: Archaeological Institute of America.

Snodgrass, A.

1985   The new archaeology and the classical archaeologist. *American Journal of Archaeology* 89: 31–37.

2002   A paradigm shift in classical archaeology? *Cambridge Archaeological Journal* 12: 179–93.

Terrenato, N.

2002   The innocents and the sceptics: *Antiquity* and classical archaeology. *Antiquity* 76: 1104–11.

Trigger, B. G.

1989   *A History of Archaeological Thought.* Cambridge: Cambridge University Press.

Victor, K. L., and M. C. Beaudry

1992   Women's participation in American prehistoric and historical archaeology: a comparative look at the journals *American Antiquity* and *Historical Archaeology*. In C. Claassen (ed.), *Exploring Gender through Archaeology.* Monographs in World Archaeology 11: 11–21. Madison: Prehistory Press.

Webb, J. M., and D. Frankel

1995   Gender inequity and archaeological practice: a Cypriot case study. *Journal of Mediterranean Archaeology* 8(2): 93–112.

Zeder, M. A.

1997   *The American Archaeologist: A Profile.* Walnut Creek: AltaMira Press.

Zimmerman, L. J., K. D. Vitelli, and J. Hollowell-Zimmer (eds.)

2003   *Ethical Issues in Archaeology.* Walnut Creek: AltaMira Press.

Zuckerman, H.

1991   The careers of men and women scientists: a review of current research. In H. Zuckerman, J. R. Cole, and J. T. Bruer (eds.), *The Outer Circle: Women in the Scientific Community,* 27–56. New York: Norton.

1998   Accumulation of advantage and disadvantage: the theory and its intellectual biography. In C. Mongardini and S. Tabboni (eds.), *Robert K. Merton and Contemporary Sociology,* 139–61. New Brunswick: Transaction Publishers.

4 The Landscapes of Modern Greek Aegean Prehistory

Stelios Andreou

Abstract

Implicitly at the start and more explicitly later, Aegean prehistory came to be regarded in Greece as the prehistory of the Greek nation. This has affected the configuration of the temporal and spatial boundaries of the prehistoric landscapes, epistemic scopes and practices, political economy, and academic standing of the discipline. The paper discusses the development of the main premises and quests that have shaped the discipline of Aegean prehistory in Greece and traces their reproduction and change through an examination of trends in academic journals, the academic status of prehistory, and state policies.

Introduction

In June 2004 the Greek Ministry of Culture held examinations, the first since 1993, for the appointment of 46 new archaeologists to the Division of Prehistoric and Classical Antiquities of the state Archaeological Service. Some 700 candidates reached the final stage of the competition, among them several holding or working towards PhD or MA degrees in Aegean prehistory. The candidates were examined in the architecture and topography of ancient monuments between 3000 BC and the 3rd century AD, vase- and monumental painting of the same period, ancient history, epigraphy, and numismatics. With the exception of one question on the Mycenaean acropolis of Tiryns, the rest focused on the Archaic and Classical periods and had a strong art-historical orientation. Among other things, the event demonstrates the marginal position that the study of prehistory still holds, in relation to classical archaeology, among state archaeological authorities. The dominant opinion about what the past of Greece consists of entails the selection of only certain prehistoric periods to be included in the discussion; earlier eras are not considered to have remains that can be classified as architecture, monuments, or art and are thus regarded as irrelevant for the understanding of ancient Greek artistic developments. With few notable exceptions, this opinion has prevailed among state officials for more than a century. Since archaeology in Greece is a field controlled by the state, the above stance had, and still has, significant impact on the development of the research agenda, the practice, and the political economy of the study of prehistory by Greek archaeologists.

The overpowering hold of classical archaeology over Aegean prehistory is not unique in the case of Greece and has been discussed elsewhere (Cullen 2001:

4   14; Kotsakis 1991). Several authors have also considered the particular importance and the role of classical archaeology in the construction of national identity in Greece and the effects of this role on the course of modern Greek archaeological thought and practice (Kotsakis 1991; Morris 1994; Hamilakis and Yalouri 1996; Kotsakis 1998). I would like, however, to touch briefly on some factors that—under the social and political circumstances that obtained during the time when Aegean prehistory developed in Greece—seem to have had a long-lasting impact on the construction of the agenda and the practice of Greek prehistorians. These factors did not lead to any radical changes. In fact it is equally important to point out some recurring themes that generate a sort of Greek tradition in Aegean prehistory, not always easily distinguishable from other traditions. It is important to remember that, until recently, the number of practitioners was small and interaction easier. Nevertheless, looking through the articles and reports of Greek archaeologists in both Greek and foreign academic journals, one can discern some shifts in the focus on different aspects of the past, on different regions and periods, and on different groups of finds and topics (tables 4.1 and 4.2). Before proceeding, I should note that the use of the terms 'Aegean prehistory,' 'Aegean archaeology,' and 'Aegean civilization' is not very common in Greek archaeological circles, and they are not always meaningful to the Greek public. When used, in lectures or conversations, they often require a definition (Platon 1970). The terms 'Greek prehistory,' 'prehistory,' 'prehistoric archaeology,' and (more rarely) 'protohistory' are used instead.

Tsountas's Prehistoric Landscape

Christos Tsountas is widely accepted as one of the founding figures of Aegean prehistory, and his pioneering contributions between 1886 and 1909 to the establishment of the Mycenaean, Early Cycladic, and Neolithic cultures of Greece are generally recognized and appreciated (McDonald and Thomas 1990; Morris 1994; Fitton 1996). The extent to which several of his interpretations and ideas influenced the thought of later generations of modern Greek prehistorians and the perceptions about the Greek prehistoric past still prevalent in Greek society has yet to be properly studied and assessed.

At Mycenae, Tsountas undertook the task of clarifying the many important issues that Schliemann's impressive and intriguing finds had left unresolved. To this end, he extended and organized the available archaeological information, presented a comprehensive picture of life and culture in the Mycenaean Age and, with as much accuracy as possible, drew the temporal and spatial boundaries of the Mycenaean culture (Tsountas 1893). Apart from the wealth of new information, however, what was significant for the future course of Aegean prehistory, and particularly for the views and practices of Greek archaeologists, were his conclusions about the Greek identity of the Mycenaean culture. Sixty years prior to the decipherment of Linear B, Tsountas had declared the Greekness of the ethnic identity of the Mycenaeans and of the Mycenaean culture (Tsountas and Manatt 1897).

Table 4.1. Articles by Greek authors in Greek academic journals

Journal	Years	Papers by Greek authors	Papers in Aegean prehistory	Aegean prehistory as % of total
Anthropologika	1980–81	14	9	64.3
	1982–85	33	13	39.4
Archaiologika Analekta Athinon	1983–89	99	22	22.2
	1990–2001	82	11	13.4
Archaiologiki Ephimeris	1952–61	125	15	12.0
	1962–71	98	18	18.4
	1972–81	157	18	11.5
	1982–91	84	16	19.0
	1992–2001	74	13	17.6
Archaiologiko Ergo sti	1987–91	184	26	14.1
Makedonia kai Thraki	1992–2001	467	86	18.4
Archaiologiko Deltio	1962–71	129	13	10.0
	1972–81	100	13	13.0
	1982–91	72	9	12.5
	1992–99	61	7	11.5
Praktika tis Archaiologikis	1952–61	314	79	25.2
Etaireias	1962–71	189	52	27.5
	1972–81	281	92	32.7
	1982–91	209	53	25.4
	1992–2001	120	30	25.0
Kretika Chronika	1952–61	15	9	60.0
	1962–71	3	2	66.7
	1972	4	2	50.0
Thessalika	1952–61	17	8	47.1
	1962–71	11	4	36.4
Totals		**2,942**	**620**	**21.1**

4　Table 4.2. Articles by Greek authors in foreign academic journals

Journal	Years	Papers by Greek authors	Papers in Aegean prehistory	Aegean prehistory as % of total
American Journal of Archaeology	1952–61	9	1	11.1
	1962–71	7	3	42.9
	1972–81	4	2	50.0
	1982–91	–	–	0
	1992–2002	6	2	33.3
Archäologische Anzeiger	1962–71	5	1	20.0
	1972–81	8	3	37.5
	1982–91	18	3	16.7
	1992–2001	9	–	0
Athenischer Mitteilungen	1955–61	19	2	10.5
	1962–71	25	2	8.0
	1972–81	19	1	5.3
	1982–91	22	4	18.2
	1992–2001	39	–	0
Annual of the British School at Athens	1952–61	3	1	33.3
	1962–71	7	3	42.9
	1972–81	10	8	80.0
	1982–91	24	14	58.3
	1992–2001	51	35	68.6
Bulletin de correspondance hellénique	1952–61	13	1	7.7
	1962–71	32	3	9.4
	1972–81	20	3	15.0
	1982–91	54	8	14.8
	1992–2002	32	12	37.5
Journal of Mediterranean Archaeology	1992–2001	3	3	100.0
Totals		**439**	**115**	**26.2**

Even more, he tried to show that the Mycenaean culture was indigenous and had developed locally through a long-term process of interactions and assimilations among the various cultures that had matured locally. According to Tsountas, this local process reached back to the Neolithic. His other two projects, in the Early Bronze Age Cyclades and in Neolithic Thessaly, along with a wealth of other information, provided support for the reconstruction of a cultural history that joined the civilization of ancient Greece with the Neolithic into one unified whole. It was pointed out, however, that several cultural transformations had occurred along the way. Cultural unity was documented by long-lasting traits such as the 'megaron' and was clearly defined in space, with boundaries that more or less coincided with the political boundaries of the Greek state of the time. For Tsountas, in accordance with the ideas of his time, the unity between the ancient Greeks and the Mycenaeans was both cultural and racial, but, judging from the common features in the material culture, the earlier inhabitants of the region also belonged to a related stock (Tsountas 1898; 1899; 1909).

Tsountas's research considerably enriched the picture of the prehistoric Aegean and authoritatively situated the prehistoric periods and their finds at the start of Greek history. He actually did what Konstantinos Paparrigopoulos, Greece's 'national historian,' had refused to do a few years earlier—perhaps due to the customary distrust of the historian toward the archaeological facts—in his ethnogenetic account in the *History of the Greek Nation* (completed in 1885; Kotsakis 1998: 51–52). Tsountas thus established a new view of the Greek past. Along with other intellectuals of the later 19th century, Tsountas was adding something new to the several other aspects that were enriching the unified and unbroken Greek identity at the instigation of Paparrigopoulos's work. Often these new facets were controversial and stirred violent reactions among intellectuals and the public (Dimaras 1977a; 1977b; Kyriakidou-Nestoros 1978). The Mycenaean era, and then the periods of the epic and Classical Greece, represented for Tsountas ages of Greek renaissance, preceded and followed by dark ages (Tsountas and Manatt 1897; Tsountas 1909). His proposition enhanced the already established genealogy of the ethnic identity of the Greeks, adding at least one more illustrious and very different phase to the history of Hellenism and demonstrating the great antiquity of the nation, along with its perseverance and versatility. Despite some occasional references to Lubbock's evolutionary archaeology and his adherence to many of the methodological premises of classicism, in spirit and in practice Tsountas's approach was more in line with the nationalist, culture-historical archaeology that was rising in Europe at the time (Trigger 1989). In this respect, he could be considered the 'founding father' of the archaeological approach, which still remains strong among Greek prehistorians. It is indicative of the long-lasting impact of his contribution, after all, that both direct and indirect references to Tsountas's authority and to his interpretations of the development of the prehistoric cultures of Greece, and their various aspects and meanings, continued to appear in the works of Greek archaeologists up until

4

4   the 1990s (e.g., Theocharis and Mylonas, in Christopoulos *et al.* 1970; Mylonas 1983; Vasilikou 1995; Iakovidis 1995).

Perhaps better than any theoretical appraisal, Tsountas's approach to the prehistoric past is aptly placed in the context of his personality and the intellectual situation of his time by K. Romaios:

> Generally speaking, Tsountas did not regard archaeological places, as every foreign scholar does, as merely an invaluable and sacred focal point of the universal civilization, but also as our own places, which either from a distance or from a closer examination speak to us always about our national history. The unscientific patriotic ideology was not mixed up inside him nor did it affect his precise investigative mind, but neither was it something beyond and forgotten or unvoiced as if ordinary and unconcerned. (Romaios 1941; trans. in part by Kotsakis [1998: 48], with an addition by Andreou)

Not all of Tsountas's views received a positive response from, or made an impression upon, the international scholarly community (Morris 1994). It seems, however, that his own concern, despite his early collaboration with Manatt, was mostly with the Greek front. His findings gained value in the context of national history because they demonstrated the variable strengths, the perseverance, and the ability of the nation to survive and to change. Tsountas's prehistoric landscape was spatially and temporally well defined by a network of places that were producing one unified narrative. It was an ethnic landscape that contributed to the creation of a Greek identity. As such, it was always revered by Greek archaeologists even if, as we shall see, it was soon partly transformed under the influence of new finds, new ideas, and the readjustment of priorities.

Aegean Prehistory in the Context of Western Civilization

A new place entered forcefully into the prehistoric Aegean landscapes with Evans's impressive finds at Knossos and the implications of his ideas concerning the Minoan civilization. They introduced new spatial and temporal meanings that formed a challenge to the setting of Tsountas's construct. Evans created his narrative based on an archaeological record of impressive quantity and quality, which also included components attractive for archaeologists trained in the tradition of classicism: works of art, writing, and religious iconography. At the same time, his all-encompassing approach, the forceful style of his text, along with the imposing material reconstruction of the Knossos palace, created a view of the Minoan past that remained dominant and without many effective challenges until recent years (Hamilakis 2002). A leading feature in his account was his reconstruction of Minoan Crete as the cradle of Western civilization. Crete, according to Evans, was ideally placed in the sea and possessed the means to transform the despotic Oriental civilization into the humane Occidental one. Furthermore, in accordance with his evolutionary views, Minoan civilization constituted the roots of classical civilization (Evans 1912; 1916). These ideas thus created a new landscape for Aegean prehistory, which encompassed all the meanings and values related to Western civilization and made reference to a much broader identity than merely the ethnic identity of the Greeks. At the same time, Evans championed the idea of the complete fusion between the Minoan and Mycenaean civilizations, which for him supported the notion of the Minoan domination of the mainland. Despite his views—unfavorable for the Greek case—about the ethnicity of the Minoans and the Mycenaeans, international recognition and the proposed relationship of Cretan antiquities to European civilization turned the Minoan past into important symbolic capital for the construction of Greek national identity (McDonald and Thomas 1990). It seems that, as a result of Evans's reconstructions, the Minoan civilization, in its ability to address the international community, acquired values similar to those of classical civilization for the issue of national identity.

There are some indications that Tsountas's ethnic landscape lost some of its force during the competition with Evans's European landscape, at least among Greek classicists (Kavadias 1909; Karollidis 1925). One wonders if the very limited participation of Greek archaeologists in the investigation and interpretation of the prehistoric past of the mainland between 1910 and 1950 is somehow related to this shift in the configuration of the prehistoric landscape. The shift, however, likely affected the motivation of Greek archaeologists for research into the Neolithic and the Early Bronze Age for many years to come (cf. figure 4.2). This part of Tsountas's narrative had been effectively undermined by the glamour of the Cretan finds and by the force and weight of Evans's ideas. It is noteworthy, on the other hand, that some important projects did take place during the same period in Crete (e.g., Chatzidakis 1921; Xanthoudides 1928).

Investigation of the origins of historical Greece continued in the southern mainland during the first half of the century, by a small group of foreign archaeologists with a classics background. They stood closer to the views of Tsountas than to Evans's colonialist propositions or to the views of several classicists who felt content with the spontaneity of the Greek phenomenon (Wace 1956). Ethnicity was again considered an essential component for the documentation of the autonomy of the mainlanders (McDonald and Thomas 1990). Characteristic of this group of Aegean prehistorians was the positivistic faith that careful stratigraphically oriented excavations, rigorous typologies, and chronotypological studies would permit the identification of successive turning points at which different ethnic groups merged and accumulated their best innate qualities to create the 'peculiar physical and mental characteristics of the Hellenic stock' (Blegen 1941; Cullen 2001). This meant that, despite an emphasis on the Mycenaean period, an important component of research was also directed toward earlier periods of mainland prehistory, including the Neolithic (Runnels 2001). Epic and the legends in ancient Greek texts often

4

formed the basis for the reconstruction of quasi-historical events, which were used to explain changes in the archaeological record. The new investigation of mainland prehistory and the emphasis on questions of origins thus further strengthened the bonds of Aegean prehistoric research with the theoretical and methodological canons of culture-historical archaeology.

By the beginning of the second quarter of the century, then, the frameworks for the study and interpretation of the prehistory of Greece—one focusing on Crete and the other on the mainland—had been worked out in terms of research questions and methodology and were actually followed with few changes until the 1970s. With the exception of Tsountas's early work, they had been created by foreign archaeologists. Greek contributions to discussions of the cultural history of the mainland were remarkably few before the Second World War (e.g., Mylonas 1930). It seems that the need for a tightly bound and unified national narrative, the main objective of Greek archaeological research at the time, was adequately served by the framework that had been provided through the blending of Tsountas's Greek prehistoric past with Evans's illustrious European past. The landscape had been curtailed in time, through the silent abolition of the Neolithic and the Early Bronze Age, but had gained in space. Evidently, the details of the ethnicity of the various cultures of the prehistoric Aegean, which were being investigated and ardently discussed by foreign archaeologists at this time, did not interest Greek archaeologists very much. After all, the Classical period and classical art always remained the main priority and the main focus of Greek archaeological research.

The Prehistory of the Greek Nation:
The Reformulations of Tsountas's Landscape

The situation changed radically in the 1950s and the 1960s. The pace of archaeological work in Greece grew rapidly under the pressure of fast and ill-planned development, which endangered many archaeological sites (Petrakos 1987; Kotsakis 1991). What is important, however, is the initiation by the Archaeological Society of some large-scale research projects that focused on the Bronze Age. There was renewed interest in Mycenae, starting with the excavation of Grave Circle B and continuing with a long series of campaigns in the settlement and on the citadel. Long-term projects also started in Messenia, the palace of Zakro in Crete, and later at Akrotiri on Thera. Smaller projects and rescue excavations at Bronze Age sites increased as well (Petrakos 1987). Prehistory, it seems, was rising in the relative ranking of the periods of the past among archaeologists, the Greek state, and eventually the public; but the main emphasis by far was on the Late Bronze Age and on the southern and central mainland.

An important development that should be related to these changes, and that affected both Greek and foreign archaeologists working in Greece, is the decipherment of the Linear B script and the demonstration that an early form of Greek was used during the Mycenaean period (Ventris and Chadwick 1953; 1956; Terrenato

2002). The wide significance of these deciphered records for an understanding of the economic, political, and many other aspects of the structure of the Mycenaean states is quite apparent. The issue of the ethnicity of the Mycenaeans, however, was another significant aspect of the decipherment—one that had particular importance for foreign and Greek Aegeanists alike, although for slightly different reasons.

For Blegen, Wace, and other Aegean archaeologists, the main objective during the early years of research in Aegean prehistory was to use the chronotypological approach of cultural history in order to trace the development of Classical Greece, a development viewed as a unique and exceptional phenomenon at the foundation of Western civilization (Blegen 1941; Wace 1956). Ethnicity was considered an innate and essential factor of the uniqueness of this culture, and language a crucial criterion for the recognition of ethnicity. Chronological issues and quasi-historical questions never ceased to occupy the interest of foreign Aegean prehistorians in the following years, but at the same time the discipline started to redirect its objectives and methods. In the 1970s—and not without great reluctance—there began attempts to keep up with wider changes in archaeological thought and practice. As a result, new interdisciplinary and regional approaches were introduced to cope with research questions and interpretations that, with growing frequency, came to focus on economic, political, and social aspects of prehistoric life in the Aegean (Fitton 1996; Cullen 2001; Davis 2001b).

For modern Greeks, the ideological implication of the decipherment was different. Language was again identified with ethnicity, and the confirmation of the Greekness of Mycenaean civilization allowed the official annexation of the Mycenaean period to a continuous and unbroken national history, thus elevating the Greeks to the status of one of the two most ancient people in the world. This had been suggested 60 years earlier by Christos Tsountas, but it now took the form of an historical fact, one that was recognized and spelled out to the international community in the words of Carl Blegen (1967: 16):

> Nonetheless it [the definite recognition of the Mycenaeans as Greeks through the decipherment] demonstrates the inherent strength of the Greek people and their astonishing power for survival: they still exist and flourish today, retaining their distinctive character, their language, their exclusiveness along with their cohesiveness, despite intense individualism. Apart possibly from the Chinese, there are few, if any, other comparable peoples in their tenacity to endure.

And Blegen continued with a revised version of Paparrigopoulos's narrative:

> In their long history they have at least three times blossomed out into world leadership in culture: in the Late Mycenaean Age, in the Classical period and in the heyday of the Byzantine Empire . . . they have always in the end absorbed the marauders and imposed their own Greek spirit,

4   their way of thinking and their culture, on the fusion of the Hellenised survivors that remained.

In this scheme of an illustrious national past, the Minoan civilization was also included, on the basis of its fusion with the Mycenaean, as proposed by Evans. This view, too, was considered an historical fact. It is no coincidence that Blegen's statement was included in the first paragraphs of the introduction to the new *History of the Greek Nation,* was repeated by Greek archaeologists in official ceremonies, and has even entered official school textbooks (Marinatos 1967; Christopoulos *et al.* 1970; Kasvikis 2004). The overwhelming emphasis of Greek prehistoric research—particularly between the 1950s and the 1970s, but to some extent even in the 1980s—on the Late Bronze Age of the southern and central mainland and on Crete, as opposed to other periods and regions of Greece, is not a coincidence either (figures 4.1 and 4.2). The international recognition granted to this early phase of the national narrative was sufficient to awaken the interest of the Greek state. As a result, it was possible for archaeologists to justify the diversion of a larger share of archaeological activity and funding to the investigation of Late Mycenaean and Late Minoan antiquities.

This, then, was a research framework for Greek prehistory that was defined by nationalist priorities of the Greek state but strongly influenced by the research objectives and ideas of foreign archaeologists working in Greece. It is noteworthy that the framework of this period was enclosed by narrower temporal and spatial boundaries than those proposed in Tsountas's ethnocentric scheme at the beginning of the century (Tsountas 1909).

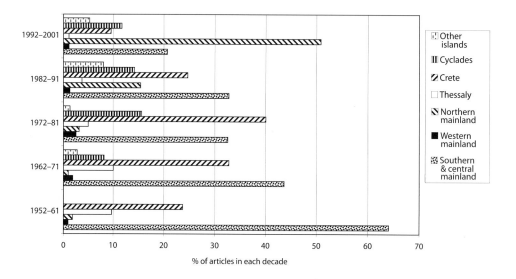

Figure 4.1. Regional emphasis of articles by Greek authors in Greek and foreign journals.

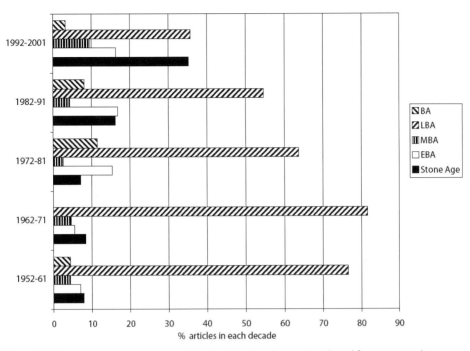

Figure 4.2. Chronological emphasis in articles by Greek authors in Greek and foreign journals.

Dimitris Theocharis tried to present an alternative version of the prehistoric landscape, in which several components of Tsountas's framework were reintroduced. After all, at that time he was reexcavating Neolithic Sesklo, one of the principal *places* of the initial landscape of Greek prehistory. His scheme encompassed all the earlier phases of prehistory and had wide geographical boundaries covering the whole of the Aegean. Like Tsountas, he stressed the indigenous character of cultural developments; but, rejecting a static notion of ethnicity, he underlined the strength of tradition and the power of the natural environment to shape a distinctive Greek character that was dynamic and was constantly accepting influences and being transformed (Theocharis, in Christopoulos *et al.* 1970). Theocharis's prehistory was also preoccupied with the origins of a group that had a continuous and unbroken history inside some well-defined spatial boundaries, and so it was actually reintroducing an ethnocentric landscape. Thus it is probably not a coincidence that Sesklo was the large-scale excavation of a Neolithic site that was supported by the Archaeological Society during the 1960s and the 1970s (Petrakos 1987).

Theocharis's framework, moreover, provided encouragement for a wider research agenda involving, for example, the investigation of environmental, economic, or social issues. In this respect, it differed considerably from the strictly historicist version of Aegean prehistory that was predominantly practiced by Greek archaeologists up until the late 1970s (figures 4.3 and 4. 4). With few exceptions,

4

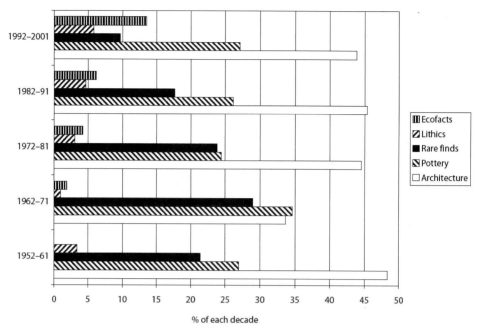

Figure 4.3. Finds of interest in articles in Aegean prehistory. Greek authors in all journals.

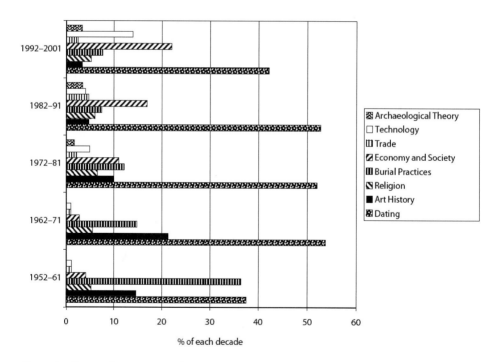

Figure 4.4. Topics of interest in articles in Aegean prehistory. Greek authors in all journals.

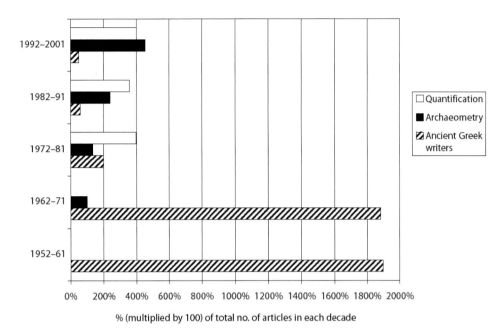

Figure 4.5. Special approaches in Aegean prehistory. Greek authors in all journals.

their emphasis was primarily on (1) the typological classification of pottery or metals, for reasons of dating and the recognition of cultural groups, contacts, and relationships; and (2) studies that shared several objectives and methodologies in common with classical archaeology (e.g., detailed descriptive approaches to architecture and burials, and art-historical and iconographic discussions of rare finds such as jewelry, frescoes, glyptic, or other objects of artistic value). During the same period, this historicist tradition also entailed the use of ancient sources to interpret finds (figure 4.5).

Recent Developments

Some significant changes in the directions and the practices of modern Greek prehistory are indicated by data collected from the later volumes of relevant academic journals.

First of all, there has been a significant increase during the last three decades in the number of articles written by Greek authors on topics concerning Aegean prehistory (figure 4.6). The increase, which is more evident in the past decade, probably indicates a growing group of Greek specialists or, more generally, a growing group of archaeologists interested in prehistoric topics; it should be noted, nonetheless, that the proportional level of interest in Aegean prehistory has not changed significantly during the last 50 years (figure 4.7). On the other hand, a growing number of Greeks now publish on Aegean prehistoric topics in foreign academic journals (figures 4.6 and 4.7). This perhaps has to do with the policies

4

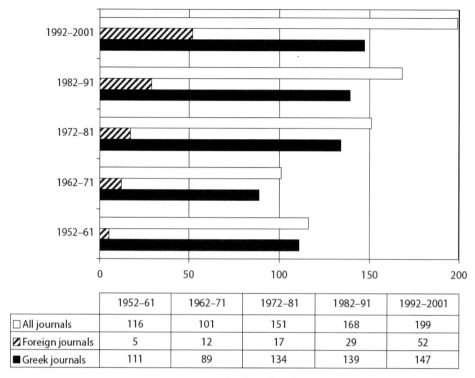

	1952–61	1962–71	1972–81	1982–91	1992–2001
☐ All journals	116	101	151	168	199
▨ Foreign journals	5	12	17	29	52
■ Greek journals	111	89	134	139	147

Number of articles

Figure 4.6. Articles in Aegean prehistory by Greek authors.

of the traditional Greek archaeological journals, which may not encourage the publication of articles in this subfield; it may also be related to the less isolationist policies of the foreign schools in Greece or to the increased number of people who study Aegean prehistory in Europe. The net result, however, is easier access for Greek archaeology to the international community. As regards the *Annual of the British School at Athens*, it seems that, among Greeks at least, it has been elevated to the academic journal *par excellence* for Aegean prehistory (table 4.2; cf. Cherry and Talalay, this volume, figure 2.1).

     During the last three, and particularly the last two, decades, important shifts have occurred in the regional and the chronological focus of prehistoric research by Greek archaeologists (figures 4.1 and 4.2). There is a proportionate increase in research that focuses on the Aegean islands and, during the past decade, on Northern Greece (Macedonia and Thrace), an area that had been largely ignored, by Greek and foreign research alike, as irrelevant to the objectives of Aegean prehistory. Similarly, one observes a considerable retreat in the research monopoly of the Late Bronze Age, accompanied by a rise of interest in the Early Bronze Age and particularly in the Neolithic and Palaeolithic (the former much more than the latter). I should add that the growth of research on the Neolithic period is related to

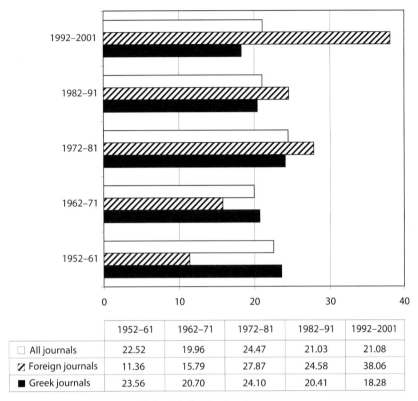

	1952–61	1962–71	1972–81	1982–91	1992–2001
☐ All journals	22.52	19.96	24.47	21.03	21.08
▨ Foreign journals	11.36	15.79	27.87	24.58	38.06
■ Greek journals	23.56	20.70	24.10	20.41	18.28

% of all articles by Greek authors

Figure 4.7. Proportion of articles in Aegean prehistory by Greek authors.

the new emphasis on Northern Greece, since it is there that most of the investigated Neolithic sites occur.

In a recent article, Kotsakis (1998) has discussed at length the strong political incentives behind the emphasis on archaeological research in Macedonia during the 1980s and 1990s and the considerable rise in state funding that this situation involved. What is important is that while the political interests and expectations were specifically oriented to the Classical period, prehistoric research benefited considerably from this opportunity as well. In this case, it was the growing interest of archaeologists in the prehistory of the region that led them to divert a share of the funding to the investigation of earlier periods.

It is true that a large proportion of prehistoric research over the past two decades has still been oriented toward the traditional objectives of cultural history and classical archaeology that dominated the activities of Greek prehistorians during the 1950s and 1960s. Recent trends in archaeological thought have so far had only a small impact on research issues and strategies of investigation, while the number of discussions of theoretical topics among Greek archaeologists is even

4   smaller (figure 4.4). Nevertheless, there are signs of change to be seen in the growing number of new categories of finds that are attracting the attention of researchers
and in the increase in interdisciplinary research related to Greek projects (figures
4.3 and 4.5). Furthermore, there is now greater interest in interpretative issues that
go beyond quasi-historical explanations and touch upon aspects of the economic
and social life of prehistoric communities (figure 4.4).

One of the reasons underlying these indications of change and the rising
interest in Aegean prehistory in Greece is the series of radical changes that have
taken place in the academic landscape of prehistoric archaeology during the last
two decades. It is remarkable that the first professor of prehistoric archaeology at
the University of Thessaloniki, Nikolaos Platon, was appointed only in 1966, and
until 1982 there was just one teaching position in the School of Philosophy of that
time. During the past decade the number of teaching positions in prehistory within
the Department of History and Archaeology (created in 1982) has increased to
six. This change has been accompanied by an almost equal increase in the number
of field projects, which also involve undergraduate and graduate students. In fact,
during the past decade the number of permanent teaching positions in prehistoric
archaeology in various universities throughout Greece (usually, but not always, in
departments of history and archaeology) has increased to at least 25. Currently,
there are three graduate programs, which accept about two dozen or more graduate students specializing in this subdiscipline. In addition, the University of Athens
lists about 60 PhD candidates in prehistoric archaeology, and another 26 are at various stages of their work at the University of Thessaloniki. Among them are several
members of the Archaeological Service, and this, I think, is an encouraging sign of
change in attitudes and emphasis among state archaeologists. At the same time a
considerable number of students are studying prehistory abroad.

Significant problems remain. In many departments, training in archaeology
suffers from a lack of infrastructure—libraries, training, and research laboratories.
Universities are still very much dominated by classical archaeology, in terms of the
number of courses taught, the general directions of the curriculum, and research
priorities. Because of the lack of prospects for future employment in archaeology,
students often have to turn to employment as teachers in secondary education, a
prospect that creates obstacles for the full development of anthropologically oriented programs in archaeology.

In terms of research, one should add the important contribution of the
Archaeometry Laboratory at Demokritos, which, since the 1980s, has facilitated
the development of interdisciplinary projects in a number of directions. On the
other hand, there is an apparent shrinking of the role that the Athens Archaeological Society had as the major agent of prehistoric research until the last quarter of
the 20th century; it seems that economic difficulties have forced the redirection of
priorities. At the same time, the availability of a number of other sources of funding—including public works and salvage projects, local authorities, the universities,

and the Institute for Aegean Prehistory—has encouraged a shift of the majority of archaeological activity away from the Archaeological Society.

4

In every respect, the situation is now very different from the time when there existed in the Archaeological Service only a handful of archaeologists investigating the prehistory of the Aegean, often against the general trend that discouraged estrangement from the privileges of classical archaeology, and with very few means and without much formal training. There is no doubt that there have been important shifts in the research objectives and the practice of prehistoric archaeology in Greece during the past two decades, and changes in the training of archaeologists have contributed significantly. The community has grown and diversified in terms of interests and professional specialties. There are important causes for discomfort, however, and I cannot finish with optimistic remarks. A growing number of young scholars has received and is receiving specialized training in various subfields of prehistoric and interdisciplinary research, but with thin prospects for future employment, despite the pressing needs of Aegean prehistory for such research. The priorities that determine the attitudes and policies of the Ministry of Culture toward archaeological practice and of which an example was given at the start of this paper do not allow room for much optimism. Similarly, the lack of flexibility, of funding, and of actual interest in upgrading and introducing innovations in archaeological training and research within the universities does not encourage hopes of improvement in the situation in the near future.

Acknowledgments

I would like to thank the organizers of the workshop for inviting me to participate and for their warm hospitality in Ann Arbor. I would also like to thank them for their unending patience regarding the completion of this paper.

References

Blegen, C. W.
   1941   Preclassical Greece. In *Studies in the Arts and Architecture*. University of Pennsylvania Bicentennial Conference: 1–14. Philadelphia: University of Pennsylvania Press.
   1967   The Mycenaean age. In D. W. Bradeen, C. G. Boulter, A. Cameron, J. L. Caskey, P. Topping, C. R. Trahman and J. M. Vail (eds.), *Lectures in Memory of Louise Taft Semple*, 1–41. Princeton: Princeton University Press.
Chatzidakis, I.
   1921   *Etude de préhistoire crétoise: Tylissos à l'époque minoenne, suivi d'une note sur les larnax de Tylissos.* Trans. I. Chatzidakis, with the collaboration of L. Franchet. Paris: P. Geuthner.
Christopoulos, G., I. Bastias, K. Simopoulos, and C. Daskalopoulou (eds.)
   1970   *Ιστορία του Ελληνικού Έθνους.* Αθήνα: Εκδοτική Αθηνών.

4 Cullen, T.

2001 Introduction: voices and visions of Aegean prehistory. In T. Cullen (ed.), *Aegean Prehistory: A Review. American Journal of Archaeology* supplement 1: 1–18. Boston: Archaeological Institute of America.

Davis, J. L.

2001 Classical archaeology and anthropological archaeology in North America: a meeting of minds at the millennium? In G. M. Feinman and T. D. Price (eds.), *Archaeology at the Millennium: A Sourcebook*, 415–37. New York: Kluwer Academic/Plenum.

Dimaras, K. T.

1977a *Νεοελληνικός διαφωτισμός.* Αθήνα: Ίκαρος.

1977b Η διακόσμηση της Ελληνικής ιδεολογίας. In G. Christopoulos, I. Bastias, K. Simopoulos, and C. Daskalopoulou (eds.), *Ιστορία του Ελληνικού Έθνους,* 405–9. Αθήνα: Εκδοτική Αθηνών.

Evans, A.

1912 The Minoan and the Mycenaean element in Hellenic life. *Journal of Hellenic Studies* 32: 277–97.

1916 New archaeological lights in the origins of civilization in Europe: its Magdalenian forerunners in the South-West and Aegean cradle. In *President's Address in the British Association for the Advancement of Science,* 1–23. Newcastle-on-Tyne.

Fitton, J. L.

1996 *The Discovery of the Greek Bronze Age.* Cambridge, Mass.: Harvard University Press.

Hamilakis, Y. (ed.)

2002 *Labyrinth Revisited: Rethinking 'Minoan' Archaeology.* Oxford: Oxbow.

Hamilakis, Y., and E. Yalouri

1996 Antiquities as symbolic capital in modern Greek society. *Antiquity* 70: 117–29.

Iakovidis, S.

1995 Introduction. In D. Vasilikou, *Ο Μυκηναϊκός Πολιτισμός,* xi–xii. Αθήναι: Η εν Αθήναις Αρχαιολογική Εταιρεία.

Karollidis, P.

1925 Introduction. In K. Paparrigopoulos, *Ιστορία του Ελληνικού Έθνους,* 109–24. Αθήναι: Ελευθερουδάκης.

Kasvikis, K.

2004 Αρχαιολογικές αφηγήσεις και εκπαίδευση. Unpublished PhD thesis, Department of History and Archaeology, University of Thessaloniki.

Kavadias, P.

1909 *Προϊστορική Αρχαιολογία.* Αθήναι: Η εν Αθήναις Αρχαιολογική Εταιρεία.

Kotsakis, K.

4

1991   The powerful past: theoretical trends in Greek archaeology. In I. Hodder (ed.), *Archaeological Theory in Europe*, 65–90. London: Routledge.

1998   The past is ours: images of Greek Macedonia. In L. Meskell (ed.), *Archaeology under Fire: Nationalism, Politics, and Heritage in the Eastern Mediterranean and Middle East*, 44–67. London: Routledge.

Kyriakidou-Nestoros, A.

1978   *Η θεωρία της ελληνικής λαογραφίας*. Αθήνα: Εταιρεία Σπουδών Νεοελληνικού Πολιτισμού και Γενικής Παιδείας.

Marinatos, S.

1967   Οι επέτειοι διδάσκουν το έθνος και τα έθνη. *Επιστημονική Επετηρίς Φιλοσοφικής Σχολής Αθηνών* 17: 1–10.

McDonald, W. A., and C. G. Thomas

1990   *Progress into the Past: The Rediscovery of Mycenaean Civilization*. 2nd ed. Bloomington: Indiana University Press.

Morris, I.

1994   Archaeologies of Greece. In I. Morris (ed.), *Classical Greece: Ancient Histories and Modern Archaeologies*, 8–47. Cambridge: Cambridge University Press.

Mylonas, G. E.

1930   Οι προϊστορικοί κάτοικοι της Ελλάδος και τα ιστορικά ελληνικά φύλα. *Αρχαιολογική Εφημερίς*: 1–29.

1983   *Mycenae, Rich in Gold*. Athens: Ekdotike Athenon.

Petrakos, V.

1987   *Η εν Αθήναις Αρχαιολογική Εταιρεία. Η ιστορία των 150 χρόνων της 1837–1987*. Αθήνα: Η εν Αθήναις Αρχαιολογική Εταιρεία.

Platon, N.

1970   Ο προανακτορικός μινωικός πολιτισμός. In G. Christopoulos, I. Bastias, K. Simopoulos, and C. Daskalopoulou (eds.), *Ιστορία του Ελληνικού Έθνους*, 108–21. Αθήνα: Εκδοτική Αθηνών.

Romaios, K.

1941   Ανασκαφή στο Καραμπουρνάκι Θεσσαλονίκης. In *Επιτύμβιον Χ. Τσούντα*, 358–87. Αθήναι: Η εν Αθήναις Αρχαιολογική Εταιρεία.

Runnels, C.

2001   The Stone Age of Greece from the Palaeolithic to the advent of the Neolithic. In T. Cullen (ed.), *Aegean Prehistory. A Review. American Journal of Archaeology* supplement 1: 225–58. Boston: Archaeological Institute of America.

Terrenato, N.

2002   The innocents and the sceptics: *Antiquity* and classical archaeology. *Antiquity* 76: 1104–11.

4   Trigger, B. G.

1989   *A History of Archaeological Thought*. Cambridge: Cambridge University Press.

Tsountas, Ch.

1893   *Μυκήναι και μυκηναίος πολιτισμός*. Αθήναι: Βιβλιοπωλείο της Εστίας.

1898   Κυκλαδικά. *Αρχαιολογική Εφημερίς* 1898: 10–211.

1899   Κυκλαδικά II. *Αρχαιολογική Εφημερίς* 1899: 73–134.

1909   *Αι προϊστορικαί ακροπόλεις Διμηνίου και Σέσκλου*. Αθήναι: Η εν Αθήναις Αρχαιολογική Εταιρεία.

Tsountas, Ch., and J. I. Manatt

1897   *The Mycenaean Age: A Study of the Monuments and Culture of Pre-Homeric Greece*. Boston and New York: Houghton, Mifflin.

Vasilikou, D.

1995   *Ο Μυκηναϊκός πολιτισμός*. Αθήνα: Η εν Αθήναις Αρχαιολογική Εταιρεία.

Ventris, M., and J. Chadwick

1953   Evidence for Greek dialect in the Mycenaean archives. *Journal of Hellenic Studies* 73: 84–103.

1956   *Documents in Mycenaean Greek*. Cambridge: Cambridge University Press.

Wace, A. J. B.

1956   Forward. In M. Ventris and J. Chadwick, *Documents in Mycenaean Greek*, xxi–xxxv. Cambridge: Cambridge University Press.

Xanthoudides, S.

1928   *The Vaulted Tombs of Mesara: An Account of Some Early Cemeteries of Southern Crete*. London: Hodder and Stoughton.

5 Embedding Aegean Prehistory in Institutional Practice: A View from One of Its North American Centers

Jack L. Davis and Evi Gorogianni

Abstract

This paper considers relationships between institutional practice and the creation of institutional policy from the perspective of our own academic department at the University of Cincinnati (UC), a center for the study of Aegean prehistory in North America. We conclude that, although the program in Aegean prehistory at UC for historical reasons came to possess the human and material resources needed to develop independently of the practices of the American School of Classical Studies at Athens, it has continued, nonetheless, to be enmeshed by the same ideology of Hellenism that promoted the creation of both ASCSA and the field of Aegean prehistory as a whole. This structural reality continues to promote a gap between archaeological practice by Aegean prehistorians and prehistorians working in other areas of the Mediterranean.

Critical Disciplinary History and Aegean Prehistory at the University of Cincinnati
There is much to be gained for Aegean prehistory as a discipline, as for classical archaeology in general, from a critical examination of institutional histories. The present form of American archaeology practiced in the Mediterranean is in no way an inevitable, natural, or self-evident development but has been molded by decisions made by individuals at particular points in time in response to specific social and political circumstances (concerning such issues elsewhere in the world, see, e.g., Wobst and Keene 1983; also Kuhn 1970; Soffer 1983). Today such decisions have become part of a system of beliefs and policies (an unwritten academic *habitus*, in the terminology of Bourdieu; cf. Bourdieu 1977: ch. 2) that are unconsciously shared.

Critical histories of classical archaeology have largely focused on the development of the discipline as a whole, with an 'aim to set individual archaeologists and institutions into their social and political contexts' (Morris 1994: 9; also Morris 2000: ch. 2; Shanks 1996: ch. 4, in particular; Dyson 2002). Relatively little attention has been paid to the particular roles that significant institutions of classical archaeology have played in the process of disciplinary reproduction, while those specific to Aegean prehistory have been almost entirely neglected (but see Cullen 2001; Kennell 2002; Hamilakis 2002; McEnroe 2002; Preziosi 2002; Voutsaki 2002; and papers by Andreou, Cherry and Talalay, and Cullen in this volume). We would argue that this has been a mistake.

Elsewhere (Davis 2003), one of the authors of this chapter has recently

5 studied the operation of disciplinary reproduction as a reflection of the practices of the American School of Classical Studies at Athens (hereafter, ASCSA), the corporate body charged by Greek law with the responsibility for overseeing all archaeological activity by Americans in Greece. It is thus our intention to examine here some of the same issues as in that paper, in particular the relationships between institutional practice and the creation of institutional policy, but from the perspective of our own academic department, a long-time supporting member of ASCSA, whose history has often been closely entwined with it.

In so doing, we offer some of our own thoughts concerning the history of the practice of archaeology of the prehistoric Aegean by members of the Department of Classics of the University of Cincinnati (hereafter, UC), and the development of its academic program. This case study will serve as a platform from which we can address the issues of principal concern to the organizers of the workshop, the products of which are being presented in this volume.

A focus on UC, although this may at first glance appear to readers to be somewhat hubristic, seems justified in that it has been, and continues to be, a center of graduate education for Aegean prehistory in North America. Gerald Cadogan, in a memoir of Mervyn Popham written for the British Academy (Cadogan 2004: 354), has asserted, with reference to the Classics Department of UC, that 'Since well before the war, this department had been the jewel in the university's crown, thanks to generous funding from Louise Taft Semple. . . . The surprising result was that this Midwestern . . . university led the United States in study of the Aegean Bronze Age by some 40 years.'

UC was not, in fact, the unqualified leader of Aegean prehistory in the United States since archaeologists, such as Boyd Hawes and Seager, were sponsored in Crete by eastern universities long before Carl W. Blegen arrived at Cincinnati (see Allsebrook 1992; Becker and Betancourt 1997; Muhly 2000). Still, as documented by the survey conducted in 1994 in conjunction with a second edition of the *International Directory of Aegean Prehistory* (hereafter, *IDAP*; see Cherry and Davis 1995a and, for the complete results of the survey, Cherry and Davis 1995b; a third edition of *IDAP* is available on-line at http://classics.uc.edu/nestor/IDAP/isearch.lasso), UC is one of a handful of North American universities that dominate the American job market in Aegean prehistory. Since Jerome Sperling submitted his thesis in 1937 (Sperling 1937), UC has granted 26 doctoral degrees for dissertations concerned with aspects of Aegean prehistory. In 2004 ca. 14 of these individuals held academic positions in the United States, while others were active in the field in other ways.

In this paper we include discussion of the following topics, among others:

(1)   The ways in which the requirements of UC have responded to, and have influenced, the development of the institutional policy of ASCSA. The origins of the so-called 'sponsored' excavations of ASCSA, and the long-term effects on Aegean prehistory in the United States of the so-called Capps-

Hill Affair, including the fossilization of the dichotomy between the program of ASCSA and the activities of its member institutions.

(2)   The structure and focus of instruction in Aegean prehistory at UC. Meanings of the terms 'Bronze Age' and 'Aegean Prehistory' will be considered within the context of the program of UC.

We conclude that, although the program in Aegean prehistory at UC for historical reasons came to possess the human and material resources needed to develop independently of the practices of ASCSA, it has continued, nonetheless, to be enmeshed by the same ideology of Hellenism that promoted the creation of both ASCSA and the field of Aegean prehistory as a whole. This structural reality continues to promote a gap between archaeological practice by Aegean prehistorians and prehistorians working in other areas of the Mediterranean.

The History of Aegean Prehistory at the University of Cincinnati: A Primer
It is worth recalling just how UC rose to prominence in Aegean prehistory by recounting a few basic facts in departmental history. In 1910–11, William T. Semple (PhD, Princeton) was hired in UC's Department of Greek after he had completed supplemental graduate studies in Rome and at Halle (figure 5.1). In 1917, Semple had married Louise Taft (figure 5.2). As head of a classics department (newly created in 1920), with her help, Semple embarked on a lifelong mission to create through the investment of their own personal fortune an academic department that, in the words of J. L. Caskey (1963: 81), 'saw the study of classical antiquity as a single undertaking, not to be divided sharply into separate compartments. The historical and archaeological approaches to the subject were not less important than the linguistic and literary and not ancillary, but integral components of the classical discipline.'
Semple soon enticed new scholars to Cincinnati, including James Penrose Harland. The addition of new faculty made it possible for the first time in 1924–25 to offer a separate curriculum in each of four subfields, Greek, Latin, ancient history, and archaeology, and it was in this context that Harlan offered the first instruction in Aegean prehistory in 1923–24: an undergraduate course entitled 'Homer and Ancient History.' Harland's special field of interest was the archaeology and prehistory of early Greece. He had been a student at ASCSA in later 1914 and, in 1920–21, returned there after completing his PhD at Princeton (a work later published as Harland 1925).
Harland's arrival in Cincinnati was an important component in Semple's vision for the department, and it is no coincidence that the first excavations funded by the University of Cincinnati in Greece were inaugurated in the following year, at Nemea (figure 5.3). In 1923, UC also became a cooperating member of ASCSA, nearly 40 years after the foundation of the latter institution. But first steps toward

5

Figure 5.1. William T. Semple at Troy, 1935 (courtesy of the Department of Classics, University of Cincinnati).

Figure 5.2. Louise Taft Semple (courtesy of the Department of Classics, University of Cincinnati).

the creation of a program of archaeological fieldwork by UC had been already taken in 1921, when there seems first to have been discussed the possibility of organizing a dig in Greece that would be sponsored financially by UC and directed by the staff of ASCSA (Davis 2004).

Three annual campaigns of large-scale excavation were conducted within the Sanctuary of Zeus at Nemea in 1924, 1925, and 1926–27. Carl W. Blegen (figure 5.4), then Assistant Director of ASCSA, organized the project, while in 1926–27 Harland represented the University of Cincinnati in a collaborative exploration of the nearby prehistoric mound of Tsoungiza (cf. Wright 1990: 618).

Cincinnati, ASCSA, and the Capps-Hill Affair
The relationship between ASCSA and UC has been a curious one with regard to the sponsorship of archaeological expeditions. Unlike any other of the foreign schools in Greece, ASCSA was founded as a consortium of academic institutions and has

5

Figure 5.3. Temple of Zeus at Nemea during excavations, 1927 (courtesy of the Department of Classics, University of Cincinnati).

no official relationship with the government of the United States. On the other hand, since its establishment in 1881, ASCSA has directly controlled most excavations organized by American universities in Greece.

This authority of ASCSA to do so met its first serious challenge in 1927, as a direct result of actions taken by UC. Bert Hodge Hill, Director of ASCSA (figure 5.4), was dismissed in 1926, at the culmination of a long-standing quarrel with Edward Capps, Chairman of the Managing Committee of ASCSA (figure 5.5). Blegen, Hill's best friend, became Acting Director of ASCSA for the 1926–27 academic year, in somewhat acrimonious circumstances (for a sanitized version of the events, see Lord 1947: 190–92). Blegen then replaced Harland at UC in the fall of 1927. With his arrival in Cincinnati, Semple had both the money and technical expertise required to break the umbilical cord that had previously tied his department to ASCSA.

The potential effects of Blegen's move to Cincinnati were of particular concern to Capps, when in 1928 a decree was issued by the Greek government that would have permitted foreigners to excavate in Greece independently of the foreign schools of archaeology. Capps suspected a conspiracy involving Blegen, Hill, and Konstantinos Kourouniotes, Director of Antiquities of Greece, and he lobbied hard for suspension of the decree. Ultimately, in August 1928, Kourouniotes was blackmailed by Capps into agreeing 'that no American Archaeologist would be

5

Figure 5.5. Edward Capps, Chairman of Managing Committee of ASCSA, 1918–39 (after Lord 1947: facing p. 130; courtesy of the American School of Classical Studies at Athens).

Figure 5.4. Carl W. Blegen (left) with Bert Hodge Hill (right, seated) during Tsoungiza Excavations, Nemea, 1924 (courtesy of the Nemea Excavations, University of California at Berkeley).

permitted to excavate in Greece in cooperation with a Greek, independent of ASCSA' (Lord 1947: 205) and was said by Rhys Carpenter, the new Director of ASCSA who represented Capps in negotiations with Kourouniotes, 'to have radiated a considerable amount of heat' in a private interview.

It is clear from documents in the archives of UC and ASCSA that this incident was the direct result of the conflict between Hill and Capps. Negotiations among Kourouniotes, Blegen, and Hill were under way during Blegen's acting directorship in early 1927. A letter from Capps dated February 19, 1927, had requested that Kourouniotes assure him that 'no new concessions of any nature for archaeological work in Greece—I mean particularly excavations—will be granted by the Archaeological Service of the government to any other American organization or to any American individual.' Capps threatened that 'the granting of any—which I don't think you would be likely to do without consultation with the American School in any event—would in the present circumstances place in jeopardy the whole Agora undertaking as far as the American School is concerned' (UA-83-15,

Box 1, folder 9; *ADM* Box 701/1, folder 4: Capps to Kournouniotes, February 19, 1927, and Kourouniotes to Capps, March 31, 1927, where assurances are given to Capps that permits will only be issued to Americans via ASCSA; *ADM* 318/1, folder 6, Capps to Kourouniotes, March 8, 1927; cf. *ADM* Box 318/1, folder 4: Capps to Carpenter, January 2, 1928, where the entire affair is summarized in detail).

Kourouniotes, however, did not yield, and the decree was issued the following year (*ADM* 318/2, folder 1, Carpenter to Capps, February 27, 1928; *ADM* 318/1, folder 6, Capps to Carpenter, March 19, 1928; *ADM* 318/1, folder 6, Capps to Executive Committee, March 24, 1928). In a letter of July 18, 1928, Kourouniotes clarified for Blegen matters pertaining to cooperative projects between Greek archaeologists and foreigners: viz., a permit would be awarded in the name of a Greek archaeologist, with a notation that an excavation would be conducted together with a foreign archaeologist. The nationality of the foreigner would be of no concern, and he might pay part or all of the expenses of the excavation, as agreed with the Greek archaeologist (UA-83-15, Box 1, folder 30).

Under the terms of the decree, a permit was granted in 1928 for Hill and Kourouniotis to excavate jointly at Eleusis (*ADM* Box 701/1, folder 2, Nikoloudes to Hill, April 25, 1928), but, after Capps's protest, it was retracted. On August 23, 1928, Kourouniotes wrote to Hill, expressing his deep regrets that this cooperative research could not be executed because of complaints from the Managing Committee of ASCSA and hoping that Hill would understand the difficult political circumstances in which he, Kourouniotes, found himself (UA-83-15, Box 1, folder 29 and *ADM* 701/1, folder 2; cf. *ADM* 318/1, folder 6, Capps to Carpenter, August 21, 1928, and Kourouniotes to Capps, August 21, 1928).

ASCSA then, for the first time, quickly took steps to regularize and formalize procedures for fieldwork conducted under its auspices by member institutions (ASCSA 1927–28: 21). Until the 1920s, control of excavations does not appear to have been a serious concern, and the organization of American fieldwork in Greece was similar to that of other foreign schools. Excavations were directly managed by ASCSA and were supervised by its director, other officers of the School, or its students (excavations by whom were described as being 'under the auspices of the School' and were partly funded by ASCSA). Its sole collaborations were organized with the Archaeological Institute of America.

But a different model for American archaeological research in Greece began to evolve after UC's entry on the Greek scene and when, also in the early 1920s, the Fogg Museum proposed joint excavations at Colophon, in Asia Minor (regarding Colophon, see Davis 2003; concerning various collaborative projects funded by UC, see Davis 2004). While Capps welcomed the influx of new money, from the start he envisioned threats to the authority of ASCSA, as well as political risks. The disastrous consequences of the Colophon project did not set his mind at ease.

The collaboration at Colophon between ASCSA, represented by Hill and Blegen, and the Fogg Museum, represented by Hetty Goldman, operated under the

5

aegis of the Greek administration that governed western Turkey from 1920 to 1922. The capture and destruction of Izmir/Smyrna by the forces of Ataturk in September 1922, and the embarrassing results for ASCSA when it was discovered by Turkey that the School had been complicit in the illegal exportation of antiquities from western Asia Minor, ended its sponsorship of fieldwork in Turkey. These events had lasting consequences for the practice, by its members, of both archaeology in general and Aegean prehistory in particular (Davis 2003).

The fact that archaeological operations of ASCSA retreated within the borders of the Greek state and that, in the 1930s, its financial resources were concentrated in the Athenian Agora and at Corinth meant that early American interests in Minoan Crete were not pursued further. (The position of financial stability that ASCSA enjoyed, even during the Great Depression, should be contrasted with that of the Archaeological Institute of America, its parent organization; see Dyson 2002.) Excavations at Corinth and in the Athenian Agora were primarily concerned with the classical Greek and Roman past, and on the Greek mainland, ASCSA again played an active role in sponsoring predominantly prehistoric investigations only much later at Lerna (1952–59), during the directorship of John L. Caskey, an Aegean prehistorian trained by Blegen at UC.

The Creation of a Program in Aegean Prehistory at UC

The arrival of Blegen in Cincinnati in 1927–28 in one fell swoop stripped Capps of the assets of UC that had previously been available in support of the projects of ASCSA (since Blegen now directly controlled access to funding by the Semples) and ensured that a strong American tradition in Aegean prehistory would continue independently of ASCSA. With the exception of the years of World War II, there has hardly been a year when UC has not funded the excavation of a prehistoric site in Greece, Turkey, Cyprus, or Albania. At the same time, instruction in Aegean prehistory has been a significant component in graduate and undergraduate education at UC, although its scope, focus, and intensity have varied, as can be seen from the following review based on data gleaned from a comprehensive survey of annual university catalogues for the years 1927–2003.

From 1927 until 1960, Blegen was normally the only faculty member at UC who offered instruction in Aegean prehistory (although, for one academic year [1942–43], Georg Karo, a refugee from the Nazis, came to Cincinnati). Blegen developed several graduate courses with a substantial or total prehistoric component: 'The Origins of the Greeks,' 'The Mycenaean Age,' 'Homer and the Homeric Age,' 'The Mycenaeans and the Homeric Age,' 'Preclassical Greece,' and 'Problems of Preclassical Greece.' The teaching of Aegean Prehistory lapsed with American involvement in World War II, as Blegen and his graduate students left to serve their country, but it returned to the curriculum in 1948–49. From then until 1960, when he retired, Blegen four times offered a graduate course entitled 'Preclassical Greece' or 'The Mycenaean Age.' It seems clear that the term 'preclassical' was a particular favorite, as in the title of his well-known lecture delivered at the University of Pennsylvania on the occasion of its bicentennial (Blegen 1941).

Instruction in Aegean prehistory was intensified when Jack Caskey arrived in 1959–60. Caskey, unlike Blegen, rarely taught anything but graduate seminars in 'Preclassical Greece' and 'The Mycenaean Age.' In 1970, the addition of a second prehistorian, Mervyn Popham, led to a further increase, and typically two to three courses per year were offered at both the graduate and undergraduate levels. The term 'Aegean Archaeology' was introduced to the curriculum for the first time as the title for two of Popham's courses: 'Aegean Archaeology and Art' and 'Techniques and Problems of Aegean Archaeology.' After his arrival in 1973–74, Cadogan taught a 'Survey of Pre-Classical Aegean Archaeology,' 'The Mycenaeans,' 'The Archaeology of Cyprus until the Coming of the Greeks,' and 'The Emergence of Classical Greece (1000–700),' while Caskey continued to teach a seminar in 'Pre-Classical Greece.'

Although new to UC in the 1970s, the use of 'Aegean' to describe the prehistory of Greece was hardly new. Aegean archaeology is represented at least as early as Hall's *Aegean Archaeology: An Introduction to the Archaeology of Prehistoric Greece* (1915) (see also Casson 1927), Aegean prehistory at the latest by Chadwick's paper, 'The Greek Dialects and Greek Prehistory' (Chadwick 1956). Other Linear B specialists were using the term (e.g., Palmer 1961 and see the parallel use of the word in German [e.g., Schachermeyr 1951]).

Expansion of subject matter and a growth in the number of graduate courses ultimately resulted in the creation of a separate PhD track within the Department of Classics. When it first hit the books in 1972–73, this specialization was entitled 'Pre-Classical Aegean Archaeology.' By the 1970s, the use of the adjective 'Aegean' to describe Greek prehistory had become increasingly common, and its appearance in several highly visible venues no doubt had much to do with its widespread dissemination (e.g., Crossland and Birchall 1973; Betancourt 1976).

Blegen and Caskey, we suspect, favored the term 'Preclassical Greece' because it permitted them to encompass Crete, the Greek mainland, and the Greek islands under a single heading, with a nod, where appropriate, to the Troad. 'Aegean Prehistory,' although the polysemic nature of the term might serve as a focus for contested national claims (see Margomenou *et al.*, ch. 1, this volume), also seems to us to be a remarkably good way of describing our field of study. Subject matter today embraces geographical areas well outside the boundaries of the Greek state, and objectives have become increasingly detached from explication of the Homeric texts (as demonstrated by the absence of instruction in 'Homeric Archaeology' at UC since World War II) or the origins of the Greeks.

It is the geographical vagueness that promoted more widespread use of the term 'Aegean Prehistory' in the titles of courses at UC since the 1970s, and the phrase has been enshrined in the name of the Institute for Aegean Prehistory and in the title of the bibliographical newsletter, *Nestor* (now officially *Nestor: The Monthly*

5 *Bibliography of Aegean Prehistory and Related Areas*).[1] But at UC the term 'Aegean Prehistory' has itself yet officially to be applied to the PhD degree granted by the Department of Classics. Instead, in 1982–83 the track within the PhD program that is concerned with Aegean prehistory was changed from 'Preclassical Aegean Archaeology' to 'Bronze Age' and is still so called in 2003. The motivation for this change was definitely a desire for geographical flexibility, in particular the quest for a term that could comfortably include Crete, the Greek mainland, and Cyprus. However, Gerald Cadogan, who was in part responsible for the change to 'Bronze Age,' notes (pers. comm.): 'We also wanted to have a more clearly diachronic approach so as to show the continuity from (Neolithic and) Bronze Age to Classical—which of course was the stated aim of the Department.'

It is clear to us in reviewing the history of instruction in Aegean prehistory at UC that, along with greater specialization and the expansion of the methodological, theoretical, geographical, and chronological boundaries of the subject matter included in the Bronze Age degree program, this 'stated aim of the Department' is being increasingly neglected at Cincinnati. This is a universal phenomenon. A telling piece of evidence in support of this supposition is that Morris (2000: 40), in his recent elaboration of Renfrew's (1981) 'Great Divide' concept, singles out the gap between Aegean prehistory and classical archaeology as one of the more lamentable in Mediterranean studies. Such a development raises real concerns about the present relevancy of instruction in Aegean prehistory in any classics department.

Aegean Prehistory and UC: Past and Future

It should be clear from the preceding discussion that the development of one major program in Aegean prehistory, that of the Department of Classics at UC, has reflected developments in the field as a whole, while it has influenced the direction of the practice of Aegean prehistory in America and by Americans. The departure of Blegen from ASCSA in 1927 deprived that institution of its most renowned Aegean prehistorian and of a major source of funding that had previously been available for collaborative fieldwork.

The failure of plans to establish a regular field school at Colophon encouraged ASCSA to concentrate its energies in Corinth and in the newly conceived Agora Excavations, where prehistory was not a major component or focus of fieldwork. Capps was interested in maintaining large-scale permanent excavations, not the short-term exploratory endeavors of which Blegen was so fond.

On the other hand, at Cincinnati Blegen now directly controlled the finances required to launch research programs independently of ASCSA. It initially was his plan to continue excavating in Greece and to organize a series of soundings at Peloponnesian sites other than those in the Corinthia. Hayioryitika was to be only the first component of that venture, and his notebook for 1929 records visits to various sites in Arcadia and Messenia (Blegen Notebook 1929: 9–22; Petrakis 2002). But the resources of the University of Cincinnati also gave Blegen the ability to launch a large-scale expedition to Troy, at the same time as ASCSA was retreating from Turkey to Greece. Still, it is clear from the nature of the academic program that was offered at the University of Cincinnati from 1927 to 1960 that Blegen's concept of Aegean prehistory remained closely bound to the tenets of contemporary Hellenism and was concerned with areas outside Greece principally when they had an impact on a more strictly Greek prehistory or on the interpretation of Greek literary texts.

Semple's own vision for UC was that it should boast an integrated classics department in which philology, history, and archaeology would coexist and would contribute intellectually in a joint pursuit of *Altertumswissenschaft*. From the beginnings of the department there was a strong interest in Aegean prehistory, even prior to Blegen's arrival, and subsequent hiring decisions continued to emphasize this specialization. Men such as Harland, Blegen, and Caskey seem to have had little doubt as to the significance of Aegean prehistory within the wider discipline of classics. Their methods, approaches, and concerns were in common with those of their colleagues, and it was easy to see the relevance of Aegean prehistory within the overall context of Hellenism. In a period when the 'Greekness' of the prehistoric remains of the Greek mainland remained to be proven by means of the decipherment of Linear B, Aegean prehistorians could be seen as pioneers pushing Greek claims over the lands of the Greek nation deep into the remote past by demonstrating continuities in material culture (Tsountas and Manatt 1897; Haley and Blegen 1928; Renfrew 1964; Kotsakis 1998; Karimali 2001; Voutsaki 2002; Voutsaki 2003; Voutsaki in press).

Thus the focus of instruction was on Homeric archaeology, pre-classical Greece, and the origins of the Greeks. Courses in Anatolian, Cypriot, or Near Eastern prehistory were noticeably absent from the curriculum, even though Blegen was intimately familiar with the subject matter and knew well the archaeologists working in these parts of the world. In large part, the topics emphasized in instruction at UC were determined during Blegen's tenure by a desire to present to students an Aegean prehistory that was, in Cadogan's words, in keeping with 'the stated aim of the department': i.e., to emphasize the pre-classical foundations of classical Greece. This remained the case long after his retirement.

In the longer term, however, the resources of the department have given it the ability to follow developments in the field of Aegean prehistory internationally and outside the discipline of classics. While ASCSA has continued to restrict its own operations to the territory of modern Greece, archaeologists at UC have directed fieldwork in Turkey, Albania, and Cyprus (Davis 2004). Although archaeology within the borders of modern Greece very much remains the focus of instruction, the increasing use of terms such as 'Bronze Age' and 'Aegean' to refer to courses and programs at UC does seems to reflect decreasingly parochial and less Hellenocentric attitudes toward the field of Aegean prehistory.

At the same time, an expansion in the geographical and chronological

5

scope of instruction and fieldwork has created a certain tension at UC, as in other American institutions, between Aegean prehistory and the curricula of the departments in which its programs are embedded. In particular, their relevance to the field of classics is no longer taken for granted, as it must have been by scholars of Blegen's generation. In the initial stages of the development of Aegean prehistory, literature and physical remains were considered to be organically related to each other: archaeology was the tangible representation of earliest Greek literature. The recent explosion in the amount of research in Aegean prehistory that is conducted annually and the broadening of the range of topics that seem relevant for investigation by Aegean prehistorians have brought attention to a wide variety of cultural remains that are increasingly removed chronologically and spatially from the central themes of the Homeric texts.

Even at sites such as Mycenae, Sparta, and Troy, which figure prominently in the works of Homer, there has been a tendency to examine archaeological discoveries without reference to texts. While an unsystematic survey of faculty and students within our own department suggests that our colleagues in philology, history, and historical Greek and Roman archaeology are largely supportive of what we do and feel that our research is an integral part of a graduate education in classics, it is important to note that the situation at Cincinnati is unusual in that some two-thirds of its graduate students are specializing in archaeology. One suspects that, even then, an acceptance of Aegean prehistory in our department may rest more on tradition than on any rational grounds.

The opinions of our colleagues seem to us, nonetheless, of considerable importance, inasmuch as the ways in which our fellow students and faculty in a classics department choose to regard us situates us (as prehistorians) and the field of Aegean prehistory in a grid of power relations among other constituencies, all of which are trying to defend the interests of their own members and accordingly to change or maintain the state of affairs in the field of classics (cf. Bourdieu 1988: 18). And such considerations would seem all the more important in departments without venerable traditions in Aegean prehistory.

Inasmuch as some two-fifths of practitioners of Aegean prehistory in the United States are based in classics departments, it is likely that for the foreseeable future the shape of Aegean prehistory there will continue to be molded by the needs of PhDs to find employment in classics. Research topics in the sciences are, for example, unlikely to be favored for dissertations, and a focus on viewing Aegean prehistory as the study of pre-classical Greece will not evaporate soon. The situation of Aegean prehistory in departments of classics will also continue to constrain the geographical expansion of research conducted in the United States by inhibiting the admission to graduate programs of students from countries such as Turkey, Bulgaria, Macedonia, and Albania, who might otherwise play significant roles in shaping an Aegean prehistory that is not defined by the borders of modern Greece. Students from these nations can rarely demonstrate the competence in reading ancient Greek or Latin that is still a fundamental requirement for admission to most graduate programs in classical archaeology in the United States.

Disciplinary Practice from the Bottom Up

It has not been our intention to imply that the present conditions in which Aegean prehistory is practiced in our department are in any way representative of the discipline as a whole. Indeed, it is obvious that the program of Aegean prehistory in it has followed a trajectory that is in many regards unique and that has been molded in part by the availability of an extraordinary permanent endowment and the interests of the faculty who have specialized in Aegean prehistory.

On the other hand, the nature of fieldwork and instruction at UC has been greatly influenced by developments in other American programs, and in those of Europe, at the same time as it has been constrained in its evolution by the role that classicists continue to expect it to play within the discourse of Hellenism. It was, after all, the decision of Semple and his colleagues in a newly created Department of Classics to emphasize fieldwork and instruction in Aegean prehistory, first by bringing Harland, then Blegen, to Cincinnati, and then by reinforcing these initial decisions by continuing to hire scholars with similar interests. In this regard, Aegean prehistorians in Cincinnati find themselves in a situation that differs little from that of most other Aegean prehistorians in the United States.

The main impetus for this particular paper stems at the most general level from a desire to understand why things are the way they are in our field. As Bourdieu has stressed, studying the realm in which we work brings nothing but benefits for our research, since it raises our epistemological vigilance, a tenet pursued in his various studies of the French educational system (Bourdieu 1973; 1977; 1988; Bourdieu and Passeron 1979; in the same vein, see the sociological studies of American universities in Brown 1973). Despite the various criticisms that his work has received, we nevertheless remain convinced that the examination of institutional histories and the sociopolitical conditions determining the shape and structure of our discipline is a very powerful tool in our scholarly toolkit (e.g., Wylie 1983; Soffer 1983; Schlanger 2002: 128–30; Kaesar 2002: 172; Maischberger 2002: 210).

Although classical archaeology has been slow to embrace postmodern perspectives (Morris 2000: 72), a few scholars *have* accepted Bourdieu's challenge to produce analytical disciplinary histories that would help them comprehend 'what they are motivated to see and not to see' (Bourdieu 1988: 150). Stephen L. Dyson, a former president of the AIA, was virtually the first classical archaeologist in the US to compose disciplinary critiques in this genre (Dyson 1981; 1989; 1998). (In the United States scholarly analysis of the sociopolitical conditions concerning the production of archaeological knowledge and the reproduction of structures of power within the discipline has also been a concern of anthropological archaeologists since the early 1980s; see Gero *et al.* 1983.) Mostly in the style of so-called

5   Crisis Literature, his experiential insights into the practices of classical archaeology reflect the general atmosphere that classical archaeologists, and with them Aegean prehistorians, still confront in the United States.

Dyson has explained the nature of the crisis that he and many others, ourselves included, believe exists in classical archaeology: namely, that it has fallen out of step with other fields of archaeology in both its methods and theory. The parameters of discourse in the genre of Crisis Literature have by now been well established (for other examples, see Snodgrass 1987: 1–35; Davis 1994; 2001; Morris 1994; 2000). Common to studies of this type is an emphasis on the complex power relations that exist within those institutions where classical archaeologists are trained or in the institutions abroad that are responsible for representing American archaeologists in the nations of the Mediterranean in which they conduct fieldwork. Such studies have typically revealed multiple hierarchies of power within which classical archaeologists are subordinated and coerced into following traditional practices and that preclude or inhibit contact with other aspects of the academic world outside the discipline, whether in the United States or elsewhere.

For the most part, Crisis Literature has been concerned with classical archaeology as a whole rather than with the individual bodies that comprise the discipline. More recently, however, histories of particular institutions that have practiced archaeology in Mediterranean lands have appeared. In the United States, examinations of the AIA (Allen 2002; Dyson 2002) and of ASCSA (Davis 1994; 2003) have deconstructed the ideology that has fueled the creation of institutional policy and the narratives that have been shaped within these organizations—factors that mold the practice of archaeology by classical archaeologists in the United States.

As yet, however, the specific institutions of Aegean prehistory have received little attention, despite the intense interest in recent years in writing biographies of significant early 'heroes' of our field (e.g., Harden 1983; McDonald and Thomas 1990; Allesbrook 1992; Momigliano 1995; 1996; 1999; Traill 1995; Fitton 1996; Becker and Betancourt 1997; McGillivray 2000). Nor have there yet been published studies of those individual academic programs that have shaped disciplinary practice. This is as true for classical archaeology as for Aegean prehistory, and, indeed, within archaeology as a whole such studies have been uncommon, and often informal (but see Tilley 1989; Sabloff 1998).

We hope in this paper to have begun to fill this void, by providing a case study of one of the many programs that have nourished the field of Aegean prehistory in North America. They, as much as, perhaps even more than, our professional organizations and foreign schools, structure the way in which we think and work, and a holistic critique of disciplinary practice demands attention to them. An understanding of the histories of these programs thus seems essential to comprehending the forces that have created and nurtured the field of Aegean prehistory and that continue to determine the meaning of 'Aegean' for archaeologists. In the words of Alison Wylie (1983: 120):

5

Thus, reflective awareness of context makes it clear that, to some extent, we create the waters in which we swim. This insight has special significance because it immediately opens up the possibility not only of apprehending but of acting on these conditions of existence. It is awareness of this, the possibility of achieving some measure of emancipation from and control over these conditions, that . . .

we may take to be the principal purpose of our contribution to this volume.

Acknowledgments
We are grateful to the organizers of the 2003 Kelsey Museum workshop, 'Prehistorians Round the Pond: Reflections on Aegean Prehistory as a Discipline,' John Cherry, Laurie Talalay, and Despina Margomenou, for including us in the gathering in which an earlier version of this paper was orally delivered. We also thank the staff of the University Archives of the University of Cincinnati, in particular Kevin Grace, for facilitating our access to records of Carl Blegen that are curated there, the staff of the Archives of the American School of Classical Studies at Athens, Natalia Vogeikoff-Brogan (Archivist) and Evi Sikla, for many pleasant days spent examining the correspondence of Bert Hodge Hill and Carl Blegen that belongs to their collection, and Stephanie Kennell and Sophia Voutsaki for copies of their papers. Finally, we are extremely grateful to Jennifer Glaubius for assistance in preparation of illustrations.

Note
1.   The term 'Aegean Prehistory' was commonly in use at Indiana University in the 1970s and appeared in the title of the first edition of the *International Directory of Aegean Prehistorians* (Petruso and Talalay 1984). Cf. also the prominence of the term 'Aegean' in the title of the 'New York Aegean Bronze Age Colloquium,' founded in 1973.

References
Special abbreviations:

ADM	American School of Classical Studies at Athens Archives, ADM REC Series, Athens, Greece.
ASCSA 1927–28	Forty-Seventh Annual Report of the Managing Committee of the American School of Classical Studies at Athens, 1927–1928.
Blegen Notebook 1929	Carl W. Blegen, Pylos Notebook for 1929 and 1939. Original in Archives of ASCSA. Microfilm in Archives of the Department of Classics of the University of Cincinnati.
UA-83-15	University of Cincinnati, Archives and Rare Books, Carl W. Blegen Papers UA-83-15

5 Allen, S. H.
     2002   The archaeology of the AIA: an introduction. In S. H. Allen (ed.), *Excavating Our Past: Perspectives on the History of the Archaeological Institute of America,* 1–25. Boston: Archaeological Institute of America.
Allsebrook, M.
     1992   *Born to Rebel: The Life of Harriet Boyd Hawes.* Oxford: Oxbow Books.
Becker, M. J., and P. P. Betancourt
     1997   *Richard Berry Seager: Pioneer Archaeologist and Proper Gentleman.* Philadelphia: University of Pennsylvania, Museum of Archaeology and Anthropology.
Betancourt, P. P. (ed.)
     1976   *Temple University Aegean Symposium* 1. Philadelphia: Department of Art History, Temple University.
Blegen, C. W.
     1941   Preclassical Greece. In *Studies in the Arts and Architecture,* 1–14. Philadelphia, University of Pennsylvania Press.
Bourdieu, P.
     1977   *Outline of a Theory of Practice.* Cambridge: Cambridge University Press.
Bourdieu, P.
     1988   *Homo Academicus.* Cambridge: Polity Press.
Bourdieu, P., and J.-C. Passeron
     1979   *The Inheritors: French Students and Their Relation to Culture.* Chicago: University of Chicago Press.
Brown, R. (ed.)
     1973   *Knowledge, Education, and Cultural Change: Papers in the Sociology of Education.* London: Tavistock Publications.
Cadogan, G.
     2004   Mervyn Reddaway Popham. *Proceedings of the British Academy* 120: 345–61.
Caskey, J. L.
     1963   Necrology. *American Journal of Archaeology* 67: 81–82.
Casson, S.
     1927   *Essays in Aegean Archaeology Presented to Sir Arthur Evans in Honour of his 75th Birthday.* Oxford: The Clarendon Press.
Chadwick, J.
     1956   The Greek dialects and Greek prehistory. *Greece and Rome* (series 2) 3: 38–50.
Cherry, J. F., and J. L. Davis
     1995a   *International Directory of Aegean Prehistorians.* 2nd ed. Ann Arbor and Cincinnati: University of Michigan and University of Cincinnati.

1995b   Aegean prehistory in 1994: results of the IDAP survey questionnaire. pdf file accessible at http://classics.uc.edu/nestor/IDAP/isearch.lasso.

Crossland, R. A., and A. Birchall (eds.)

1973   *Bronze Age Migrations in the Aegean: Archaeological and Linguistic Problems in Greek Prehistory.* Proceedings of the First International Colloquium on Aegean Prehistory. London: Duckworth.

Cullen, T.

2001   Introduction: voices and visions of Aegean prehistory. In T. Cullen (ed.), *Aegean Prehistory: A Review. American Journal of Archaeology* supplement 1: 1–18. Boston: Archaeological Institute of America.

Davis, J. L.

1994   Regional studies in Greece: a *vade mecum?* In P. N. Kardulias (ed.), *Beyond the Site: Regional Studies in the Aegean Area,* 398–405. Lanham: University Press of America.

2001   Classical archaeology and anthropological archaeology in North America: a meeting of minds at the millennium? In G. M. Feinman and T. D. Price (eds.), *Archaeology at the Millennium: A Sourcebook,* 415–37. New York: Kluwer Academic/Plenum.

2003   A foreign school of archaeology and the politics of archaeological practice: Anatolia, 1922. *Journal of Mediterranean Archaeology* 16: 145–72.

2004   *Mediterranean Expeditions: Archaeological Field Research by the Department of Classics. A Brief Overview Compiled on the Eightieth Anniversary of the First Departmental Excavations at Nemea in 1924.* Cincinnati: Department of Classics, University of Cincinnati.

Dyson, S. L.

1981   A Classical archaeologist's response. *Bulletin of the American Schools of Oriental Research* 242: 7–13.

1989   Complacency and crisis in late twentieth century Classical archaeology. In P. Culham and L. Edmunds (eds.), *Classics: A Discipline and Profession in Crisis,* 211–20. New York: University Press of America.

1998   *Ancient Marbles to American Shores: Classical Archaeology in the United States.* Philadelphia: University of Pennsylvania.

2002   The Archaeological Institute of America between the wars. In S. H. Allen (ed.), *Excavating our Past: Perspectives on the History of the Archaeological Institute of America,* 157–68. Boston: Archaeological Institute of America.

Fitton, J. L.

1996   *The Discovery of the Greek Bronze Age.* Cambridge, Mass.: Harvard University Press.

Gero, J. M., D. M. Lacy, and M. L. Blakey (eds.)

1983   *The Socio-politics of Archaeology.* Research Reports 23. Amherst: Department of Anthropology.

5

5   Haley, J. B., and C. W. Blegen
      1928   The coming of the Greeks. *American Journal of Archaeology* 32: 141–54.

Hall, H. R.
      1915   *Aegean Archaeology: An Introduction to the Archaeology of Prehistoric Greece.* London: Philip Lee Warner.

Hamilakis, Y.
      2002   What future for the 'Minoan' past? Re-thinking Minoan archaeology. In Y. Hamilakis (ed.), *Labyrinth Revisited: Rethinking 'Minoan' Archaeology*, 2–28. Oxford: Oxbow Books.

Harden, D. B.
      1983   *Sir Arthur Evans, 1851–1941: 'A Memoir.'* Oxford: Ashmolean Museum.

Harland, J. P.
      1925   *Prehistoric Aigina: A History of the Island in the Bronze Age.* Paris: H. Champion.

Kaisar, M.-A.
      2002   On the international roots of prehistory. *Antiquity* 76: 170–77.

Karimali, L.
      2001   Όψεις και αναγνώσεις της Νεολιθικής Εποχής· Η περίπτωση του Αιγαίου. *Αρχαιολογία και Τέχνες* 60: 67–71.

Kennell, S.
      2002   Schliemann and the foreign schools. *Pharos* 10: 135–56.

Kotsakis, K.
      1998   The past is ours: images of Greek Macedonia. In L. Meskell (ed.), *Archaeology under Fire: Nationalism, Politics, and Heritage in the Eastern Mediterranean and Middle East*, 44–67. London: Routledge.

Kuhn, T. S.
      1970   Reflection on my critics. In I. Lakatos and A. Musgrave (eds.), *Criticism and the Growth of Knowledge*, 231–78. Cambridge: Cambridge University Press.

Lord, L. E.
      1947   *History of the American School of Classical Studies at Athens 1882–1942: An Intercollegiate Project.* Cambridge, Mass.: American School of Classical Studies at Athens.

MacGillivray, J. A.
      2000   *Minotaur: Sir Arthur Evans and the Archaeology of the Minoan Myth.* New York: Hill and Wang.

McDonald, W. A., and C. G. Thomas
      1990   *Progress into the Past: The Rediscovery of Mycenaean Civilization.* 2nd ed. Bloomington: Indiana University Press.

McEnroe, J. C.

    2002   Politics and archaeology 1898–1913. In Y. Hamilakis (ed.), *Labyrinth Revisited: Rethinking 'Minoan' Archaeology*, 59–72. Oxford: Oxbow Books.

Maischberger, M.

    2002   German archaeology during the Third Reich, 1933–45: a case study based on archival evidence. *Antiquity* 76: 209–18.

Momigliano, N.

    1995   Duncan Mackenzie: a cautious canny Highlander. In C. Morris (ed.), *Klados: Essays in Honour of J. N. Coldstream. Bulletin of the Institute of Classical Studies* supplement 63: 163–70. London: Institute of Classical Studies, University of London.

    1996   Evans, Mackenzie, and the history of the Palace at Knossos. *Journal of Hellenic Studies* 116: 166–69.

    1999   *Duncan Mackenzie: A Cautious Canny Highlander and the Palace of Minos at Knossos. Bulletin of the Institute of Classical Studies* supplement 72. London: Institute of Classical Studies, University of London.

Morris, I.

    1994   Archaeologies of Greece. In I. Morris (ed.), *Classical Greece: Ancient Histories and Modern Archaeologies*, 8–47. Cambridge: Cambridge University Press

    2000   *Archaeology as Cultural History: Words and Things in Iron Age Greece.* Malden: Blackwell.

Muhly, J. D. (ed.)

    2000   *Crete 2000: A Centennial Celebration of American Archaeological Work on Crete (1900–2000).* Athens: American School of Classical Studies at Athens and the INSTAP Study Center for East Crete.

Palmer, L. R.

    1961   *Mycenaeans and Minoans: Aegean Prehistory in the Light of the Linear B Tablets.* London: Faber and Faber.

Petrakis, S. L.

    2002   *Ayioryitika: The 1928 Excavations of Carl Blegen at a Neolithic to Early Helladic Settlement in Arcadia.* Philadelphia: Institute for Aegean Prehistory Academic Press.

Petruso, K. M., and L. E. Talalay (eds.)

    1984   *International Directory of Aegean Prehistorians.* Bloomington: Program in Classical Archaeology.

Preziosi, D.

    2002   Archaeology as museology: rethinking the Minoan past. In Y. Hamilakis (ed.), *Labyrinth Revisited: Rethinking 'Minoan' Archaeology*, 30–39. Oxford: Oxbow Books.

5 Renfrew, C.

    1964   Crete and the Cyclades before Rhadamanthus. *Κρητικά Χρονικά* 18: 107–41.

    1981   The Great Tradition versus the Great Divide: archaeology as anthropology? *American Journal of Archaeology* 84: 287–98.

Sabloff, P. L. W.

    1998   *Conversations with Lew Binford: Drafting the New Archaeology*. Norman: University of Oklahoma Press.

Schachermeyr, F.

    1951   Die ägäische Frühzeit (Kreta und Mykenai). *Anzeiger für die Altertumswissenschaft* 4: 5–30.

Schlanger, N.

    2002   Ancestral archives: explorations in the history of archaeology. *Antiquity* 76: 127–31.

Shanks, M.

    1996   *Classical Archaeology of Greece: Experiences of the Discipline*. London: Routledge.

Soffer, O.

    1983   Politics of the Palaeolithic in the USSR: a case of paradigms lost. In J. M. Gero, D. M. Lacy, and M. L. Blakey (eds.), *The Socio-politics of Archaeology*. Research Reports 23: 91–105. Amherst: Department of Anthropology, University of Massachusetts.

Snodgrass, A. M.

    1987   *An Archaeology of Greece: The Present State and Future Scope of a Discipline*. Berkeley: University of California Press.

Sperling, J.

    1937   Troy I. Unpublished PhD dissertation, Department of Classics, University of Cincinnati.

Tilley, C.

    1989   Discourse and power: the genre of the Cambridge inaugural lecture. In D. Miller, M. Rowlands, and C. Tilley (eds.), *Domination and Resistance*, 41–62. London: Unwin Hyman.

Traill, D.

    1995   *Schliemann of Troy: Treasure and Deceit*. New London: John Murray.

Tsountas, Ch., and J. I. Manatt

    1897   *The Mycenaean Age: A Study of the Monuments and Culture of Pre-Homeric Greece*. Boston and New York: Houghton, Mifflin.

Voutsaki, S.

    2002   The Greekness of Greek prehistory: an investigation of the debate 1876–1900. *Pharos* 10: 105–22.

2003   Archaeology and the construction of the past in 19th century Greece. In H. Hokwerda (ed.), *Constructions of the Greek Past: Identity and Historical Consciousness from Antiquity to the Present*, 231–55. Gronigen: Egbert Forsten.

in press The Hellenization of the prehistoric past. In S. Voutsaki and P. Cartledge (eds.), *Ancient Monuments and Modern Identities: The History of Archaeology in 19th and 20th Century Greece*. London: Ashgate.

Wobst, H. M., and A. S. Keene

1983   Archaeological explanation as political economy. In J. M. Gero, D. M. Lacy, and M. L. Blakey (eds.), *The Socio-politics of Archaeology*. Research Reports 23: 79–89. Amherst: Department of Anthropology, University of Massachusetts.

Wright, J. C., J. F. Cherry, J. L. Davis, E. Mantzourani, S. B. Sutton, and R. F. Sutton Jr

1990   The Nemea Valley Archaeological Project: a preliminary report. *Hesperia* 59: 579–659.

Wylie, M. A.

1983   Comments on the 'socio-politics of archaeology': the de-mystification of the profession. In J. M. Gero, D. M. Lacy, and M. L. Blakey (eds.), *The Socio-politics of Archaeology*. Research Reports 23: 119–30. Amherst: Department of Anthropology, University of Massachusetts.

6 The Aegean Prehistorian's Role in Classical Studies Today

Bryan E. Burns

Abstract

This paper explores connections between Aegean prehistory and other subfields of classical studies in a reconsideration of the Aegean prehistorian's present disciplinary situation. I examine the ways that Aegeanists in particular have been encouraged to cross the boundaries that separate archaeological specialties and highlight recent archaeological inquiries in order to present current options and new directions in classical archaeology.

My chief goal is to move away from the continued description of classical studies in terms of its tradition and to reframe the current discipline as a home for the various topics and themes pursued within Aegean prehistory and other subfields. Today's discipline of classics should be defined less in terms of its own heritage and more by the collection of methods brought to bear on the diverse cultures of the ancient Mediterranean.

Introduction

I was invited to participate in the 2003 Kelsey Museum workshop to share my perspective on Aegean prehistory as a junior faculty member in an American classics department. Other archaeologists, housed in departments of anthropology or art history and in regional programs such as Near Eastern studies or Mediterranean archaeology, have their own tales to tell. Many discussions within Aegean studies about the intellectual health of our specialty focus on creating a dialogue among these various disciplines. It is equally important, however, to maintain an awareness of the various strengths that contribute to classical studies and the ways in which archaeology can participate.

Self-reflection hit classics and Greek archaeology hard in the 1980s and 1990s, leading to publications that warmly welcomed New Archaeology (Snodgrass 1985; Dyson 1993), surveyed the history of classical archaeology (Morris 1994; Dyson 1998), expressed concern for the survival of an isolated field (Culham and Edmunds 1989), and demonstrated the possible benefits of a theoretically informed approach (Snodgrass 1987; Spencer 1995; Shanks 1996). These works were motivated by the concern to maintain one's territorial existence in the academic landscape, as well as to negotiate, shift, or break down disciplinary boundaries. Some scholarly divisions intensified during the middle of the twentieth century, such as the distinction between archaeologist and historian (Morris 1997: 119) or the more

6

general divisions between humanities and science or New World and Old World studies (cf. Renfrew 1980: 292). With reference to Aegean archaeology, however, the first disciplinary rifts developed along chronological lines and were encouraged by those seeking to protect the Classical period from its newly discovered predecessors—the Minoan and Mycenaean eras—and their promoters.

Though Heinrich Schliemann was heralded as the founder of a whole new field of archaeological study, reaction to his initial discoveries and claims were mixed. Initial judgments, such as those in the *Edinburgh Review* and *Quarterly Review*, typically lauded his energy and persistence but criticized his connections of artifacts to classical deities and legendary heroes as part of a tendency to aggrandize his discoveries. Schliemann's use or misuse of Homer in his interpretation of finds at Troy, Mycenae, and Tiryns was countered by close readings of the material culture described in the *Iliad* and *Odyssey*, which were marshaled to demonstrate the distance between prehistoric and later periods (Gardner 1882; Jebb 1886). The assertion that Homeric Greece was more akin to the culture of the Classical period justified a view of the Bronze Age as peripheral to classical studies proper.

The additional dramatic discovery of Knossos, and Sir Arthur Evans's promotion of himself and the Minoan culture, exacerbated a growing fear of the Bronze Age in some camps. Charles Waldstein, art historian and excavator of the Argive Heraion, found the burgeoning field of Aegean prehistory a direct threat to classical archaeology. He cautioned his contemporaries that 'we are in danger of losing the sense of proportion, of losing sight of the true essence of classical antiquity, owing to the newness and the consequent vividness of interest pertaining to the prehistoric aspect of classical study' (Waldstein 1909: 519). His solution was a clear disciplinary focus: 'the head and forefront of classical studies will always be the highest literature, art and philosophy of the ancient Greeks and Romans,' at the expense of Aegean prehistory which should be relegated to the 'wider departments of Anthropology and Ethnology' (520). Contrary to Waldstein's recommendations, Aegean prehistory has found a place within classical studies, which has, however, led to its isolation from other fields.

My aim in this paper is not to trace the development of disciplinary divides but rather to see where we stand today, what gulfs remain, and what bridges are available. Below, I reconsider two aspects of the Aegean prehistorian's position *vis-à-vis* classical studies: first in its role as a disciplinary intermediary with the more theoretically dynamic field of anthropological archaeology; and second, as the cultural connection-maker between the prehistoric Aegean and the text-rich periods of later Greece. Following this assessment of Aegean prehistory's own tradition, I offer an alternative model for the Aegeanist's contributions to classical studies today. My goal is to move away from the continued description of classical studies in terms of its tradition and to reframe the current discipline as a home for the various topics and themes brought by Aegean prehistory and other subfields. Today's discipline of classics should be defined less in terms of its own heritage and more by the collection of methods brought to bear on the diverse cultures of the ancient Mediterranean. Thus, the connections that I promote are not those made through the rubric of similarities and continuities but through explicit comparisons and an emphasis on the cultural and chronological context of dynamic interactions.

Aegeanists as Archaeologists Crossing the Disciplinary Divide

Colin Renfrew (1980) characterized the state of classical archaeology in terms of the 'Great Tradition' and the 'Great Divide.' His influential paper established the 'tradition' as shorthand for classical studies—including philology, history, and art history—and the 'divide' for the enduring distance between classical and anthropological archaeologies. Having authored a major study that was already of interest to both traditional Aegeanists and New Archaeology processualists (1972), Renfrew spoke with authority when he asserted that classical and anthropological archaeology have much to gain from each other. With further examples of publications, data sets, and common themes of inquiry drawn from Bronze Age Aegean (1980: 296–97), Renfrew set a precedent for Aegean scholars to continue crossing the divide with fruitful results.

This ambassadorial role has become customary for the Aegeanist, as demonstrated in recent articles commissioned as updates on classical archaeology for a decidedly non-classicist audience. John Bennet and Michael Galaty's 1997 article 'Classical archaeology' was written for the *Journal of Archaeological Research*, a periodical whose emphasis on archaeological method and science rarely includes Mediterranean case studies. As indicated by their subtitle, 'recent developments in the archaeology of the prehistoric Aegean and regional studies,' Bennet and Galaty focused selectively on the earlier periods of the classical past. Their review of literature and issues presented the study of the Aegean in terms accessible to archaeologists working in other regions. But the virtual exclusion of historical periods was a missed opportunity.

Jack Davis (2001) attempted a more chronologically balanced review of the field for a millennial collection assembled by the editors of the *Journal of Archaeological Research*. Davis set a negative tone from the beginning, judging that Renfrew's great divide 'remains an enormous gulf' and naming one obstacle to enlightened anthropologists working on the 'untapped gold mine' of classical data: the 'gigantic mound of literature' produced by such long-term excavations as Corinth and the Athenian Agora (2001: 416–18). Seeking to forge bonds, Davis courted the anthropologists with lengthy appraisals of problems in prehistory—the Greek version (2001: 421–29), followed by a nod to studies on the rise of the Greek *polis* and the expansion of Roman imperial power (2001: 429–30). His affirmation of classical archaeology, however, gives little indication of the value of classical texts to these studies of social complexity in more historical periods.

As the previous Aegean reviewers (Renfrew, Bennet and Galaty, and Davis) have noted, classical studies is enlivened by the incorporation of theory and a

6   comparative method. The lament that much of classical archaeology continues in a course independent from the trends of anthropological, art-historical, literary, or sociological development should not lead to greater isolation. The quantity of assembled literature should not be presented as an obstacle to non-classicists (Davis 2001: 420); most primary texts are widely available in English translations (Renfrew 1980: 289), and publications from the long-standing excavations are available in nearly every research library across the country. Increasingly, these texts, reports, and growing archives are further accessible through web sites and electronic collections. I emphasize that the 'great tradition,' rather than a hindrance, provides stable foundations for today's scholars, many of whom are in touch with the currents of anthropological and archaeological theory.

The formation and organization of complexity is an area of research common to the archaeologies of all stratified societies, and the development of this topic within classical archaeology has certainly kept pace with anthropology. The emergence of the Minoan palace in Bronze Age Crete and the rise of the Greek *polis* during the Iron Age received major treatment with the applications of New Archaeology (Renfrew 1972; Snodgrass 1977) and continue to receive processualist attention (Cherry 1984; Morris 1987; Dabney and Wright 1990; Morgan and Whitelaw 1991; Whitley 1991). While focusing on the specifics of ancient Greece, this body of work, as a whole, compares favorably with the individual case studies of other geographical regions (Arnold and Gibson 1998; Covey 2003; Papadopoulos and Leventhal 2003). Comparative analysis seeking to redefine and elaborate categories of chiefdoms and states (Wright 1994; Feinman 1998) may lead to some questions about how well the cultural organizations of the prehistoric Aegean meet the qualifications of state-level society (Small 1999). This inquiry is matched, however, by major efforts to understand better the nature of the Greek *polis*, including a comparative evaluation of city-state scale and structure across world cultures (Hansen 2000). Both classical and anthropological archaeologists have questioned the presumed importance of time and place in state formation (Cherry 1983; Spencer 1990) and also critiqued the dominance of evolutionary schemata over perceptions of social change (Morris 1992b; Yoffee 1995).

Archaeological approaches to the dynamics within the mature Greek city-state, usually Athens, have developed through the more postprocessual questions about various forms of power and agency. Recent advances have turned away from the major monuments of public spaces, contemplating more personal venues such as the relation of individuals to domestic architecture (Nevett 1995; Morris 1999) and material culture (Stewart 1997; Neer 2002). These studies have much to draw on, not least of which is the corpus of literary and documentary texts directly relevant to the wide range of art and artifacts preserved from classical Greek cities. They are also well served by the typological studies and inventories that have traditionally dominated classical scholarship, including textual concordances, reports of large-scale excavations, and catalogue-driven monographs. The background of classical philology, history, and archaeology provides comprehensive data for new consideration. The classifications of Corinthian pottery produced by Payne (1931) and more recently Amyx (1988), for example, were not designed for, but have ably furnished, the more postmodern musings of Michael Shanks (1995; 1999).

Drawing on the full range of the tradition's resources, classical archaeologists have also brought a nuanced perspective to the study of time, a special province of archaeological studies. In part, this stems from the diachronic perspective surface survey has brought to landscape studies, a field also charged by questions of identity, ethnicity, and memory (Cherry *et al.* 1991; Whitley 1998; Alcock 2002). Looming large in the Greek landscape were the sites and monuments of earlier generations, especially the Bronze Age citadels connected with local heroes, from the Iron Age on (Nilsson 1932; van Leuven 1996). Focused excavations, or the full report of earlier excavations, have clarified the relationship between these phases at various sites. Within the Argolid, for example, clear distinctions are now evident among cases once thought similar: Tiryns, where Building T was built directly atop the palatial megaron in LH IIIC (Maran 2000); Mycenae, where a more significant distance in time and form separates the Archaic temple from palatial remains (Klein 1997); and the Argive Heraion, where the temple terrace mimicking Bronze Age masonry was part of the Archaic construction program (Antonaccio 1992). Broader interpretive studies have presented patterns for Iron Age through Roman activity at a variety of Bronze Age monuments or ruins (Antonaccio 1994; Mazarakis Ainian 1997; Alcock 2002: esp. 99–131; Prent 2003), suggesting possible meanings and dynamics that are far more compelling than simple continuity.

This attention to the accretion of monuments, ruins, and memories over time has spurred reflection on how to approach the past in the present, as well as the past in the past (Fotiadis 1995; Hamilakis and Yalouris 1996; Bradley and Williams 1998). A growing awareness of the active refashioning of the past's monuments suggests that perceived continuities in the archaeological record were shaped through acts of interpretation, identification, and even reconstruction. With that in mind, I return to the debated relationship between prehistoric and historical eras of ancient Greece, for this too was a venue for reshaping the past.

Aegeanists as Classicists Crossing the Chronological Divide

Whether Aegean prehistory properly held a place within classical studies was a question initially framed in terms of finding the Bronze Age origins of Greek culture and determining the ethnic identity of Mycenaeans and Minoans (Hall 2002: 30–55). Percy Gardner once described the importance of the *Journal of Hellenic Studies*, under his own editorship, as deriving chiefly from the study of prehistory:

> The *Journal* contains much good work in the field of really Hellenic literature, history, and art; yet perhaps its contributions to the Greek origins and the record of pre-Hellenic Greece have been even more remarkable.

6   In a Darwinian age the search into origins has a strong attraction, and
one cannot regret a tendency which has done so much to make known
what one may call the prolegomena to Greek history and antiquities.
(Gardner in Jebb 1904: lxxii)

Gardner's appreciation for prehistory appears tempered by his distinction between
prehistory and 'really Hellenic' subjects. Some seven years later, upon stepping
down from the presidency of the Society for the Promotion of Hellenic Studies,
Gardner clearly came to regret his earlier generosity. He expressed a fear, similar
to Waldstein's (above), that Hellenic studies would lose their focus if students' enthusiasm for the new discovery of early phases might lead them 'to overvalue mere
antiquity, to care more for the root than for the leaves and the fruit' (Gardner 1911:
lix). Asserting that greater understanding of the Minoan and Mycenaean civilizations indicated how distinct the Late Bronze Age was from Homeric and historical Greece, he sounded an ominous warning not to reach too far: 'the chasm div-
ing pre-historic from historic Greece is growing wider and deeper; and those who
were at first disposed to leap over it now recognize that such feats are impossible.'
Gardner's warning went unheeded; directly following his speech the Society elected
Arthur Evans as his successor.

Evans offered a direct response to Gardner's plea for a renewed classical
concentration, with an essay appropriate for the 'days of origins.' He claimed that
'scientific study of Greek civilization is becoming less and less possible without
taking into constant account that of the Minoan and Mycenaean world that went
before it' (1912: 277). Evans, of course, emphasized the Minoan and promoted a
unity that was based not on the observation of Hellenic origins in the Bronze Age
but phrased instead in terms of non-Hellenic survivals in Homeric and classical
Greece. Evans's argument for the continued existence of the Great Goddess of Minoan Crete in later art and religion balanced with similar connections promoted
by Schliemann, such as his identification of 'cow-faced idols' with Homer's *Hera
Boöpis* (1880: 10–22). A tradition was now firmly established, and connections
between the Aegean Bronze Age and later periods of classical antiquity were assembled (Nilsson 1932), despite the growing conviction that the Dark Age divided
Homer from the Mycenaeans (Morris 1997).

Readings of Mycenaean iconography through Greek religion and the histo-
ricization of myths through archaeology continued into current scholarship as well.
A number of influential scholars support specific connections between later myths
and Bronze Age texts, topography, and material culture, if not events. The remarkable similarity between Homeric descriptions and Bronze Age art is envisioned as
evidence for later society's recorded memories of the Mycenaean era (Shear 2001)
or, alternatively, for shared poetic traditions between the Late Bronze Age and Iron
Age (Morris 1989). Other specific connections have been bolstered by Linear B
evidence. Emily Vermeule, for example, compiled a body of archaeological and

textual evidence in support of a Bronze Age 'Seven Against Thebes' (1987) that nearly proves too compelling to resist. Similarly, Sarah Immerwahr's parallel of the Theseus myths with the regional dynamics of Mycenaean Attica and the relations between Athens and Crete (1971: 156) may find further support in the Linear B tablet from Knossos that suggests a link with the city of Athens (Gulizio *et al.* 2001).

Similarities, to be sure, existed between Bronze Age and Iron Age Greece. Connections can be drawn between periods of classical antiquity, and continuities do exist across time and space. Documented similarity in agricultural and pastoral practices (Forbes 1976; Snyder and Kippel 2000; Palmer 2001) and more fundamental aspects of material culture (Snodgrass 2002) may be part of common strategies for survival in the Greek landscape. At a basic level, these likenesses unite prehistory and the classical tradition, and they have been employed variously to legitimize the place of Aegean prehistory within Greek archaeology, as well as the modern Greek state and the larger Western tradition (Morris 1997; Peckham 2001). This chain of similarities, however, makes dangerous underpinnings for the contemporary field of classical studies. I say that, in general, because emphasizing the sameness of cultures or chronological periods flattens the richness of antiquity into a static continuum. In terms of archaeological interpretation, common images and objects do not necessarily have the same significance in distinct contexts; various activities might leave the same partial trace in the archaeological record. With respect to this particular issue of the 'Dark Age,' continuities in Greek culture are arguably the product of repeated artistic and cultural influence from the eastern Mediterranean (Morris 1992a), but the various connections between specific places in different periods should not be reduced to a general common culture or phenomenon. Instead, we should strive to define the particular nature of interactions across time and space, which demonstrate that the past was a valuable resource, alongside other external sources of inspiration and power.

The inclusion of prehistory can do much more than expand the chronological range of a field already supplied by historical periods with tremendous amounts of data from diverse cultures. When connected with later periods in classical studies, the Bronze Age need not be presented in terms of origins. In general, I prefer to take an anthropological approach and make comparisons not to find origins or show continuity but to understand what is particular to each culture. In exploring various themes within Greek archaeology, Bronze Age examples provide for a methodological consideration of how to use material culture, in isolation or in combination with textual material. Whether those texts are Linear B tablets, Homeric poetry, or later histories, the time and place of their authorship must be carefully considered. Just because the Greeks placed various inventions and events in an heroic past does not mean that we should look for the origins of Archaic and Classical Greek culture in the Bronze Age.

6   Well before the decipherment of Linear B demonstrated that many of the
Olympian gods had sanctuaries in the Late Bronze Age, Nilsson (1927) portrayed
Greek religion as descending from the prehistoric Aegean. The discovery of Bronze
Age material at major sanctuaries prompted theories of Mycenaean founding, although often this material was unstratified or from secondary deposits—as recently demonstrated for Aegina and Isthmia (Pilafidis-Williams 1998; Morgan 1999:
295–343). Stronger indications are found at Eleusis, where Michael Cosmopoulos
(2003) has asserted independent evidence for the religious character of a Bronze
Age structure; there exists, however, no evidence for direct continuity between
the cults of the Mycenaean megaron and the Archaic telesterion (Darcque 1981).
Perhaps the best-known case for the continued rebuilding of a cult space is the
temple at Ayia Irini on Keos, with phases that likely ran unbroken from the Middle
Bronze Age through Hellenistic periods (Caskey 1986). It would appear, however,
that there were significant changes in the focus of ritual activity, as suggested by
the reappearance of the terracotta head from a 15th-century BC female statue as
an object of worship in the 8th-century shrine. Rather than being recognized as an
image akin to a Minoan goddess, this head is far more likely, and no less interestingly, to be identified with Dionysos, the deity worshipped at the shrine from the
Archaic period onward.

Associations continue to be made, apparently to add prestige or character
to prehistoric finds that need no embellishment. To some extent, this might be
described as a 'fear of anonymity,' stemming from the lack of known personalities
from the Bronze Age proper and the perceived pressures of tourism and the popular press (Darcque 2003). The excavation of a settlement near the rock-cut tholos
tombs of Pellana, for example, sheds important light on the history of Mycenaean
Laconia, independent of an alleged connection with Helen and Menelaus (Spyropoulos 2002). Similarly, the newly discovered sanctuary site at Ayios Konstantinos
on Methana commands attention because of its extensive and well-preserved remains in a somewhat peripheral location. It is altogether unnecessary for the excavator, Eleni Konsolaki, to link worship here to the later 'earth-shaker' Poseidon or
to promote this as the sanctuary 'from which the most prominent cults of Troeze-
nia originated' (2002: esp. 35–36). Bronze Age sanctuaries are implicated not only
in claims about the origins of Greek religion but also in the study of the ancient
Olympics and the initiatory practices of Dorian pederasty.

Bronze Age sports are often brought into the search for the origins of the
Olympic games. Compared to the athletic events of the early Olympics and those
recorded in Homer, such as those held for the funeral of Patroklos, the activities depicted in Minoan and Mycenaean art appear somewhat removed (Vermeule 1987:
141; Renfrew 1988). The hypothesis that games at Olympia developed in connection with the funerary cult of the hero Pelops dates the beginnings earlier than the
traditional date of 776 BC, but no evidence exists for Bronze Age activity in the
Pelopeion or Mycenaean cult at the site, in general (Eder 2001). Their dissociation

from the Olympics, however, hardly exhausts the possible lessons to be learned from the prehistoric representations of athletic competition. Mycenaean scenes of chariot racing and processions, for example, need not be connected with any later tradition (Mylonas 1951; Rystedt 1988) in order to be seen as an important device for elite self-representation in the various contexts of the Shaft Grave stele, palatial wall-paintings, or on ceramic vessels.

The publication of a remarkable ivory figurine from Palaikastro in eastern Crete also calls upon its iconography to bridge time and space. This single artifact is the most compelling evidence for the classification of a town shrine 100 m and 1,700 years away from a later cult of Diktaian Zeus (MacGillivray *et al.* 2000). Identification of the 'Palaikastro kouros' as an early appearance of this youthful Cretan Zeus folds into the argument that Cretan initiation of the Archaic period (Dover 1978: esp. 185) has a Minoan precedent (Koehl 1986). This project is akin to a search for the origins of Greek homosexuality (Halperin 1997: 40–43; cf. Dover 1978: 194). While depictions of age differences in Aegean art do suggest initiatory groupings, evidence of same-sex desire is lacking. Such nuanced aspects of sexuality are challenging to recover in prehistory, just as true access to the emotions of any ancient individual, even in historical periods, is difficult (Dixon 1997). Other aspects of gendered life are well explored through archaeological evidence (Donald and Hurcombe 2000; Arnold and Wicker 2001; Nelson and Rosen-Ayalon 2002), but those looking for material correlates of love and desire might remember Emily Vermeule's realization that 'murder and incest are not archaeologically datable' (1987: 128). Murder, at least in some cases, is archaeologically detectable; but when it comes to the more ephemeral aspects of past lives, it is little wonder that prehistorians are so drawn to historical parallels.

Conclusion

This paper has concentrated on divisions and differences, some of which don't need to be bridged or resolved. There are limits to what we can know about the past, especially the prehistoric past. In pushing those limits, we must branch out widely in order to find new approaches, appropriate questions, and creative parallels. Our inquiries, however, should not always find the same answers. Models borrowed from other places and periods will not fit perfectly, and it is in the gaps that we may find the most important elements of each culture. The ambassadorial role Aegeanists are able to play should not only be directed out toward anthropology but maintained within classics as well. We should strengthen classical archaeology as a whole by engaging with later periods as well as prehistoric ones, not in terms of origins and sameness but to better understand the diversity of the ancient world. By demonstrating specific differences between Bronze Age and Iron Age Greece, for example, we can better appreciate the efforts through which classical Greece laid claim to its heroic past.

The field of classics has shown itself to be remarkably flexible, enduring the increasing specialization of subfields and the inclusion of cultures and topics

6 once thought to be too marginal—geographically, chronologically, or intellectually. Today, classical studies encompasses cultures that were in conflict with one another and cultures that have little in common. Aegean archaeologists have wandered off into the world of anthropology, among other jungles, but as a group we remain with at least one foot planted in the field of classics. We do not need to justify that position by emphasizing the prehistoric foundations of high classical cultures. Rather, we will help make classics firm and fertile ground by valuing our contribution, as well as others'.

If accepted as an area study, classics is free to expand the chronological range of the discipline and to emphasize the complexity and diversity of the ancient Mediterranean. The growth of classical studies to include new approaches and methods of research leads one to ask whether Aegean prehistory must continue to play an intermediary role across the disciplinary divide. I hope the answer is yes, but not just for Aegeanists; classicists of all types should be conversant with method and theory of disciplines relevant to their own specialization. That, of course, raises the question of what holds together these varied studies of dissociated cultures—and I hope there are many contradictory answers.

References

Alcock, S. E.
> 2002   *Archaeologies of the Greek Past: Landscape, Monuments, and Memories.* Cambridge: Cambridge University Press.

Amyx, D. A.
> 1988   *Corinthian Vase-painting of the Archaic Period.* Berkeley: University of California Press.

Antonaccio, C. M.
> 1992   Terraces, tombs, and the early Argive Heraion. *Hesperia* 61: 85–105.
> 1994   Placing the past: the Bronze Age in the cultic topography of early Greece. In S. E. Alcock and R. Osborne (eds.), *Placing the Gods: Sanctuaries and Sacred Space in Ancient Greece*, 79–104. Oxford: Clarendon.

Arnold, B., and D. B. Gibson (eds.)
> 1998   *Celtic Chiefdom, Celtic State: The Evolution of Complex Social Systems in Prehistoric Europe.* Cambridge: Cambridge University Press.

Arnold, B., and N. L. Wicker (eds.)
> 2001   *Gender and the Archaeology of Death.* Walnut Creek, Calif.: AltaMira Press.

Bennet, D. J. L., and M. Galaty
> 1997   Classical archaeology: recent developments in the archaeology of the prehistoric Aegean and regional studies. *Journal of Archaeological Research* 5: 75–120.

Bradley, R., and H. Williams (eds.)
> 1998   *The Past in the Past: The Reuse of Ancient Monuments* (*World Archaeology* 30.1). London: Routledge.

Caskey, M. E.

6

    1986   *Keos* II: *The Temple at Ayia Irini*, Part 1: *The Statues*. Princeton: American School of Classical Studies at Athens.

Cherry, J. F.

    1983   Evolution, revolution, and the origins of complex society. In O. Krzyszkowska and L. Nixon (eds.), *Minoan Society*, 33–45. Bristol: Bristol Classical Press.

    1984   The emergence of the state in the prehistoric Aegean. *Proceedings of the Cambridge Philological Society* 30: 18–48.

Cherry, J. F., J. L. Davis, and E. Mantzourani.

    1991   *Landscape Archaeology as Long-Term History: Northern Keos in the Cycladic Island from the Earliest Settlement until Modern Times*. *Monumenta Archaeologica* 16. Los Angeles: UCLA Institute of Archaeology.

Covey, R. A.

    2003   A processual study of Inka state formation. *Journal of Anthropological Archaeology* 22: 333–57.

Dabney, M. K., and J. C. Wright

    1990   Mortuary customs, palatial society and state formation in the Aegean area: a comparative study. In R. Hägg and G. C. Nordquist (eds.), *Celebrations of Death and Divinity in the Bronze Age Argolid*, 45–53. Stockholm: Svenska Institutet i Athen.

Darcque, P.

    1981   Les vestiges mycéniens découverts sous le Télésterion d'Eleusis. *Bulletin de correspondance hellénique* 105: 593–605.

    2003   Από το θησαυρό του Ατρέα στο Παλάτι του Μενελάου: ο τρόμος της ανωνυμίας στη μυκηναϊκή αρχαιολογία. *Αρχαιολογία* 86: 24–30.

Davis, J. L.

    2001   Classical archaeology and anthropological archaeology in North America: a meeting of minds at the millennium? In G. M. Feinman and T. D. Price (eds.), *Archaeology at the Millennium: A Sourcebook*, 415–37. New York: Kluwer Academic/Plenum Publishers.

Dixon, S.

    1997   Continuity and change in Roman social history: retrieving 'family feeling(s)' from Roman law and literature. In M. Golden and P. Toohey (eds.), *Inventing Ancient Culture: Historicism, Periodization, and the Ancient World*, 79–90. London: Routledge.

Donald, M., and L. Hurcombe (eds.)

    2000   *Gender and Material Culture in Archaeological Perspective*. New York: St. Martin's Press.

Dover, K. J.

    1978   *Greek Homosexuality*. Cambridge, Mass.: Harvard University Press.

6 Dyson, S. L.

1993 From New to New Age Archaeology: archaeological theory and Classical archaeology—a 1990s perspective. *American Journal of Archaeology* 97: 195–206.

1998 *Ancient Marbles to American Shores: Classical Archaeology in the United States*. Philadelphia: University of Pennsylvania Press.

Eder, B.

2001 Continuity of Bronze Age cult at Olympia? The evidence of the pottery from the Dark Age sanctuary. In R. Hägg and R. Laffineur (eds.), *POTNIA: Deities and Religion in the Aegean Bronze Age. Acts of the Eighth International Aegean Conference at Göteborg University, 12–15 April 2000* (*Aegaeum* 22): 201–9. Liège: Université de Liège; Austin: University of Texas at Austin.

Evans, A. J.

1912 The Minoan and Mycenaean element in Hellenic life. *Journal of Hellenic Studies* 32: 277–97.

Feinman, G.

1998 Scale and social organization: perspectives on the archaic state. In G. Feinman and J. Marcus (eds.), *Archaic States*, 95–133. Santa Fe: School of American Research Press.

Forbes, H.

1976 'We have a little of everything': the ecological basis of some agricultural practices in Methana, Trizinia. In M. Dimen and E. Friedl (eds.), *Regional Variation in Modern Greece and Cyprus. Annals of the New York Academy of Science* 268: 236–50.

Fotiadis, M.

1995 Modernity and the past-still-present: politics of time in the birth of regional archaeological projects in Greece. *American Journal of Archaeology* 99: 59–78.

Gardner, P.

1882 The palaces of Homer. *Journal of Hellenic Studies* 3: 264–82.

1911 Annual report of the council [of the Society for the Promotion of Hellenic Studies]. Session 1910–11. *Journal of Hellenic Studies* 31: xlv–lxvi.

Gulizio, J., K. Pluta and T. Palaima

2001 Religion in the Room of the Chariot Tablets. In R. Hägg and R. Laffineur (eds.), *POTNIA: Deities and Religion in the Aegean Bronze Age. Acts of the 8th International Aegean Conference at Göteborg University, 12–15 April 2000* (*Aegaeum* 22): 453–61. Liège: Université de Liège; Austin: University of Texas at Austin.

Hall, J. M.

2002 *Hellenicity: Between Ethnicity and Culture*. Chicago: Chicago University Press.

Halperin, D. M.
    1997   Sex before sexuality: pederasty, politics, and power in classical Athens.
            In M. Duberman (ed.), *Queer Representations: Reading Lives, Reading
            Cultures*, 37–53. New York: New York University Press.

Hamilakis, Y., and E. Yalouri
    1996   Antiquities as symbolic capital in modern Greek society. *Antiquity* 70:
            117–29.

Hansen, M. H. (ed.)
    2000   *A Comparative Study of Thirty City-State Cultures: An Investigation
            Conducted by the Copenhagen Polis Centre.* Copenhagen: The Royal
            Danish Academy of Sciences and Letters.

Immerwahr, S. A.
    1971   *The Athenian Agora XIII: The Neolithic and Bronze Ages.* Princeton:
            American School of Classical Studies at Athens.

Jebb, R. C.
    1886   The Homeric house, in relation to the remains at Tiryns. *Journal of
            Hellenic Studies* 7: 170–88.
    1904   Meeting in celebration of the twenty-fifth anniversary of the Society
            for the Promotion of Hellenic Studies. *Journal of Hellenic Studies* 24:
            l–lxxiii.

Klein, N.
    1997   Excavation of the Greek temples at Mycenae. *Annual of the British
            School at Athens* 92: 247–322.

Koehl, R.
    1986   The Chieftain Cup and a Minoan rite of passage. *Journal of Hellenic
            Studies* 106: 99–110.

Konsolaki, E.
    2002   A Mycenaean Sanctuary on Methana. In R. Hägg (ed.), *Peloponnesian
            Sanctuaries and Cults. Proceedings of the Ninth International Sympo-
            sium at the Swedish Institute at Athens, 11–13 June 1994*: 25-36. Stock-
            holm: Svenska Institutet i Athen.

MacGillivray, J. A., J. M. Driessen and L. H. Sackett (eds.)
    2000   *The Palaikastro Kouros: A Minoan Chryselephantine Statuette and Its
            Aegean Bronze Age Context.* London: British School at Athens.

Maran, J.
    2000   Das Megaron im Megaron: Zur Datierung und Funktion des Anten-
            baus im mykenischen Palast von Tiryns. *Archäologischer Anzeiger*:
            1–16.

Mazarakis Ainian, A.
    1997   *From Rulers' Dwellings to Temples: Architecture, Religion and Society
            in Early Iron Age Greece (1100–700 B.C.).* Studies in Mediterranean
            Archaeology 121. Jonsered: Paul Åströms Förlag.

6   Morgan, C.
          1999   *Isthmia, Excavations by the University of Chicago under the Auspices of the American School of Classical Studies, Vol. VIII: The Late Bronze Age Settlement and Early Iron Age Sanctuary.* Princeton: The American School of Classical Studies at Athens.

Morgan, C., and T. Whitelaw
          1991   Pots and politics: ceramic evidence for the rise of the Argive state. *American Journal of Archaeology* 95: 79–108.

Morris, I.
          1987   *Burial and Ancient Society: The Rise of the Greek City-State.* Cambridge: Cambridge University Press.

          1994   Archaeologies of Greece. In I. Morris (ed.), *Classical Greece: Ancient Histories and Modern Archaeologies*, 8–47. Cambridge: Cambridge University Press.

          1997   Periodization and the heroes: inventing a dark age. In M. Golden and P. Toohey (eds.), *Inventing Ancient Culture: Historicism, Periodization, and the Ancient World,* 96–131. London: Routledge.

          1999   Household archaeology and gender ideology in Archaic Greece. *Transactions of the American Philological Association* 129: 305–17.

Morris, S. P.
          1989   A tale of two cities: the miniature frescoes from Thera and the origins of Greek poetry. *American Journal of Archaeology* 93: 511–35.

          1992a   *Daidalos and the Origins of Greek Art.* Princeton: Princeton University Press.

          1992b   Greece beyond East and West: perspectives and prospects. In G. Köpcke and I. Tokumaru (eds.), *Greece between East and West: 10th–8th Centuries B.C.*, xiii–xviii. Mainz: Philipp von Zabern.

Mylonas, G. E.
          1951   The figured Mycenaean stelai. *American Journal of Archaeology* 55: 134–47.

Neer, R. T.
          2002   *Style and Politics in Athenian Vase-painting: The Craft of Democracy, ca. 530–460 B.C.E.* Cambridge: Cambridge University Press.

Nelson, S. M., and M. Rosen-Ayalon (eds.)
          2002   *In Pursuit of Gender: Worldwide Archaeological Approaches.* Walnut Creek, Calif: AltaMira Press.

Nevett, L. C.
          1995   Gender relations in the classical Greek household: the archaeological evidence. *Annual of the British School of Archaeology at Athens* 90: 363–81.

Nilsson, M. P.
          1927   *The Minoan-Mycenaean Religion and Its Survival in Greek Religion.* Lund: C. W. K. Gleerup.

1932   *The Mycenaean Origin of Greek Mythology.* Berkeley: University of
          California Press.

Palmer, R.
  2001   Bridging the gap: the continuity of Greek agriculture from the My-
          cenaean to the historical period. In D. W. Tandy (ed.), *Prehistory and
          History: Ethnicity, Class and Political Economy*, 41–84. Montreal: Black
          Rose Books.

Papadopoulos, J. K., and R. M. Leventhal (eds.)
  2003   *Theory and Practice in Mediterranean Archaeology: Old World and New
          World Perspectives.* Cotsen Advanced Seminar 1. Los Angeles: Cotsen
          Institute of Archaeology, University of California, Los Angeles.

Payne, H. G. G.
  1931   *Necrocorinthia: A Study of Corinthian Art in the Archaic Period.* Ox-
          ford: Clarendon Press.

Peckham, R. G.
  2001   *National Histories, Natural States: Nationalism and the Politics of Place
          in Greece.* London: I. B. Tauris.

Pilafidis-Williams, K.
  1998   *The Sanctuary of Aphaia in the Bronze Age.* Munich: Hirmer Verlag.

Prent, M.
  2003   Glories of the past in the past: ritual activities at palatial ruins in Early
          Iron Age Crete. In R. M. Van Dyke and S. E. Alcock (eds.), *Archaeolo-
          gies of Memory*, 81–103. Oxford: Blackwell.

Renfrew, C. A.
  1972   *The Emergence of Civilisation: The Cyclades and the Aegean in the Third
          Millennium BC.* London: Methuen.

  1980   The great tradition versus the great divide: archaeology as anthropol-
          ogy? *American Journal of Archaeology* 84: 287–98.

  1988   The Minoan-Mycenaean origins of the panhellenic games. In W. J. Ra-
          schke (ed.), *Archaeology of the Olympics*, 13–25. Madison: University
          of Wisconsin Press.

Rystedt, E.
  1988   Mycenaean runners—including *apobatai.* In E. French and K. Wardle
          (eds.), *Problems in Greek Prehistory*, 437–42. Bristol: Bristol Classical
          Press.

Schliemann, H.
  1880   *Mycenae: A Narrative of Researches and Discoveries at Mycenae and
          Tiryns.* New York: C. Scribner's Sons.

Small, D. B.
  1999   Mycenaean polities: states or estates? In W. A. Parkinson and M. L.
          Galaty (eds.), *Rethinking Mycenaean Palaces: New Interpretations of an
          Old Idea*, 43–47. Los Angeles: Cotsen Institute of Archaeology, Univer-
          sity of California, Los Angeles.

6   Shanks, M.

    1995   Art and archaeology of embodiment: some aspects of Archaic Greece. *Cambridge Archaeological Journal* 5: 207–44.

    1996   *Classical Archaeology of Greece: Experiences of the Discipline.* London: Routledge.

    1999   *Art and the Early Greek State: An Interpretive Archaeology.* Cambridge: Cambridge University Press.

Shear, I. M.

    2000   *Tales of Heroes: The Origins of the Homeric Texts.* Athens: Caratzas.

Snodgrass, A. M.

    1977   *Archaeology and the Rise of the Greek State.* Cambridge: Cambridge University Press.

    1985   The new archaeology and the classical archaeologist. *American Journal of Archaeology* 89: 31–37.

    1987   *An Archaeology of Greece: The Present State and Future Scope of a Discipline.* Berkeley: University of California Press.

    2002   The rejection of Mycenaean culture and the oriental connection. In E. A. Braun-Holzinger and H. Matthäus (eds.), *Die nahöstlichen Kulturen und Griechenland an der Wende vom 2. zum 1. Jahrtausend v. Chr. Kontinuität und Wandel von Strukturen und Mechanismen kultureller Interaktion,* 1–9. Möhnesee: Bibliopolis.

Snyder, L. M., and W. E. Kippel

    2000   Dark age subsistence at the Kastro site, east Crete: exploring subsistence change and continuity during the Late Bronze Age–Early Iron Age transition. In S. J. Vaughan and W. D. E. Coulson (eds.), *Palaeodiet in the Aegean. Papers from a Colloquium Held at the 1993 Meeting of the Archaeological Institute of America in Washington D.C.,* 65–83. Oxford: Oxbow Books.

Spencer, C.

    1990   On the tempo and mode of state formation: neo-evolutionism reconsidered. *Journal of Anthropological Archaeology* 9: 1–30.

Spencer, N. (ed.)

    1995   *Time, Tradition, and Society in Greek Archaeology: Bridging the 'Great Divide.'* London: Routledge.

Spyropoulos, T.

    2002   Το μυκηναικό Ανάκτορο του Μενελάου και της Ελένης στην Ομηρική Λακεδαίμονα Πελλάνα. *Corpus* 39: 20–31.

Stewart, A.

    1997   *Art, Desire, and the Body in Ancient Greece.* Cambridge: Cambridge University Press.

van Leuven, J.

1996   The Nilssonian origin of Mycenaean mythology. In E. De Miro, L. Godart, and A. Sacconi (eds.), *Atti e memorie del secondo congresso internazionale di micenologia.* Incunabula Graeca 98: 923–38. Rome: Gruppo editoriale internazionale.

Vermeule, E. T.

1987   Baby Aigisthos and the Bronze Age, *Proceedings of the Cambridge Philological Society* 213: 122–52.

Waldstein, C.

1909   Classical archaeology and prehistoric archaeology. In *Fasciculus Joanni Willis Clark dicatus*, 517–28. Cambridge: Typis academicis impressus.

Whitley, J.

1988   Early states and hero cults: a re-appraisal. *Journal of Hellenic Studies* 108: 173–82.

1991   *Style and Society in Dark Age Greece: The Changing Face of a Pre-Literate Society, 1100–700 BC.* Cambridge: Cambridge University Press.

1998   From Minoans to Eteocretans: the Praisos region 1200–500 B.C. In W. G. Cavanagh, M. Curtis, J. N. Coldstream, and A. W. Johnston (eds.), *Post-Minoan Crete. Proceedings of the First Colloquium on Post-Minoan Crete Held by the British School at Athens and the Institute of Archaeology, University College London, 10–11 November 1995*: 27–39. London: The British School at Athens.

Wright, H. T.

1994   Pre-state political formations. In G. Stein and M. Rothman (eds.), *Chiefdoms and Early States in the Near East: The Organizational Dynamics of Complexity*, 67–84. Madison: Prehistory Press.

Yoffee, N.

1995   Too many chiefs? (or safe texts for the 90s). In N. Yoffee and A. Sherratt (eds.), *Archaeological Theory: Who Sets the Agenda?*, 60–78. Cambridge: Cambridge University Press.

6

7 Greek Modernists' Discovery of the Aegean

Artemis Leontis

Abstract

This paper traces Greek modernists' discovery of the Aegean. The story begins with the 'back to roots' movement in the 1920s, which looked to vernacular art and architecture of the Aegean for timeless aesthetic. A turning point came in the 1930s with Odysseus Elytis and other modernists, who placed the Aegean at the center of their conceptual atlas of Greece. By doing this they reconfigured national space. They replaced the irredentist idea of recovering lost Byzantine territories — the Megali Idea, *undone by the Asia Minor Disaster of 1922—with a smaller, self-sustaining idea of Greece. At the same time, they deepened notions of Greek tradition. Modernists' Aegean discovery compensated for geopolitical loss with historical depth. For while archaeology was finding in the Aegean a reservoir of artifacts from prehistoric times, poets and artists were drawing from that reservoir to lengthen and strengthen the Greek sense of continuity.*

The Aegean, a watery region flanked on two sides by the ends of two continents, is a fluid environment taking its color from the sky above and the life that reflects itself on the sea's surface. Though fluid, the Aegean is not an amorphous, inert container but an active force pervading human society. It occupies real geographical space. Yet its significance changes, depending on the times and the beholder. The Aegean has inspired a range of visions: sea travelers have seen it as a dangerous passageway leading from the Mediterranean to the Black Sea, archaeologists as a rich storehouse of a long line of past achievements, and vacationers as a place of restful forgetfulness.

The Aegean acquired significance for artists, intellectuals, and, in turn, the general public, beginning in the 1920s and continuing through the 1980s. During the interwar period, a group of Greece's modernists discovered the Aegean. Whereas the Aegean barely appeared in Greek works of the previous decades, suddenly during the 1920s in painting and the 1930s in literature, it made a dramatic debut. As a group of artists turned from other geographical settings to the Aegean for inspiration, it began to work on their imaginations in unexpected ways that suited the ideological, artistic, and even emotional needs of their era. It gave them a new set of artifacts of the Greek past to mine. It offered a different set of past events from those—some of them very painful—that had occupied their precursors. It laid the foundations for a new narrative about Greece. It offered a new set of icons.

7   Gradually, the Aegean archipelago came to occupy a disproportionately large place in conceptualizations of Greek history and space.

'Prehistorians Round the Pond,' a workshop on the present state of archaeology of the Aegean emphasizing the history of that rather youthful discipline, inspired me to think about the parallel and nearly contemporaneous history of Greek artists' engagement with the region. I began to think about visions of the Aegean that appeared in Greek writing during the second quarter of the 20th century. I pieced together evidence of the Aegean's dramatic appearance in the arts during that period and explored the version of Greece's story made possible by the new literary atlas of Greece that put the Aegean at its center. This work is the product of those reflections.

A word about my own approach. While literature is my primary area of study, I work through sources that include not just poetry and prose but painting, sculpture, and architecture in order to grasp changing representations of place. A key word in my reading of Greek literature is *topos*: ο τόπος μου, my place, my home. A *topos* is a commonplace, of course, but in contemporary Greek usage τόπος is also the term used to invoke the self-presence of Hellenism. *Topos* is where the Greek feels at home. It is a place of intimacy because it is a place of return. It is a homeland. Repetition is key. Repeated invocations, repeated images, and repetitively evocative descriptions of a place make it a commonplace, while they also produce the illusion of a self-revealing presence.[1]

The Aegean is a *topos*. In general usage the Aegean marks an island-filled passageway between the Mediterranean and the Black Sea, which is bounded on the east and west by two sometimes warring coastlines. In today's popular Greek imagination the Aegean also stands for a rich literary and artistic heritage of great depth, from prehistory to the present. To seek out the Aegean is to reach down into the deepest reservoir of Greek history. It is to bring to mind prehistoric icons of the human body. It is to dwell on the beginnings of Greek literature and music. It is to recall the shores where Homer first composed his verses, Sappho wrote her poems, and Alcaeus composed and played. And it is to suggest that today's artists, humble successors of those great forebears, continue vital, unbroken traditions of writing, composing, playing, and dancing. The Aegean evokes all of these things in the Greek imagination today, thanks in large part to writers who began publishing in the 1930s, artists who worked closely with them, and architects who explored vernacular architecture in order to uncover the roots of both classical and modern building forms. They were the first in the modern era to turn to the region for inspiration and to associate with it images of sun, sea, whitewashed buildings, waves, wind, love, and life, which feed our imaginations to this day.

The Aegean did not always represent these things. As an artistic *topos*, 'Aegean' has a brief modern history. It appears in the interwar era, specifically in the 1920s in the visual arts and the 1930s in writing. Certainly the Aegean preexists those decades—and certainly it was depicted or mentioned in works prior to the

7

period I take up. It formed the backdrop in paintings of ships anchored in harbors or traveling in the open sea or maneuvering in naval battles during the Greek revolution, scenes all popular from the mid-1800s to the early 1900s. But it was not yet a signifier of something as large or important or moving as it would later become. Its fair-weather colors had not yet found their palette. It was not yet that special part representing the whole of Greece. Nor did it contain the jugular vein of Greek identity, a long sinuous thread of historical-cultural continuity from the distant past to the luminous present. Other places stood for the continuity of the Greek spirit. From 1844 to 1922, for example, Constantinople signified the greatness that Greek civilization had once achieved and the power and territorial limits it aspired to reach again.

Two poems from that period give to the Aegean a small part; in the one case, its omission stands as a foil to later literary practices. In *Πατρίδες* [*Homelands*] (1895), a set of 12 sonnets mapping the 'ancient, immovable *topoi* in the depths of my soul' (poem 9, lines 3–4), poet Kostis Palamas (1859–1943) mapped out his imaginary homeland, from Patras to the stars, but only briefly mentioned the Aegean.[2] He rendered it 'blue, a sapphire-bearing treasure' (poem 6, lines 5–8), just as Palamas's successors would later see it. But he gave it a diminutive role: the Aegean takes up just one in 48 stanzas, or four of 168 lines, a place proportionate to its size but not to the role it would come to play in the works of Palamas's literary descendents.

Kostas Karyotakis (1896–1928) did not even mention the Aegean in *Θάλασσα* [*Sea*] (1919),[3] a symbolist poem that gave its own color, meaning, and feelings to the sea. Karyotakis's picture was decidedly different from the one that would evolve after he abruptly exited the society of poets by taking his life in 1928. His sea was green and stormy, its deep, opaque waters threatening to swallow those who dared to traverse them. This was not a place where the past made itself transparently visible but instead one where the present faced the dark threat of its demise. Especially worthy of note is the fact that the poem's presiding consciousness did not expect ever to enjoy the calm sunny seascape following a storm.

Clear, bright, calm, and blue did not enter into Karyotakis's picture of the sea. Such an image would have to wait for a poet of a different sensibility, a different era. In literature it is tempting to point to a single herald of change. Odysseus Elytis (1911–96), called the 'sun-drinking poet,' happily embraced the name ποιητής του Αιγαίου [poet of the Aegean]. He was proud of his family's Lesbian origins. He sought the company of other Αιγαιοπελαγήτες [people from the Aegean Sea], as he called his fellow writers from Samos, Chios, Lesbos, as well as Smyrna and other coastal towns of Asia Minor. He singled out Greek artists of all eras with origins in the Aegean: Sappho of Lesbos, Archilochus of Paros, Homer of Chios, and Heraclitus, all from Greek antiquity, and the naïve painter Theophilos, also from Lesbos but a generation older.

Elytis deliberately turned to the Aegean as a source of inspiration in 1934.

7   His essay, 'Το χρονικό μιας δεκαετίας' ['Chronicle of a Decade'], which chronicles the decade of the 1930s, describes the artistic impasse he had been facing until that year, when he read Yorgos Theotokas's essay, 'Ώρες αργίας' ['Leisure Hours'] (1931). Theotokas's rhetorical question, 'Really, is there anything in the world more moving than the Aegean?,' inspired Elytis to take a new direction. Elytis (1982: 262) commented:

> This was the first time I saw someone trying to conceptualize a more general spirit having to do with the seafaring nature of Greece. Since this idea found nourishment in my own genuinely personal experience, I felt that it flooded me and asked of me to find for it, the language of a contemporary sensibility, a new poetic idiom in thousands of possible variations.

A few months later, Elytis helped plan the 1935 issue of the influential journal of his day, *Τα νέα γράμματα* [*New Letters*]. There he published *Του Αιγαίου* [*Of the Aegean*].[4] With this set of three poems, Elytis delivered a new literary landscape. In the first poem, abstract and concrete nouns—love, archipelago, gull, song, voyage, nostalgia, a young woman, and homecoming—formed the building blocks of a new world. The second poem described the rising sun, which in the third poem played with key elements of the sea: sand, wind, waves, shells, and a hundred shades of blue. Words found in this publication became trademarks of Elytis's powerful art 'of the Aegean,' interchangeable signifiers of identity calling to mind not just the Aegean Sea but all of Greece and a metaphysical world transcending Greece.[5]

Elytis's poem had a startling effect. In contrast to the still fashionable trend of imitating Karyotakis's bitingly satirical verse, Elytis presented images of fresh, shocking brightness. He rejected Karyotakis's pessimism and painted over his darker hues. For a readership thirsting for something new, Elytis offered a stark contrast. His poems immediately struck a chord.

No matter how important Elytis is to the Aegean discovery in the second quarter of the 20th century, the story of how artists found in the Aegean 'a field of miraculous assimilative energy, the εργαστήριο [laboratory] of nuclei of art ... the wise digestive track of Hellenism ... the depths of the collective unconscious' (Elytis 1982a: 414–15) neither begins nor ends with him. As art critic Eleni Vakalo put it, the 'generation of the 1930s,' a loosely affiliated group to which Elytis belonged, 'inscribed its history in all artistic domains' (Vakalo 1983: 35). For the first time in modern Greek intellectual and artistic life, people working in different media became aware of one another's work and cultivated the terrain together. Evidence of an Aegean turn can be found in everything from painting, drawing, and architecture to poetry, fiction, non-fiction, and music over a period of several decades. In music, for example, Nikolas Skalkotas composed an ode to the Aegean entitled *Θάλασσα* [*Sea*] in 1949. Then in 1960, Manos Hatzidakis devoted half his long composition entitled *Ελλάς χώρα των ονείρων* [*Greece Land of Dreams*] generally to *H γη* [*The Earth*] and the other half to nothing less specific than *To Αιγαίο* [*The Aegean*].

I shall make three points about this development, offer a few examples from different media to support those points, and conclude by piecing together the idea of Greece that emanates from the Aegean center.

My first point concerns volume, repetition, and coordination in the artistic production of images of the Aegean across media. Elytis was not writing in a void. The Aegean fascinated his contemporaries. It was not just poets but artists who turned to the Aegean. Some of the painters (and their works) who preceded Elytis in their Aegean discovery were: Konstantinos Maleas (*Santorini*, 1920s), Michalis Oikonomou (*Hydra*, 1926–27), Agenoros Asteriades (*Hydra*, 1927), S. Papoulakes (*Agiassos Mytilini*, 1928), and Nikos Hatzikyriakos-Gikas (*Festivity on the Seashore*, 1931; *Houses on Hydra*, 1938). The Aegean became increasingly popular after the war, as is evident in the works by Efthymis Papadimitriou, Nikos Nikolaou, as well as photographers of Mykonos and Santorini in the 1940s and 1950s. While they were slower to turn to the Aegean than were their artist friends, poets followed suit. Elytis's fascination with the Aegean was ongoing, beginning with the poem discussed above, continuing with a group of poems entitled *Σποράδες* [*Sporades*, 1938] and with individual poems entitled 'Ωδή στη Σαντορίνη' ['Ode to Santorini'] and 'Μελαγχολία του Αιγαίου' ['Aegean Melancholy'], published in his first major collection, *Προσανατολισμοί* [*Orientations*, 1940], and persisting throughout his entire corpus. From 1934 to 1935 George Seferis published poems about Santorini and Hydra, the island he named in his first published collection of poems, *Στροφή* [*Strophe*, 1930]. The list continues (I give the titles in English translation) with Ioanna Tsatsos's 'Chios,' Alexander Matsas's 'Midday Contemplation at Delos' and 'Sleep at Delos' (1940); Nanos Valaoritis's 'Dawn's Lesson' (1943–44), a poem set on the shores of Naxos; Nikos Gatsos's 'Amorgos' (1941–42), a poem named for a remote Aegean island though the island never figures in the poem; and I. M. Panayotopoulos's 'Sunday of the Aegean' (1951).

Santorini, Hydra, Mytilini, Delos, Chios, Amorgos, Mykonos: an Aegeocentric set of place names gradually inscribed itself on the Greek national consciousness. The range and number of artists who made the Aegean familiar ground are great. Thus my first point is this: the Aegean was not the product of a single imagination but of many artists and writers working alongside one another. The Aegean worked its magic on a variety of artists, who shaped it into a landmark of familiarity, so that people soon identified the Aegean as Greece and Greece through the Aegean.

My second point concerns the intellectual groundwork for this topographical turn. Elytis and his group were building on foundations outlined earlier in the 1900s and filled in by the επιστροφή στις ρίζες ['back to roots'] movement of artists and architects beginning in the 1920s. The deceased 'father' of the movement was art historian Perikles Yannopoulos (1869–1910). He wanted to correct what

7   he saw as the mindless imitation of German, French, and British art. He believed that artists could be both contemporary and Greek, provided they fixed their eyes on the Greek landscape. What they needed was an indigenous aesthetic—lines, colors, images, and themes free of foreign influences, unaffected by spurious learning, true to the requirements of place, drawing on the surrounding landscape and the artistic traditions native to that setting. Accordingly, Yannopoulos studied the Attic peninsula, the purest distillation of the Greek landscape, as he saw it, characterized by a higher level of energy than the lethargic south and more intense light than the darker north. In Attica he discovered the building blocks of Greek art from antiquity to the present: καμπύλη [the curved line] and transparent φως [light] as reflected in the color of κυανούν [cyan blue]. Those elements, according to Yannopoulos, were unique to the Attic peninsula. As for technique, Yannopoulos pointed to Byzantine churches or simple houses rinsed by time: here he found prototypes for a national aesthetic.[6]

While Yannopoulos focused his gaze on the Attic peninsula, his protegés, a group of artists and architects who briefly formed the 'back to roots' movement, broadened the view to include whatever they considered natural, that is, true to a Greek setting, including vernacular architecture and art of the Aegean. One important figure in the movement was Dimitris Pikionis, who landscaped the Athenian Acropolis and Hill of the Muses in the 1950s. Pikionis had met Yannopoulos and embraced his vision. Like Yannopoulos, he eschewed influences he considered to be foreign, specifically the Frankish, Italian, and, to a lesser degree, Ottoman, all of which he identified as foreign powers, which, in occupying Greece, had grafted onto the landscape false, foreign forms. 'The imposition of their own measure . . . takes the form of a high-handed intrusion on the karma of a people, an unbearable rape of the Hellenic consciousness' (Pikionis 1985b: 208). Instead, he turned to the simple artisan, whose work Pikionis perceived as closest to a natural, unaffected form of expression and therefore capable of becoming the foundation for something higher.

In vernacular structures and decorative arts of the Aegean archipelago, visionaries such as Pikionis discovered a set of principles they considered timeless: human scale, integration of landscape and building materials, response to climate and lifestyle, correspondence among function, building requirements, and form. They detected what they saw as a continuity of building practices. To support the idea of continuity, they pointed to remains of civilizations from prehistory through the Archaic, Classical, Post-classical, Byzantine-Christian, Ottoman, and modern traditional. What gave the feeling of continuity was not just evidence of buildings from all periods or the almost continuous presence of living communities for thousands of years. It was the idea that those living communities, responding to the constant environmental factors and having at their disposal corresponding building materials, offered a cohesive, spontaneous range of answers to persistent questions about how people can live in harmony with their environment.

Figure 7.1. Pebble mosaic, detail of a mermaid holding a ship and a fish. Courtyard of J. Yoyce, Spetsae, mid-19th century (photograph: National Bank of Greece).

In their explorations of the Aegean, they drew inspiration from certain classes of buildings and materials. Dovecotes and other buildings of Tinos, for example, attracted attention because they adapted comfortably from countryside to town settings without adding cosmopolitan features that compromised their integrity, and they exhibited their function in their form. According to one architect's estimation, 'The houses were built by Tinian craftsmen who brought the traditional architectural style of the village to the town uncontaminated, using the same materials, the same methods' (Kharitonidou 1983: 276). What 'back to roots' artists and architects appreciated was the buildings' 'uncontaminated' form, as if the buildings rose naturally from the soil. Besides building structures, architectural details fascinated them: pebble mosaics decorating courtyards of 19th-century island homes (figure 7.1), for example, or a stone fanlight with incised scenes of two 18th-century merchant ships from Tinos (figure 7.2), in which Pikionis in 1925 saw 'an example of the sculptural ornament of folk art, and, with this, of nature, the true origin of sculpture. Better, not just of sculpture but of all the plastic arts' (1985a: 61). Appreciation of artifacts such as these brought into focus materials like pebbles and

7

Figure 7.2. Stone fanlight with incised scenes of two merchant ships from Tinos, 18th century (Athens Byzantine Museum).

stone, long used in the decorative arts in the region but now entering studios in the capital city.

Conditions were ripe for a revaluation of earlier works made of stone such as the prehistoric figurines found in the Cyclades. These artifacts, which during the 19th century connoisseurs had tossed aside as ugly creations of a barbaric people, acquired great value as Greek art in the first half of the 20th century. Visual artists in Greece turned to them for inspiration. There were two trends. One was the tendency to imitate the figurines or to combine their clear lines, round feminine curves, and sharp angles with traditional vernacular motifs such as the mermaid or personifications of the winds. Painter and book artist Yannis Moralis worked along these lines to produce his illustrations for Elytis's epic poem *To Αξιον Εστί* [*To Axion Esti*, 1959], George Seferis's *Δοκιμές* [*Essays*, 1962] (figure 7.3), and his *Painted Comments* for Seferis's collected poems published by Ikaros in 1965—a work that throws together architectural and sculptural fragments from different eras onto a sea-blue background. The general fascination with the lines of Cycladic

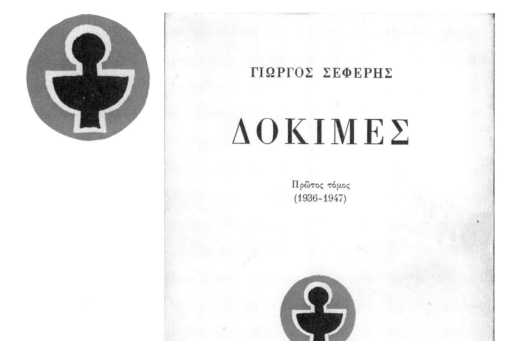

ΓΙΩΡΓΟΣ ΣΕΦΕΡΗΣ

ΔΟΚΙΜΕΣ

Πρῶτος τόμος
(1936-1947)

ΙΚΑΡΟΣ

Figure 7.3. Yannis Moralis, illustration, jacket cover for George Seferis's *Δοκιμές* [Essays] (1962).

stone sculpture is most evident in Moralis's *Girl Painting (Diptych)* (figure 7.4) and in Nikos Nikolaou's *Hydra, Spetses, Psara* (1961) (figure 7.5).

Another trend found its inspiration in the materials of Cycladic figurines, that is, in stone, and in what was imagined as the primordial encounter between prehistoric artists and their medium. At the center of that trend was artist Nikos Nikolaou, who, for a period, experimented with figurative painting on pebbles and small stones. In a critical appraisal of his work, Elytis imagined the scene of Nikolaou's creative discovery, in which Nikolaou handled 'mute' prehistoric stones and made them 'speak.' Elytis described the scene thus: one fine summer morning on the island of Aigina, Nikolaou was

7

Figure 7.4. Yannis Moralis, *Girl Painting* (diptych, acrylic on canvas, 1971) (Private Collection).

. . . taking a few steps along the seashore. Playing at first, he gradually ap-plied himself to observing the special form the large pebbles on the shore had taken after having been worked for centuries by the sea—by the hand of Chance, which had become waves or wind, sun or rust. Those stones were born as mute rocks perhaps before Homer's time, now they were all but ready to speak. It's the 'all but' that a poet [like Nikolaou] adds to produce a magical charm. . . . With Nikolaou's art you feel like you are met by the echo of the sea. (Elytis 1986: 72)

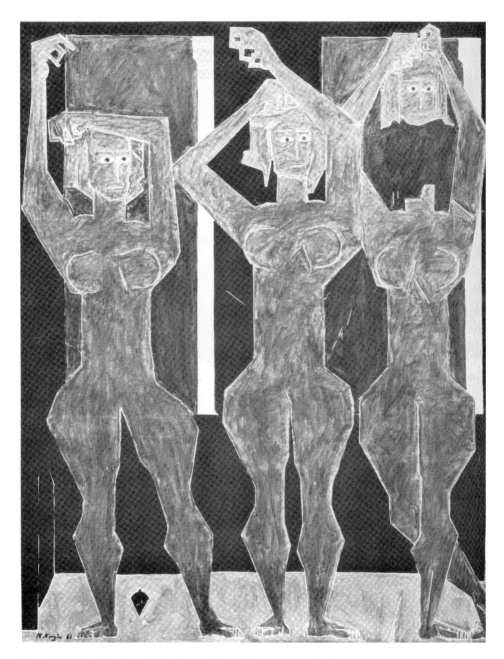

Figure 7.5. Nikos Nikolaou, *Hydra, Spetses, Psara* (oil on canvas, 1961).

My third point has to do with the Aegean's geopolitical centrality in events of the interwar period. The poetic, artistic, and critical fascination with the Aegean found support in contemporary political events. Images of the Aegean, repeated allusions to the Aegean, artistic borrowings from the art and architecture of the

7　Aegean resonated because the Aegean was at the same time a hotspot in the evolving story of Greece. The latest element in that story was the Asia Minor Disaster, which happened in 1922. This was *the* traumatic memory for many of the artists who turned to the Aegean in the 1930s for solace. It was *the* event that these artists had to put to rest.

A brief foray into Greece's recent history is necessary. First I must insert a reference to the irredentist *Μεγάλη Ιδέα* [*Great Idea*], which governed Greek foreign policy for nearly 80 years, from 1844 to 1922, and envisioned a greater Greece of two continents and four seas. The *Megali Idea* pressed for Greece to reach the geographical span of the later Byzantine Empire, with Constantinople at its political and cultural center. The idea was for the Greek state to take from the Ottoman Empire formerly Byzantine lands where Greeks still lived. That idea reached a pitch of hope, hype, and hysteria when the Greek army entered Anatolia in 1922—after having been assigned by Britain and France to protect Smyrna's Christian populations—and marched toward Ankara to face the leader of the Turkish national revolution Kemal Attaturk. A misguided military turn led to a rousing defeat of the Greeks by the Turkish revolutionary army in September of 1922. There followed the army's retreat, the burning of Smyrna, and massacres of Christians by armed Turks. Then came expulsions of Greeks from Turkey and, the next year, a treaty ending Greece's expansionist policy and requiring an exchange of populations between Greece and the new Turkish state. All this finally put the *Megali Idea* to rest.

The fallout from the disaster, which brought more than one million Orthodox Christian refugees to Greece's doorstep and sent some 300,000 Muslims to Turkey, produced a scene that would play itself out again and again in the Greek imagination. Refugees from Asia Minor and Anatolia, Greek speakers and/or Greek Orthodox Christians who were formerly Ottoman subjects, crossed to Aegean islands such as Chios or Lesbos near the coast of Asia Minor or reached Greece's port cities as strangers. Greeks of another world, violently uprooted, had to adjust to a foreign way of life.

The events put the Aegean center stage. Refugee stories straddling the Aegean's two shores entered prose works by Elias Venezis, Stratis Myrivilis, Yorgos Theotokas, Photis Kondoglou, Kosmas Politis, Elie Alexiou, and countless others. There were scenes of destruction and loss on one side, then a difficult passage, followed by the everyday experience of disorientation on the other side. On one side people were torn from their age-old homelands, on the other they found a tentative home among strangers. Lying between the lost and the not yet embraced homelands, the Aegean was their watery medium of transport, transition, and, in some cases, transformation. It was the space between the old world and the new, the familiar and the strange, the never more and the not yet. It saved people from destruction but carried them to an unwanted future for which they were not prepared.

I have now surveyed a wide range of sources in order to make several points. Elytis and others working near him were able to bring the Aegean into lasting focus because they offered bright, shining images of the Aegean. They rendered these images through different media. They offered them repeatedly. They emphasized the deep history of the region. They appended stories of Greece's recent traumas. The volume, repetition, collaborative force, historical depth, drama, and relevance of their Aegean idea produced lasting effects.

Beyond the effectiveness of their Aegean allusions on multiple levels, however, one should attend to the conceptual atlas of Greece these artists produced. Greece's modernists placed the Aegean at the center of their universe, replacing a different center that no longer held. When the *Megali Idea* that had guided the Greek Kingdom's foreign policy of expansion for 80 years collapsed with the expulsion of Greeks from Asia Minor, it was more than Greek politics that felt the aftershocks. The submersion of the *Megali Idea* somewhere between Athens and Ankara sank an idea of Greece that had sustained the nation for almost eight decades; it removed an orienting point of reference. I refer to Constantinople, the heart of the *Megali Idea*, and the lands extending south along the coast of Asia Minor and east along the Black Sea. Previously, the Greek nation-state existed in the Greek political unconscious as an incomplete organism with a metaphysical drive. There was Athens, the body's brain and nervous system, fed by healthy cells from villages, islands, and port towns in Greece. But Constantinople, the organism's heart, stood sadly outside the Greek state. The *Megali Idea* had promised to make Greece whole by making it bigger—that is to say, by aligning the Greek state with the much larger idea of the nation. The Asia Minor Disaster removed that potentiality. Therefore, the work of Greek artists and intellectuals who began reimagining Greece's political and social body so as to give it a healthy new shape was crucial. In their hands, Greece would become whole according to a new scheme. Their Greece was not a nation of latent grandeur but of a self-contained, self-sustaining completeness. What comprised its heart was not Constantinople but the Aegean. With the Aegean as its historical, emotional, and artistic center, Greece became whole, not because it expanded to fill a dream but because it found deep within itself a new inspiration for dreams.

Scenes of archaeological excavation in or near the Aegean may have spawned the idea. Some of these entered Greek literature. There was the citadel of prehistoric Asine, named in the Homeric catalog of ships and identified with a site on the coast of the Argolid in George Seferis's evocative poem, 'Ὁ βασιλιάς της Ἀσίνης' ['The King of Asine,' 1938–40]. For Seferis, the search for poetry mirrored the difficult search to fill in stubborn gaps in our knowledge about the past. There were scenes of archaeologists unearthing burial sites on Rheneia or gluing pottery in a workroom on Mykonos, which filled pages of the semi-autobiographical novel by Melpo Axiote, *Το σπίτι μου* [*My Home*, 1965]. Axiote's συγκολητής (the man who glued artifacts together—and lost his sight in the arduous process) became a metaphor for her own literary attempts to recover through narrative the picture of Mykonos as she remembered it in her childhood.

7   Elytis, however, described the process of discovery as a search for a poetic method that could give flesh to his feelings about the Greek *topos*. 'It was natural for me to yearn for a poetic method . . . capable—with my own soul's intervention—of giving flesh to the feelings that fascinated me' (1982b: 243). While he felt a calling to follow some of the more radical experiments taking place in Europe, particularly surrealism, he never shook off a belief that his art must remain true to the Greek *topos*. 'Why is it that Greek poets of every era are always occupied with our *topos*?,' he asked rhetorically. He embraced a requirement that his experiments with language align themselves with the color, shape, and history of the Greek *topos*, specifically of elements he associated with the Aegean: 'the glittering, the transparent, the watery, the fresh, the cool green, the pure' (1982b: 243).

As Elytis and others pressed onward to find that elusive artistic πρωτοπορία ['avant-garde' or 'front line'], they found themselves moving *en masse* toward the Aegean archipelago. Theirs was not the only modernist movement to converge on the Aegean. It should be noted that non-Greek modernists, especially sculptors, also drew inspiration from early Aegean art. In the Aegean, it seems, they beheld a moment of primal inspiration, as if they could see before their eyes prehistory's inhabitants marking their presence in stone or preserving their words for future generations. Greeks, too, from Pikionis to Elytis to Nikolaou, found in the Aegean a primordial moment of artistic expression.

Besides the avant-garde forms they found in Aegean art, modernists also saw the Aegean as a rich reservoir of Greek history and a preserver of life during troubled times, as it proved itself to be during the recent Disaster. Beautiful, ageless, innocent, sustaining, the Aegean quietly ebbed and flowed between Greece and its sometimes hostile neighbor. It absorbed all that had been Greek in Turkey—as it had absorbed all that was Greek during older foreign occupations. It drew into its watery embrace remnants of lost homelands and stored fragments from all layers of the Greek past. It offered victims of violence on one side secret passage to a new home on the other.[7]

And so it happened that poets, artists, and architects extended their imaginations to what became a new center of the Greek universe. Out of the Aegean, they developed a smaller, self-sustaining idea of Greece to replace the older, expansionist *Megali Idea*. They also gave Greek history a new trajectory, making the Aegean—and its scattered artifacts from prehistory—a required starting point. In other words, Aegean prehistory, about which artists who came of age in the interwar period had but a vague knowledge, entered into the story Greeks began to tell themselves as they tried to accommodate to the reality of a smaller Greece.

I would like to conclude by suggesting that the adventures in reimagining Greece after the Asia Minor Disaster not only consolidated their hold on the Greek popular imagination but also convinced the wider world that this was and remains Greece. Today Greek writers seem to be restating the obvious when they describe the

. . . centuries-long march of civilization through time in the Aegean and of influences on the Greek κορμό [trunk] and on the entire Greek nation. The Aegean is the living center of the cultural, economic, and social life of the nation, a link between different parts of the Greek εθνότητα [nation] as it radiated outward to the east and west, with emphasis always on the πνευματική [cultural-spiritual] developments and on economic activity. (Pepelases 2002: 346–47)

Descriptions such as this one are commonplace.

More interesting than the tenacious grip the idea of Aegean as 'the living center of the nation' has on the Greek imagination, however, is the possible link between literary and artistic visions of the Aegean, on the one hand, and the Aegean's archaeological study, on the other. Thus, I end with a lingering question, which I leave for people more qualified than myself to answer. Has this brief survey of modern trends been just an agreeable interlude—an Aegean vacation, if you will—to draw attention temporarily away from the concerns of prehistoric archaeology? Or does it lead archaeologists back to their discipline by another route? I am not a prehistorian. I do not claim to know anything about the disciplines of Aegean archaeology—only something about the history of the Aegean's resonance on Greek elite and popular imaginations. But I wonder if there are not some unexplored connections between archaeology's turn to the Aegean during the last century and the somewhat coterminous mining of the Aegean past by Greek artists and intellectuals during that same period. It may be more than coincidence that the Aegean began to draw the attention of archaeologists at the same time that it found a place in the center of Greek art.

Notes

1.   I develop what I call a 'topological' approach in Leontis 1995: 17–39.

2.   The 12 sonnets anchor themselves in 12 real or imaginary 'homelands': Patras (the poet's birthplace), Messolongi (scene of a great siege during the War of Independence memorialized by Greece's poet laureate Dionysios Solomos, and of Byron's death), Athens (the national capital), Corfu (a literary capital), Egypt, Mt. Athos, the Greek Kingdom (comprised of Roumeli, Moria, the Ionian islands, Epirus, and Thessaly), the Balkans, the earth's great continents, the regions of the mythical imagination, the universe, and the soul. The quotation is from the seventh sonnet, dedicated to the continents. The poems appeared in Palamas's collection *Ασάλευτη ζωή* [*Life Immovable*], published in 1895 and reprinted in countless anthologies.

3.   The poem appeared in Karyotakis's collection entitled *Ο πόνος του ανθρώπου και των πραμάτων* [*The Pain of the Human Being and of Things*], published in 1919. It is reprinted in Karyotakis 1982: 14–15.

7   4.   The poem was reprinted in Elytis's first collection, *Προσανατολισμοί* [*Orientations*], and appears in Elytis 2002: 11–12. Below is an English translation by Kimon Friar, as it appeared in Elytis 1974: 47:

> Love
> The archipelago
> And the prow of its foam
> And the seagull of its dream
> On its highest mast the sailor waves
> A song
>
> Love
> Its song
> And the horizons of its voyage
> And the echo of its nostalgia
> On love's wettest rock the betrothed awaits
> A ship
>
> Love
> Its ship
> And the freedom from care of its etesian winds
> And the jib of its hope
> On its highest undulation an island rocks
> The homecoming

5.   I owe a debt to Sherrard (1986), who analyzes Elytis's 'search for identity' in this same set of poems.

6.   Yannopoulos's aesthetic ideas appear in *Η σύγχρονος ζωγραφική* [*Contemporary Painting*] (1902), and *Η ελληνική γραμμή, το ελληνικό χρώμα* [*Hellenic Line, Hellenic Color*] (1904), both reprinted in Yannopoulos 1988: 7–65, 93–158. For a discussion of his aesthetic ideas, see Leontis 1995: 84–89, 119–21. On his contribution to the 'back to roots' movement in architecture, see Philippides 1983.

7.   Elytis develops this scene in the poem 'Μικρή πράσινη θάλασσα' ['Little Green Sea'] (1979), reprinted in Elytis 2002: 213 and appearing in English translation in Elytis 1974: 146.

References

Elytis, O.
    1974   *The Sovereign Sun: Selected Poems.* Trans. Kimon Friar. Philadelphia: Temple University Press.
    1982a   *Η σύγχρονη ελληνική τέχνη και ο ζωγράφος Ν. Χατζηκυριάκος Γκίκας* [*Contemporary Art and the Painter N. Hatzikyriakos Gikas*] [1947]. In *Ανοιχτά χαρτιά* [*Open Book*], 408–17. Athens: Ikaros.

1982b *Το χρονικό μιας δεκαετίας* [*Chronicle of a Decade*]. In *Ανοιχτά Χαρτιά* [*Open Book*], 234–329. Athens: Ikaros.

1986   *Οι θαλασσινές πέτρες του Νικολάου* [*Nikolaou's Thalassic Stones*] [1972]. Reprinted in N. Nikolaou (ed.), *Η περιπέτεια της γραμμής στην τέχνη* [*The Adventure of Line in Art*], 71–73. Athens: Th. Sakellariou and P. Mougios.

2002   *Ποίηση* [*Poetry*]. Athens: Ikaros.

Karyotakis, K.

1995   *Ποιήματα και πεζά* [*Poetry and Prose*]. G. P. Savvides, ed. Athens: Ermes.

Kharitonidou, A.

1983   Tinos. Trans. David Hardy. In *Greek Traditional Architecture,* Vol. 2: *Cyclades,* 275–305. Athens: Melissa.

Leontis, A.

1995   *Topographies of Hellenism: Mapping the Homeland.* Ithaca: Cornell University Press.

Nikolaou, N.

1986   *Η περιπέτεια της γραμμής στην τέχνη* [*The Adventure of Line in Art*]. Athens: Th. Sakellariou and P. Mougios.

Pepelases, A.

2002   *Το Αιγαίο του πολιτισμού και της ανάπτυξης* [*The Aegean of Culture and Development*]. *Η Λέξη* 169 (May–June): 344–51.

Philippides, D.

1983   Historical retrospect. Trans. David Hardy. In *Greek Traditional Architecture,* Vol. 1: *Eastern Aegean, Sporades—Ionian Islands,* 33–49. Athens: Melissa.

Pikionis, D.

1985a *Η λαϊκή μας τέχνη κι εμείς* [*We and Our Folk Art*] [1925]. In *Κείμενα* [*Texts*], 53–69. Athens: Educational Foundation of the National Bank.

1985b *Το πρόβλημα της μορφής* [*The Problem of Form*] [1950]. In *Κείμενα* [*Texts*], 204–46. Athens: Educational Foundation of the National Bank.

Sherrard, P.

1986   *Ο Οδυσσέας Ελύτης και η ανακάλυψη της Ελλάδας* [*Odysseas Elytis and the Discovery of Greece*]. *Χάρτης* 21–23 (November): 501–21.

Vakalo, E.

1983   *Ο μύθος της ελληνικότητας* [*The Myth of Hellenicity*]. *Η φυσιογνωμία της μεταπολεμικής τέχνης στην Ελλάδα* [*The Nature of Post-War Art in Greece*, 4 vols.], Vol. 3. Athens: Kedros.

Yannopoulos, P.

1988   *Άπαντα* [*Collected Works*]. Athens: Eleftheri Skepsis.

7

Commentary and Response

8   Round a Bigger Pond

Colin Renfrew

'A great sunrise . . . our Europe was first beginning to think, to be!'

It is a pleasure to be invited by the editors to add my voice (or should it be my croak?) to the debate that *Prehistorians Round the Pond* is likely to generate. They are to be congratulated for producing a thought-provoking book, which will elicit a variety of reactions. This frog, however, feels more robustly optimistic than some of the contributors. The initial rather cautious assessment (Preface, p. xiv), happily substantially modified by the editors themselves in ch. 2, was that:

> Aegean Prehistory looked to be in trouble . . . its general standing within Archaeology and perhaps in the academy as a whole in decline . . . Aegean prehistory seems to have 'won the battle but lost its charm.'

Not for this prehistorian, it hasn't. To quote Thomas Carlyle once again (ch. 1, p. 11)—with perhaps a touch of hyperbole, and written in the days before aspirations of gender equality:

> Wonder, hope, infinite radiance of hope and wonder, as of a young child's thoughts, in the hearts of these strong men!

There are grounds, I think, for trying to recapture the inspiration of Carlyle. After a brief consideration of the scale of our pond and a comment on different approaches to the Greek inheritance, I would like to assert that what Carlyle said remains valid, and that we still have much to learn that is of value from the Greek experience. Today we can see more clearly that there was not one but several 'experiences,' and multiple creative episodes from which we can hope to learn.

Which Pond?

Plato is generally believed to have been referring to the Mediterranean Sea, *mare nostrum,* as the Romans were to call it. But the late Alistair Cooke used much the same terminology and imagery to refer to the North Atlantic Ocean, so that the frogs in question were located in New York, and London, and Paris. Today even that focus may seem too localized when we are all inhabitants of the Global Village. So it may be helpful to set our geographical regions in clearer focus. My first wish for the debate that the editors and contributors to *Prehistorians Round the Pond*

8

have initiated is that its perspectives should not be too localized. Plato's pond was the Mediterranean, and there would certainly be a case for setting out to review the rarity of the occasions on which prehistorians around that pond sit down together and discuss mutual problems. The Phoenicians may have done it, from the Levant to Iberia, but today's prehistorian tends to be more restricted. So that pond is clearly not the editors' pond.

We should, I think, be reasonably clear about the very concept of 'the Aegean.' I was puzzled by the scholarly discussion in ch. 1 (pp. 2–5) about the definition of the Aegean, and indeed was disconcerted to read (p. 2):

> To those familiar with the field and its literature, what Aegean prehistory comprises is largely unproblematic: the prehistoric archaeology of the Greek mainland, the Aegean islands, and Crete.

As the British satirical magazine *Private Eye* is wont to insert: 'Something missing here, surely?—*Ed.*' No Ancient Greek would for a moment have ignored the great cities of the Ionian Coast, no Byzantinist would omit Ephesos, let alone Constantinople; and since we are all prehistorians together, what about Troy, or Iasos, or Miletos, or even Kum Tepe? That point is of course taken up in the ensuing discussion. But it ends with the decidedly unsatisfactory conclusion: 'So in determining what is and what is not "Aegean," there is a consistent negotiation and fluidity, consistent with the relativism inherent in the very term itself.' I was unaware that postmodernist relativism had taken so deep a hold in the Midwest! For me, 'the Aegean' designates and has always designated the lands around the Aegean Sea and the islands within it. I am perfectly willing to include Western Greece—the definition offered by Warren (1988, vii), namely 'modern Greece and the western coast of Turkey,' has indeed the merit of concision. That is the pond around which Aegean prehistorians sit, although the strength and vitality of Aegean prehistory as practiced in the United States reminds us that we do all also sit around that wider pond discerned by Alistair Cooke.

Inheritors? Discerning the Links between Yesterday and Today

Contributors to the workshop from which this volume came were concerned with the special relationships between prehistoric archaeology and classical studies. From the other side of the (Atlantic) pond one can perhaps discern a tension that may arise from the local North American tradition that prehistoric archaeology falls within the larger sphere of anthropology. In Europe, things are different. And in Greece, where ancient Greece is inevitably seen as directly ancestral to the modern nation state, nationalist sentiments are more difficult to avoid.

For an archaeologist born in Britain, the bad news may be that we British are the sons and daughters of a once-powerful colonial power, even if the sun has now set upon the grandeur of the empire. The good news, however, is that very few people in Britain now entirely believe in the panoply and rhetoric once associated with that empire. We accept our position as citizens of a nation that was once more powerful than it is today and respect the contributions made by a Shakespeare or a Newton, without claiming such preeminence in the present world. But at the Last Night of the Proms, when we join with gusto in the singing of *Rule Britannia* or *Land of Hope and Glory,* there is an irony that allows just a momentary suspension of disbelief with the words:

> Wider still and wider
> Shall thy bounds be set:
> God who made thee mighty
> Make thee mightier yet.

We may have believed that once, but today (except for football supporters travelling overseas) it is simply amusing in its grandiloquence. So for most of us, nationalism is no longer a preoccupation. Scotland and Wales have achieved a degree of self-government, and most of us are content that Britain has a place in the European Union. Although there are indeed fringe political parties preoccupied with the Union Jack (the British national flag) and with 'Britishness'—usually in opposition to immigration—we are not in the main today seeking archaeological insights into the nation as a national entity.

That is not to say that material culture and archaeology had no role in developing British nationalism—quite the contrary. Until the mid-twentieth century, historians like Sir Arthur Bryant could regard the Anglo-Saxon kingdoms as the founders not only of the British monarchy but almost of our constitution, and something of the same attitude may be seen in Winston Churchill's *History of the English-Speaking Peoples.* In the early nineteenth century, when the future King George IV was Prince Regent, there was a great reshaping of the symbolism of the monarchy in England and in Scotland. There Sir Walter Scott contributed to the notion of Scottishness—most of the Scottish tartans date from around that time—just as Charles Dickens and his contemporaries are responsible for much of the symbolism of the traditional British Christmas. But all that is more than a century ago, and it is easy (I hope) for a writer today to be a shade cynical about British nationalism. And when it comes to ethnicity, the aspiration today is to be multiethnic, so that the term 'heritage,' as in English Heritage (the official organization with responsibility for ancient monuments), has become suspect in Blairite political circles and has been dropped from the name of any government ministry.

For the modern Greek nation, Greekness and Greek ethnicity is perhaps a more powerful force than Britishness and British ethnicity appear to be today. That is scarcely surprising, since the War of Independence is less than two centuries behind us, and the events of 1922 less than a century. To an outsider, the vehemence of the hostility in northern Greece, only a few years ago, to the establishment of the Former Yugoslav Republic of Macedonia (FYROM) was at first surprising. But then so were the ethnic tensions in Bosnia and Kosovo, which had such appalling

8

consequences. Yet with Greece today as a member both of the European Union and of NATO, it is surely unthinkable that the borders of the nation could be called into question or come under threat. So that while it is important for any nation to respect and maintain its national identity, I am personally critical of tendencies to build up ethnicity beyond the extent required for the discharge of civic responsibilities in a modern democracy. Ethnicity was the bane of the twentieth century (see Renfrew 1996).

All that is a preamble to the observation that there is a risk in conflating the problems and preoccupations of the classicist, including the classical archaeologist, concerned with the entire classical world, with those of the historian of the modern Greek nation and its territorial anxieties. It is one thing for Oliver Dickinson (see ch. 1, p. 3) to emphasize the continuities between prehistoric and classical Greece, as I would myself be inclined to do. It is another for Stelios Andreou or Artemis Leontis in their respective chapters here to analyze the origins of Greek modernism, with the implication, through their inclusion in this volume, that this need have a significant bearing upon the practice of Aegean archaeology in a wider or more general sense. Of course there are strong continuities that link the recent past of Greece with its classical roots: continuities of language and of territory. I am not one of those who is cynical on that account and am likewise content to see the Greeks of today as the descendants, in genetic and cultural terms, of the Greeks of the classical era. But my own love of modern Greece, especially rural Greece, for its traditions and customs, for its songs and music and dance, for its architecture, for its hospitality and warmth, for its zest for life, is not dependent upon those strands of continuity with the classical past. I recognize and value also what one may term the 'orientalizing' elements in modern Greece—in the architecture, in the cuisine, in the music—which owe so much to the centuries when mainland Greece was at the western extremity of the Byzantine empire and its successor.

If the aim of the project is self-reflexivity, we should not be confusing or eliding these two worlds, the ancient and the modern, nor risk equating the 'Greekness' of the one with that of the other. One only has to reflect upon the meaning of 'ethnicity' (see Renfrew 1993; Jones 1997) to see that Greek ethnicity in the fifth century BC and the twenty-first century AD must be seen as very different things, although the former has influenced the latter. Nor should we forget that these qualities of contemporary rural Greece and its recent past have been highly valued by earlier generations of archaeologists. It was Wace and Thompson who wrote *Nomads of the Balkans* (1914), and Alan Wace was for a while curator of textiles and embroideries from the Aegean at the Victoria and Albert Museum. The distinguished Minoan scholar Stylianos Alexiou is also a specialist in traditional Cretan poetry. There are many things to celebrate in Greece today that do not form part of Greece's debt to its classical forbears.

The reasons for practicing archaeology in the Aegean go much wider than any analysis of the identity of modern Greece. Modern Greece, like traditional

8

Greece, is certainly a matter for celebration and admiration, but for this observer at least the theme of its national self-awareness is not its most interesting dimension.

What Crisis? An Optimistic Rejoinder

In the interestingly detailed paper by Davis and Gorgogianni about Aegean prehistory at the University of Cincinnati, I first made my acquaintance with the concept of 'crisis literature' (ch. 5, p. 106). After a moment's alarm, I was relieved to find that the 'crisis' was located principally 'within those [American] institutions where classical archaeologists are trained.' This is perhaps the moment for calming words. For a contrary exemplar is locally available, in the truly outstanding contributions made to Aegean prehistory by Carl Blegen and by Jack Caskey and by their colleagues and successors. They are among those, like Tsountas and Evans, or Xanthoudides and Platon, or Theochares and Mylonas—to mention only a few—whose discoveries and theories and publications have created the very subject that we are discussing. They transcended the intellectual limitations and the practical constraints of their day through the *praxis* of their fieldwork and by their energy in creating new data from which new understandings of the Aegean past could be shaped.

Aegean prehistory has a perennial fascination for a number of reasons, among which is the wealth of its materials from very early periods, from the Neolithic and before. It offers the opportunity of understanding, or at least of seeking to understand, the appearance of what may be regarded as the two earliest complex societies of Europe. Nor is there reason to balk at the academic divide which sometimes seems to separate the Bronze Age and the Iron Age, and which increasingly scholars such as Anthony Snodgrass or Ian Morris are beginning to bridge.

For surely there need be no hesitation in asserting that the world of classical Greece, naturally including Magna Graecia as well as the Ionian coast, must be one of intense interest for the modern thinker, when we can trace back to it so many of the founding elements of Western civilization—of science, of mathematics, of philosophy, of literature, of the arts, of what Merlin Donald (1991) has termed *Theoretic Culture*. Of course there were earlier discoveries in Sumer and in Egypt that likewise provided foundations, earlier foundations, for Western culture. And of course in China or in India or in Mesoamerica there were other upsurges of activity that may be regarded as comparable. But classical Greece may bear comparison with these. For those of us who, through the medium of the Renaissance, are its inheritors, it has and will continue to have a special place.

For those who see a key role for material culture in understanding social and economic, and indeed cognitive, change, it is the practice of archaeology that will offer better understanding of many of these things. If we look at Anglo-Saxon studies, to return to Britain for a moment, we may observe that a great transformation took place in the 1950s and 1960s. Until that time the rather scanty written records—the *Anglo-Saxon Chronicles*, the writings of the Venerable Bede—provided the outline for the period. But with the development of rescue archaeology and of

8   urban archaeology the picture changed. Now our understanding of Anglo-Saxon England rests as much on the archaeological data as upon those written texts, and progress continues.

Now of course the basic texts for Greek history of the classical period may never be surpassed, supported as they are by abundant epigraphic evidence. But when we go back to the sixth century BC and before, the situation is different. It already rests in large measure upon archaeology, and increasingly our perception of the origins of the *polis*, and of early Greek society, will depend upon the discovery and interpretation of material culture. Yet for too long the 'prehistorians' have held back, deferring in this field to scholars of a different formation, where the written word has primacy. It is time now to transcend this notional and largely fictitious barrier between prehistoric and historic, between preclassical and classical.

If a paradigm is needed, it may best be sought beyond Plato's pond, indeed beyond Alistair Cooke's. In Mesoamerica, there is much fresh thinking about the processes and circumstances that led there to the rise of urban society, indeed of literate society. The Aegean archaeologist (who need not be restricted by the term 'prehistorian') could take as an example the remarkable and now classic synthesis by Kent Flannery and Joyce Marcus (1983), *The Cloud People*, which outlines the origins and development of the Zapotec and Mixtec civilizations of Mexico, and which has been developed in subsequent work (Marcus and Flannery 1996).

Ultimately, the remarkable, and of course unique, qualities of the prehistoric and classical Aegean can only be understood within a broader framework. In that framework, these Aegean societies could be seen more clearly for what they were, in their differences as well as their resemblances with other civilizations and other traditions. We must not lose that sense of wonder which Thomas Carlyle evoked. For out of it will come the fresh and interesting questions that as archaeologists we can seek to answer. The pond has not lost its charm.

References

Donald, M.
   1991   *Origins of the Modern Mind*. Cambridge, Mass.: Harvard University Press.
Flannery, K. V., and J. Marcus (eds.)
   1983   *The Cloud People, Divergent Evolution of the Zapotec and Mixtec Civilizations*. New York: Academic Press.
Jones, S.
   1997   *The Archaeology of Ethnicity: Constructing Identities in the Past and Present*. London: Routledge.
Marcus, J., and K. V. Flannery
   1996   *Zapotec Civilization: How Urban Society Developed in Mexico's Oaxaca Valley*. London: Thames and Hudson; New York: Norton.

Renfrew, C. **8**

    1993   *The Roots of Ethnicity: Archaeology, Genetics and the Origins of Europe.* Rome: Unione Internazionale degli Istituti di Archeologia Storia e Storia dell'Arte in Roma (Conferenze 10).

    1996   Prehistory and the identity of Europe, or don't let's be beastly to the Hungarians. In P. Graves-Brown, S. Jones and C. Gamble (eds.), *Cultural Identity and Archaeology: The Construction of European Communities*, 125-37. London: Routledge.

Wace, A. J. B., and M. Thompson

    1914   *The Nomads of the Balkans: An Account of Life and Customs among the Vlachs of Northern Pindus.* London: Methuen.

Warren, P.

    1988   *The Aegean Civilizations.* New York: Peter Bedrick Books.

9 On Our Political Relevance?

Michael Fotiadis

The papers for the *Prehistorians Round the Pond* volume arrived in my office on the same day that *Nature* online reported news of a survey on the civilian death toll in Iraq since the invasion on March 19, 2003. The full article, 'Mortality before and after the 2003 invasion of Iraq: cluster sample survey,' had been published a few days earlier (October 29, 2004) in *The Lancet* online (Roberts *et al.* 2004). I downloaded and read on, in tandem with the *Prehistorians* papers. The sampling methods of the survey, conducted in mid-September 2004, were only as rigorous as war conditions might allow, and the resulting confidence intervals around the point estimates are wide. But, as the editor of *The Lancet* points out (Horton 2004), this was 'the first scientific study of the effects of this war on Iraqi civilians'; moreover the findings 'have immediately translatable policy implications for those charged with managing the aftermath of invasion':

> The main causes of death reported for the 14.6 months before the invasion were myocardial infarction, cerebrovascular accidents, and consequences of other chronic disorders, accounting for 22 (48%) reported deaths . . . After the war began, violence was the most commonly reported cause of death, either including (73/142 [51%]) or excluding (21/89 [24%]) the Falluja data, followed by myocardial infarction and cerebrovascular accidents (n=18) and accidents (n=13) . . . Violence-specific mortality rate went up 58-fold (95% CI 8.1–419) during the period after the invasion
> . . .
> Evidence suggests that the mortality rate was higher across Iraq after the war than before, even excluding Falluja. We estimate that there were 98,000 extra deaths (95% CI 8000–194,000) during the post-war period in the 97% of Iraq represented by all the clusters except Falluja. In our Falluja sample, we recorded 53 deaths when only 1.4 were expected under the national pre-war rate. This indicates a point estimate of about 200,000 excess deaths in the 3% of Iraq represented by this cluster. (Roberts *et al.* 2004: 5)

Elsewhere in the article we learn that of the 73 violent deaths recorded in the sample 61 were due to actions of the coalition forces and that all but three of those 'were caused by helicopter gunships, rockets, or other forms of aerial weaponry' (Roberts *et al.* 2004: 7). And in the last paragraph:

9

> US General Tommy Franks is widely quoted as saying 'we don't do body counts'. The Geneva Conventions have clear guidance about the responsibilities of occupying armies to the civilian population they control. The fact that more than half the deaths reportedly caused by the occupying forces were women and children is cause for concern . . . It seems difficult to understand how a military force could monitor the extent to which civilians are protected against violence without systematically doing body counts or at least looking at the kinds of casualties they induce. (Roberts *et al.* 2004: 7)

Now, if you are wondering, 'all this is very important, but what could Aegean prehistory possibly have to do with it?' then you have already come close to my point. We, Aegean prehistorians, are awkwardly irrelevant to the scene of Iraqi death and its census. The task falls on 'courageous scientists' (Horton 2004), folks whose institutional allegiances are with medical, nursing and public health schools. Clearly, it is not in our professional duties, commitments, or competences to count bodies, to carry out a survey of the situation (or, at least, a very laborious, convoluted, and, hence, unconvincing argument would have to be constructed to show that we share in responsibility). Despite this fact—the fact that we cannot hold ourselves guilty for evading duty, etc.—or, rather, *precisely because of this fact*—we cannot walk away from the scene 'as if it was not there': the scene keeps interpellating us, thinking absurdly through us 'you see, you are powerless, unable to do the slightest thing about the situation; you are irrelevant, impotent indeed!'

What follows here is an attempt to hail back at that absurd interpellation, to ease its harshness by engaging its absurdity in rationality—even though from the start I recognize in it the logic of the indelible stain: it is more likely that the stain will be blurred and will blend in as newer stains add themselves around it in the future than that we will manage to eliminate it by rubbing. Silence might be a better response.

Being irrelevant to matters of violence and death in our time, and to the politics that govern them, can serve as yet another measure of our discipline's standing, its centrality/marginality in the contemporary world. Such a measure seems to me just as pertinent as our relative successes vis-à-vis our brethren, the classical archaeologists, or kindred prehistorians. The point is not that 'we fail' to become engaged in key issues of our time. Rather, our world—the world of Aegean prehistorians—appears to be settled, tame, protected from upheavals in ways in which the world 'courageous scientists' venture in is not. The political stakes in Aegean prehistory today are low: no research of political significance comparable to that reported in *The Lancet* a few weeks ago is expected.

In Schliemann's time, it mattered politically a great deal whether the goods found in the Royal Tombs of Mycenae were of Asiatic or Greek origin (see, e.g., Voutsaki 2003). Later, in the 1890s and the early 20th century, it mattered politically whether the prehistoric Aegean was culturally European or Oriental (see, e.g.,

Myres 1933). From about 1900 to World War II, it was politically crucial whether Macedonia in prehistory should be counted as part of the Aegean or should instead 'go with the North' (Fotiadis 2002). And in the 1960s and early 1970s, when Nea Nikomedeia was celebrated as 'the site of the oldest dated Neolithic community yet found in Europe' (Rodden 1965: 83), the excitement again had political underpinnings: the knowledge gained was the product of international scientific cooperation and exchange free from political interest—precisely the kind of virtue by which the West (the 'Free World' of the era) demonstrated its moral difference over the East! Granted, none of these cases appears to have as acute a political significance as the recent survey of Iraqi death; the archaeologists involved in each case, for example, incurred virtually no political risks, for their conclusions suited (rather than clashed with) the policies of their home states and other powerful agencies. Still, such conclusions each time answered directly to deep-seated anxieties about human identity and difference, about collective selfhood and collective otherness, and that is hardly innocent, apolitical stuff. The conclusions thus mattered to great numbers of people, for whom they were immediately translatable to rights of collective existence, legitimacy of territorial inheritance, proofs of being unique on earth (uniquely gifted, uniquely wronged in the past, etc.), confirmation of blood ties with other groups, or moral justification for controlling geography and resources.

All these, however, are tales from the past of our discipline. The political ideals that installed themselves in the hearts of Aegean prehistorians (unbeknownst to them) and underpinned our practice since its inception in the late 19th century were, in the course of the 20th century, more or less accomplished. The Greek nation, endowed in the process with a deep past, has been a main beneficiary (see Andreou, ch. 4, with references to earlier works). It is not, however, the sole beneficiary: the European Union in 2004 owes no small debt for its existence to the late 19th-century idea of the 'unité européenne primitive . . . de l'époque de la pierre polie et du cuivre,' as Salomon Reinach expressed it in *Le mirage oriental* (1893: 55). Note that, for Reinach, this 'unité européenne' extended from Scandinavia to Portugal and Cyprus; 'the Aegean' played a most essential role, even though it had been 'discovered,' by Flinders Petrie, barely three years before the writing of *Mirage* (for Petrie's invention and its circumstances, see Phillips, in press). And a century later, at the dawn of the third millennium, the prehistoric Aegean was again given the place of honor in the exhibition 'L'Europe au temps d'Ulysse: dieux et héros de l'âge du bronze,' sponsored by the Council of Europe and shown in Copenhagen, Bonn, Paris, and Athens (Demakopoulou 1999).

It is a different matter whether the political causes in which Aegean prehistory became implicated in its 100-odd-year history were progressive or not. True, our practice has been spared of the most sinister political abuses to which other archaeologies have been put. Clearly also, its perceived political utility has always been distinctly lower than that of its more glamorous sibling, classical archaeology. From the vantage point of the early 21st century, however, the issue presents

9   itself in more complex terms—it is not unlike a dilemma: what can prevent one moment's progressive politics from becoming a later moment's conservative institution? Claiming a deep past as a prop for nation-building, for edifying 'national character,' is only steps away from enlisting that past in the service of oppressive nationalism. Knowledge that was heralded as setting thought free when it first emerged can grow into stifling orthodoxy. And, by the same token, knowledge that was scarcely noticed (appearing to be deprived of all significance) the moment it originated can be rediscovered in a different time and place as the lynchpin of the most contentious argument. (No one thinks anymore—at least, no one will insist when pressed—that knowledge of the past advances, first and foremost, like 'puzzle-solving' and is thus 'compounded' with time; see Zygmunt Bauman's elegant prose [2002: 16]: 'new ingredients do not lie quietly lie aside the old. . . . Old compounds can hold no more and are falling apart, new syntheses emerge'; see also below.) Such are the horns of the dilemma.

Consider. 'The Aegean' sprang into existence as a distinct (and, because of its anteriority to classical Greece, privileged) prehistoric culture in the last decade of the 19th century, as the sign of nationalism was ascending in the European skies. That was no mere coincidence: at the time, nationalism did not function simply as our discipline's context; most crucially, it empowered it in its very core, forming it 'from the inside,' as it were, by offering itself as an *epistemic system* (however incomplete: see Fotiadis 2002). In the succeeding century, this offspring of 1890s episteme, 'the Aegean,' became the object of intense scholarly curiosity and, progressively, the field of a disciplinary specialization. It was now constantly being defined and redefined (see Margomenou *et al.*, ch. 1; also Davis and Gorogianni, ch. 5), and that is testimony to the positivity of the concept, its capacity to set thought free. To put it in a different way, 'the Aegean'—that name—acted upon scholars like a magnet, or better, like an enigmatic and, thus, fascinating birthmark. It was around this name that scholarly energy intensified. 'What is your true nature, your descent, the secret of your nobility, you, the object they call "Aegean"?'—that is the question that exercised scholarly curiosity and upon which our discipline founded itself.[1]

As it happens, however, the object that emerged as practice outgrew its initial narrow frame was nothing like its name promised it would be. Instead of being singular, unified, and coherently rising to civilization, that object turned out to be discontinuous and highly heterogeneous, a multitude of objects indeed, with shifting boundaries, often running into the geographical frame—a liquid amalgam but no determinable essences. In fact, in light of what we know today, more than a century after the beginning, the premise of the prehistoric Aegean as a distinct culture area—a sufficiently stable, unified, complete object—is difficult to sustain. Besides, the demise, by the mid-20th century, of nationalism as an epistemic system for prehistory left the culture area concept itself suspended in the air, too weak to serve as a foundation for disciplinary knowledge and, also, politically useless except for regressive causes. If that is the case, can 'the Aegean' still set thought free today? Does it not by now appear as an arbitrary, irrational element in the midst of a rational practice? Is it not a mere vestige, a ghost from the past, deprived of all its former positivity—*a pure limit*?

The point is not that our discipline goes in the present by an anachronistic name (a name laden with 19th- to early 20th-century connotations, with meanings that no longer find empirical or theoretical support; a name that we retain 'conventionally' or 'just for historical reasons,' etc.; a name, in any case, that we can at last exchange for an alternative, up-to-date one). Names are known to impose their logic on practices and on circumstances—to have causal powers, in short—and 'the Aegean' seems to me no exception: it is the flag of our disciplinary allegiance, it commits us to the idea of 'the Aegean as a culture area' (however broadly or narrowly meant), and every time we pronounce it we are co-opted by its logic. (That is also to say, 'Aegean prehistory' is first and foremost the name of a disciplinary practice, much more than it is the prehistory of the islands and coasts bathed by the Aegean Sea.) We cannot let go of the name without at the same time letting go of our habits of thought, the dispositions to which the name engages us—in effect, letting go of our practice.

'Can a regionally defined archaeology that does not consort seriously with larger intellectual issues expect to survive in a landscape that is becoming increasingly more globalized?' ask Cherry and Talalay at the end of their contribution (ch. 2). By 'regionally defined,' certainly, they do not mean 'focused on a naturally circumscribed area,' and not only because the prehistorians' definitions of 'the Aegean' have only selectively paid attention to natural boundaries. It has been 20th-century geopolitical visions and struggles, not natural geography, that determined the geographical spread of the Aegean-as-region. When this is made clear, the question about the viability of our discipline in an increasingly globalized landscape (a landscape, that is, governed by a new geopolitical vision) becomes considerably more pointed. I also suggested above that Aegean prehistory, a disciplinary division by this name, is defined self-referentially, rather than regionally,[2] by resort to its historically emergent premise of the Aegean as a distinct, and distinguished, culture area in prehistory. Take that premise away, and Aegean prehistory makes no sense as a discipline; it is reduced to an area of expertise or erudition, that is, encyclopedic knowledge about specific places and time periods (and what the political stakes of such an 'area' would be?). It seems to me that institutions such as the American School of Classical Studies understand this very well when they require from their prospective members that they treat prehistory as a prelude to classical Greece (see Cullen, ch. 3).

Supposing that my sense, that the founding premise of our discipline is no longer tenable, were to be widely shared, what would that mean for Cherry and Talalay's question? When the object upon which they were founded dissolves, fields of knowledge can become extinct—at least in a complex sense of that word. That is, they become so transformed that the newly emerging field bears no readily recognizable resemblance to the old; moreover, much of the old knowledge now appears curious, meaningless in the new circumstances, and is rapidly consigned

9

to oblivion. Is not this the main lesson we learned from Thomas Kuhn's discussion (1970, especially ch. 10), almost half a century ago, of 'paradigm shift'? Perhaps nothing as dramatic will transpire in our field of knowledge, or, whatever paradigm shift happens, it will proceed at a glacial pace. It is nevertheless conceivable that in the future, some generations from now, mention of 'Aegean prehistory' will recall in the listener's mind the 19th and 20th centuries, much in the way that mention of 'antiquaries' today makes us think of the 17th and 18th centuries. That is not to say there will then be no prehistoric excavations, surveys, and regional projects in the lands around the Aegean Sea, but only that the object of such research will not be 'the Aegean'; its significance will not derive from improving knowledge of prehistoric life around the Aegean Sea but from illuminating entirely different objects.

But if that is placed some time in the future, what of the immediate present? What might raise the political stakes of Aegeanist practice, help it align itself with progressive political causes? Criticizing the founding premise of our discipline as *no longer* empirically and theoretically sound—in effect, *historicizing* Aegean prehistory—may require political courage (it exposes the critics to the risk of being marginalized within the discipline, for instance), but it is all too easy today. Tacitly dropping the founding premise from our practice (and under 'practice' here I include our teaching) and practicing Aegean prehistory as if it were the archaeology of a foreign country—in the way an Aegean prehistorian transplanted, for example, to Michigan's Upper Peninsula would do local, UP archaeology—seems to me a more virtuous emancipatory step, one that demands sustained intellectual labor. Were we to proceed this way, the prehistoric Aegean might become exotic again. Cullen (ch. 3) documents the discomfort of Aegean prehistorians with comparative studies. Her point is clear: comparative perspectives have a large potential for challenging the current paradigm of our discipline, 'relativizing' the Aegean, and so setting thought free again. I have for some time been intrigued by the gender inequity characteristic of our discipline for over a century (see Cullen, ch. 3): what is its cumulative *epistemic* effect? In other words, would not the texture of Aegean knowledge, our narratives about the prehistoric Aegean, change in the long term if the inequity were to be reversed or evened out?

These are only some suggestions (and they will, no doubt, appear unbearably naïve when the present becomes the past). There can be no scarcity of projects, indeed, that would raise the political stakes in our practice somewhat and help it realign itself with progressive causes. We only need remember that progressive political causes do not stay progressive for ever.

Acknowledgements

I am thankful to my friends, the organizers and editors of *Prehistorians Round the Pond*, for inviting me to join in this discussion. Creating opportunities such as this also is a progressive cause.

Notes

1.   The modernism Leontis (ch. 7) describes seems to me to have arrived among Aegean prehistorians rather late, in the 1960s and 1970s, and to have assumed the form of a taste, or even a hunt, for the primitive, now thought of as the authentic condition of the rural Aegean landscape (modern as well as prehistoric). I cannot, however, substantiate this view here (see Fotiadis 1995 for related material). I also think that the discovery of the Aegean as primitive added to the appeal of the object; it did not threaten, but proved in the end quite compatible with, its previously established noble identity.

2.   Though the two are by no means mutually exclusive: regions *are* self-referential; they create the reality that they come to designate (see Bourdieu 1991). But talk of regions gives rise to confusions, and that is why I avoided it here. I have also argued that regions, as they emerge from our regional projects, are the effects of a statist vision (Fotiadis 1993); they are 'not in the slightest respect natural' (Bourdieu 1991: 222).

References

Bauman, Z.
    2002   The 20th century: the end or a beginning? *Thesis Eleven* 70: 15–25.
Bourdieu, P.
    1991   Identity and representation: elements for a critical reflection on the idea of region. In P. Bourdieu, *Language and Symbolic Power*, 220–28. Cambridge, Mass.: Harvard University Press.
Demakopoulou. K., *et al.*
    1999   *Gods and Heroes of the European Bronze Age.* [Catalogue published on the occasion of the 25th Council of Europe Art Exhibition, 'Gods and Heroes of the Bronze Age: Europe at the Time of Ulysses.'] London: Thames and Hudson.
Fotiadis, M.
    1993   Regions of the imagination: archaeologists, local people, and the archaeological record in fieldwork, Greece. *Journal of European Archaeology* 1(2): 149–66.
    1995   Modernity and the past-still-present: politics of time in the birth of regional archaeological projects in Greece. *American Journal of Archaeology* 99: 59–78.
    2001   Imagining Macedonia in prehistory. *Journal of Mediterranean Archaeology* 14: 115–35.
Horton, R.
    2004   The war in Iraq: civilian casualties, political responsibilities. *The Lancet* on-line: http://image.thelancet.com/extras/04cmt384web.pdf.

9 Kuhn, T. S.
   1970   *The Structure of Scientific Revolutions* (2nd ed.). Chicago: University of Chicago Press.

Myres, J. L.
   1933   The Cretan labyrinth: a retrospect of Aegean research. (The Huxley Memorial Lecture for 1933.) *Journal of the Royal Anthropological Institute of Great Britain and Ireland* 63: 269–312.

Phillips, J.
   in press   Petrie, the 'outsider looking on.' In P. Darcque, M. Fotiadis, and O. Polychronopoulou (eds.), *Mythos: La préhistoire égéenne du XIXe au XXIe siècle après J.-C. Actes de la table ronde internationale d'Athènes (novembre 2002)*. Bulletin de Correspondance Hellénique, supplément. Paris and Athens: Ecole française d'Athènes.

Reinach, S.
   1893   *Le mirage oriental.* (Reprinted from *L'Anthropologie* 5–6, 1893.) Paris: G. Masson.

Roberts, L., R. Lafta, R. Garfield, J. Khudhairi, and G. Burnam
   2004   Mortality before and after the 2003 invasion of Iraq: cluster sample survey. *The Lancet* on-line: http://image.thelancet.com/extras/04art 10342web.pdf.

Rodden, R. J.
   1965   An Early Neolithic village in Greece. *Scientific American* 212: 83–92.

Voutsaki, S.
   2003   The 'Greekness' of Greek prehistory: an investigation of the debate 1876–1900. *Pharos: Journal of the Netherlands Institute in Athens* 10: 105–22.

10 Whither Aegean Prehistory?

Yannis Hamilakis

As the last contributor to this important and timely volume, I feel that in my short and modest commentary, I should attempt to bridge the gap between the authors and the reader by adopting an insider's/outsider's perspective on the themes and ideas discussed here. That is quite appropriate, given that (as I will explain) personally I am not entirely comfortable with the label 'Aegean prehistorian,' nor do I believe that many of my colleagues consider me as such: neither in my present post nor in the previous one was I employed as an Aegean prehistorian, although a lot of my work falls within that field. Yet I regard the reflections contained in this volume to be of immense importance for our 'enterprise' (whatever we want to call it), and I am grateful for the opportunity to be able to contribute in a small and slightly heterodoxical way.

As some of the contributors have intimated, this book may be seen as part of the 'crisis literature' of a subfield of classics: it deals with the impression and the anxiety that Aegean prehistory is undergoing a crisis and is in danger of being marginalized, both within the broader field of classics and in archaeology overall. But as several contributors have shown (especially Cherry and Talalay [ch. 2] and Cullen [ch. 3]), the picture is far more complicated than that. The study of Aegean prehistory attracts a growing number of researchers, and it is an extremely dynamic field in terms of research activity; yet there are signs that it is becoming more introverted than before, and it has yet to shed its image (assuming that it wants to, which is not a foregone conclusion) as a Eurocentric and, to a large extent, elitist field.

Definition Matters

It seems that Aegean prehistory as a term is a fairly recent construction. As shown in this volume, the social phenomenon that it denotes was until recently taught and practiced under different names—from Homeric archaeology, to preclassical archaeology, to Greek prehistory—revealing the complex interweaving of language, disciplinary history, and national and other identities. The reasons why the term Aegean prehistory has acquired currency in the USA, in many European countries, and increasingly in Greece too, are still not clear, but a significant factor may have to do with the fact that the most important funding source for this field in the last decade or two goes under the name of the Institute for Aegean Prehistory.

What of the 'Aegean' in Aegean prehistory? Both the introduction to this volume (ch. 1) and the elegant and insightful chapter by Leontis (ch. 7) have shown

10 that the term is not simply a geographical descriptor (for if it were, the problems of its applicability would have become immediately apparent) but an imaginary *topos*, created by the topographic desire to materialize in the land and localize in space both the national dream (cf. Gourgouris 1996) and the archaeological and other identity-signifying discourses. What perhaps is missing in this analysis is discussion of the selective and class-specific construction of this *topos*: for example, in the version of Greek national imagination produced by most modernist poets, authors, and other artists, the Aegean is defined by light, by the sun and the sea, and by the shining white Cycladic figurines; other national agents, however—such as, for example, the persecuted poets and painters of the post–World War II era—constructed a different, grim Aegean, by narrating the modern Greek experience of exile, imprisonment, and torture in the prison-islands of Makronisos, Ai-Stratis, Gyaros, Leros, and Gavdos, among others (cf. Papatheodorou 2000; Hamilakis 2002), an experience that has created its own Aegean archaeology, still to be taken up as a project. Equally, the 'Aegean' in Aegean prehistory is a selective construct that unifies and divides at the same time: archaeologically and culturally heterogeneous contexts become parts of the same discursive and disciplinary whole (see below), while other geographically pertinent locales (such as, for example, the Anatolian coast) are excluded most of the time.

The use of such a term to delineate a field of study has various consequences and implications. For a start, it assumes a relative homogeneity and coherence that define the field as distinct from others. But how coherent and homogeneous is the field of Aegean prehistory? What unites the study of an Early Bronze Age tholos tomb in southern Crete with the study of a Neolithic village on the Greek/Bulgarian border? More importantly, what makes the specialists in these two cases feel a disciplinary allegiance towards each other, as opposed to alternative allegiances—for example, the broader collectivity of those studying the Bronze Age of the eastern Mediterranean for the first, and the community of those studying the Neolithic of southeastern Europe, for the second?

If for a moment we examine and compare the 'Minoan' past, 'Cycladic' prehistory, and the Neolithic of northern Greece as three components of the field we call Aegean prehistory, the sense of homogeneity and coherence will soon fade. Even at the synchronic scale (as, for example, in the case of the Early Bronze Age of Crete and that of the Cyclades), the similarities and convergences in material culture are too insignificant to justify their selective grouping under one label, especially if the contemporary cultures of Anatolia are taken into account. The divergences become much more pronounced if we follow their respective historical trajectories, up to the present day. The Minoan past was invented in the twentieth century out of the material traces of the Bronze Age Cretan societies, as a truly modern, 'European' society, an idyllic remake of the British empire; it has been endlessly reworked and remade, providing the raw materials for various identity quests, be it those of the Victorian and Edwardian aristocracy, new-age feminists, art deco artists, or the local people of Crete; and the latter saw in the Minoan past a potent myth of identity that could be tactically deployed, at times as a precursor and at other times in opposition to the overarching national myth of the classical past. Cycladic prehistory, much less familiar and in the shadow of the powerful Minoan and Mycenaean legacies, was unfortunate enough to enjoy huge international fame after the modernist discovery of Cycladic figurines, the consequences of which are well known. An indicator of high aesthetic taste, today the Cycladic past is better known for the decorative replicas and jewelry of the Goulandris Museum than it is for the Early Bronze Age people of the Cyclades, whose material memories have been largely erased. Western modernist aesthetics often merge with the aesthetics of the nation, as in the opening ceremony of the 2004 Athens Olympic Games, where a huge replica of a Cycladic figurine exploded to give birth to an Archaic kouros, inscribing (maybe for the first time, in such a high-profile official ceremony) the Cycladic past in the narrative of the continuity of the nation. As for the Neolithic of northern Greece, the 'other' in Greek prehistory until recently (e.g., Andreou *et al.* 1996), it enjoys a flurry of activity, partly as a result of the political contingencies of competing nationalisms in the region following the breakup of Yugoslavia, and of the epoch-changing materializations of Andronikos's dream at Vergina (cf. Kotsakis 1998). Given the heterogeneity of the cultural histories we are dealing with, the diversity of disciplinary traditions, and the varied ways of present-day reworkings and recontextualizations of the specific material phenomena, it becomes clear that the invention of Aegean prehistory is a result of an homogenizing discourse that relates more to the historical contingencies in the last two centuries, whether European colonization, the nation-state, or archaeological financial concerns.

The above comments lead me to another, more fundamental point, one that relates not only to the phenomenon we call Aegean prehistory but to the archaeological phenomenon overall. As intimated above, the material traces of the people who lived during prehistory in the country presently known as Greece have had a complex and eventful life, a rich biography that we have started to disentangle only fairly recently. To put it in another way, many of these material traces have been participants in many social processes, well after their initial creation and use by the people who lived in prehistoric times. The examples here are plentiful (cf. Alcock 2002, in relation to the maintenance of the material memories of the Minoan past in later periods). These biographies and social lives take different forms, and archaeologists, in their attempts to understand them, often talk of reuse, secondary or tertiary use, or more interestingly, of acts of mnemonic recollection. But the notion of the social and cultural biography of objects, artifacts, and sites captures more than what these now commonly used terms denote: these objects and sites are not only active agents in the continuous process of social life, but they are also constantly made and remade; they are constantly in the process of becoming (cf. Gosden and Marshall 1999). In that sense, to term them 'prehistoric' is to prioritize their initial genesis and role, at the expense of all others. Is the 'Minoan' palace of Knossos to be dated to the Bronze Age or to the twentieth century, given its extensive rebuilding and rearrangement by Evans and all the

10   subsequent interventions? The premise of Aegean prehistory, therefore, is founded
on the assumption that prehistoric monuments and sites are, more or less, a discrete, closed universe, which—once later interventions have been cleared away—is
available for us to study. If we adopt a different ontology, however, which views the
material world as being constantly in flux, subject to various processes of reworking
and recontextualization, of which archaeological intervention and the subsequent
transformation into an 'archaeological record' is but one, then the separation between prehistory and history, and, in fact, the very possibility of dating monuments,
sites, and artifacts, become highly problematic.

Of course, disciplinary and academic traditions, methodological conve-
nience, training necessities, and practical concerns make most practitioners feel
the need to maintain labels such as 'prehistorian' or classical and more broadly 'historical' archaeologist. And there may be contexts where that distinction is tactically
and expediently important. Yet, as I have tried to show, ontologically there is no
justification for the perpetuation of such a rigid divide. As for epistemological reasons, the traditional arguments that consider the presence of documentary sources
as a key criterion are well and truly past their sell-by date and, in our regional
context, they are largely redundant: notwithstanding the important consequences
of documentation (cf. Moreland 2001), all texts are also material culture, and every
category of evidence poses its own specific interpretative problems, making the
need to divide disciplinary boundaries on the basis of absence or presence of texts
irrelevant. In fact, I would argue that the division between prehistory and history
has already become practically obsolete, as a number of researchers have chosen to
ignore it. This is most prominent in the field of interdisciplinary and multi-period
surface survey, and in landscape studies (cf. Cherry 2003). A number of Aegean
prehistorians have found themselves dealing with themes such as the archaeological recognition of ethnicity amongst the Arvanites who arrived in central Greece
in the Middle Ages (Bintliff 2003), the Ottoman presence in the Cyclades (Davis
1991) or Messenia (Bennet *et al.* 2000), the recent history of pastoralism or hay
management in the Pindos Mountains (Halstead 1990; 1998), or the recent social
life of classical and other monuments and their entanglement with processes of
colonial and national identities (e.g., Hamilakis 2003). I suggest that this reconfig-
uring of disciplinary identity is one of the most encouraging signs for the future; it
also begs the question whether the framing of our reflections using the disciplinary
label of Aegean prehistory is still valid or even desirable.

Cartographies of Power in Aegean Prehistory
As the editors of this volume state, the definition of disciplinary boundaries is a
political act. Aegean prehistory as practiced and understood today is a product of
a complex cartographic and chronothetic project with clear colonial-national and
Eurocentric foundations. In its earlier configurations, the field was constructed by
the colonial foundational narratives of its nineteenth- and early twentieth-century
protagonists, for whom European identity in the past and in the present was a

major preoccupation. Europeanism was expressed in diverse direct and indirect ways: through the incorporation of the Bronze Age in particular into the narrative of classical antiquity, as its mythical and heroic substratum (the 'Mycenaean' past); through the portrayal of some of the material culture of the period (such as the Minoan palaces) as thoroughly modern and European, an identity that was inscribed upon them through the technologies of naming (e.g., the palace, the villa, the grand staircase, the 'Parisian lady,' etc.) borrowed by the Western aristocratic milieus; or through the cultural evolutionist narrative that contributed not only to the homogeneity and teleological production of the prehistoric past but also to the direct connection of that past with the European present and future; at the beginning of the century, in the trenches of Crete and other localities of the region, Europe was producing, to use Preziosi's (2002) phrase, 'its future anterior.' In the process of incorporating the borderlands of Greece into the European realms, the antiquities of the Bronze Age played a major role, especially in locales such as Crete, which, by 1913 (the year it became part of Greece), had a world-renowned European civilization, seen as the first major civilization on European soil. The Cretan people, politicians, and intellectuals who fought the fight for the unification with Greece were grateful for that powerful weapon—one that contributed to the transformation of the multicultural, multiethnic island, linked as much to the East as it was to the West, first into a 'cleansed,' primarily Christian, European protectorate, and eventually into a Greek province. As Andreou (ch. 4) and Davis and Gorogianni (ch. 5) eloquently show in this volume, the colonial and national discourses and practices are mutually constituted and perpetuated, despite their occasional tensions.

This cartographic project delineated an area of study, both in terms of place and in terms of time, but it also attached to it some of the most powerful meta-narratives that are still quite prevalent, despite an increasing number of critiques: cultural evolutionism has been already mentioned; the discourse on 'civilization' is another such meta-narrative that has received much less critical attention, even though its power and present-day relevance are immense (cf. Patterson 1997). Granted, there are very few books and other studies today, especially of an academic nature, that explicitly refer to this discourse. Yet its shadow is there in the background, and it frames the position, practice, and even the reflective attempts of the field: it relies on the mostly unchallenged assumption about the prehistoric past of the Greek peninsula (and of the Bronze Age of southern Greece in particular) as the locale of the first European civilization, the foundational basis of the later classical civilization, and the precursor of Western civilization as we know it today. Some New Archaeology discourses blended the narrative of civilization with a rejection of diffusionism, a move that, despite its positive effects in emphasizing the agency of local societies, was inscribed in the often orientalizing, Europeanist project that had started in the nineteenth century (cf. Larsen 1995). Some authors in this volume (Burns [ch. 6], in particular) have explicitly addressed the narratives of continuity and have reminded us of their fallacy, but the overall implications and effects of the civilization discourse have not been addressed in this volume, or indeed

10 elsewhere. Yet this is an urgent and important project. The colonial undertones of the concept, its assumptions of cultural superiority, its race, class, and hierarchy effects, are well known and sufficiently debated in other fields. More importantly, the concept of civilization connects the colonial past with the colonial present. It is a discourse in the name of which the 'civilized' world continues to colonize the Other; it is in the name of 'civilization' that present-day brutality and terror become normalized and justified.

The contributors of this volume are aware of this colonial heritage, and some have explicitly or implicitly sought ways to overcome it. We are all implicated in the colonial present, as the human geographer Derek Gregory (2004: 256) has recently reminded us. The decolonization of the field is a complex process that demands a series of arduous tasks: the production of a new cartography that acknowledges the multiple connections of the prehistoric societies of the Aegean with their broader world of the eastern Mediterranean; the critique of the Europeanist, colonialist, and nationalist discourses, and the awareness of their political connotations in the present; and the opening up of the field to researchers of different backgrounds who come to it from diverse routes, and not simply from the familiar path of the classical heritage as constructed by the European elites. These are only some of the most urgent tasks.

Looking to the Future

With the above thoughts in mind, the reconfiguration of the field of Aegean prehistory may produce a much more open, challenging, and perhaps more effective and influential project. The abolition of rigid distinctions between prehistory and historical archaeology, and the redrawing of its imaginary map may allow a series of beneficial consequences to emerge. To start with, the link between Aegean prehistory and classical archaeology will be reformulated; it would be a mistake to continue the defensive position of emphasizing their complete separation; it would equally be a mistake to continue the present situation of subordination (in such contexts as American academia), a position that is justified on the premise that the graduates of these programs will need to find jobs primarily in classics departments and therefore will have to follow the traditional route of training in Greek and Latin. As Ian Morris (2004: 267) recently noted:

> The fear of classical archaeologists that their students will not find jobs unless they have spent years learning Greek and Latin will be justified only as long as classical archaeologists define their primary audience as other classical archaeologists, embedded in a hermetically sealed classics environment.

The link between Aegean prehistory and classical archaeology will need to be rethought in a radically different way. This engagement with classical antiquity and classical archaeology is essential, though not because of the perceived continuity in the material culture and the social phenomena associated with it (cf. Burns, ch. 6), a debatable argument that lies at the foundation of many essentialist discourses. It is crucial because of the need to confront not only the genealogy of our field but also the social and political conditions that have allowed for classics and classical archaeology to occupy such a predominant position—Eurocentricity and nationalism, above all. This exercise is not merely of an historiographic nature, and it does not simply fulfill the need to engage with the sociopolitics of the discipline. More importantly, it may lead to a total reformulation of our research frameworks and theoretical apparatuses: for example, it allows us to reposition Aegean prehistoric societies within the realm of eastern Mediterranean cultures, as opposed to their position as the substratum of European heritage and identity, the childhood of Western culture, as some of the pioneers of the field as well as their more recent followers have led us to believe. As classical archaeology today is changing, the association of Aegean prehistory with it will also allow the cross-fertilization of ideas and the testing of a number of key questions in current thinking in the humanities, such as the constructions of time, social memory and continuity, the material production of national imagination, the political effects of disciplinary discourses and practices, and the links between modernity and its foundational devices. Graduates who will be able to engage with these themes will be much better positioned in terms of employment opportunities, as they will demonstrate a competence that will be sought after in a wide range of programs and departments, from anthropology to cultural studies.

A researcher in Aegean prehistory who is not defined by a strict identity—one rigidly delineated in terms of its chronological and regional framework, and inevitably solidifying in professional terms—will be able to develop links, alliances, and connections with a wide range of fields and researchers; these alliances would now be based on broader research questions and on theoretical and methodological orientation, not on chronology or regional focus. This may entail the uncomfortable abolition of the exceptionalism of Aegean prehistory, the notion of a self-contained field that is in need of its own structures, research procedures, funding bodies, conference venues, and publication outlets; that is an attitude that has led to the introverted character of the field, as I mentioned at the beginning and as documented elsewhere by Cherry and Talalay (ch. 2). I do not deny the usefulness of some of these structures, nor do I underestimate the efforts of many people in maintaining them. Yet I would contend that a reconfigured, broad field of Aegean prehistory will have to invent ways to embed these structures and procedures in the wider, interregional, cross-cultural, and interdisciplinary debate (cf. Papadopoulos and Leventhal 2003 for one such interesting attempt to do so).

In the past, Aegean prehistory has sought to contribute to broader anthropological discussions by providing material proofs of myths of origins or, more recently, examples that could illustrate universal neo-evolutionist typologies of the 'chiefdom and state' variety. As argued above, such typologies, now heavily and widely critiqued in archaeology and anthropology, were inscribed

10

into a Western essentialist, and inevitably colonialist, project. They also homogenized and erased the specificity and diversity of human experience: the Aegean prehistoric past became merely yet another example that proved a universal rule, no more than a footnote.

Alternative Aegean prehistoric futures are, however, possible. As has recently been noted by Rowlands (2004), an emerging theme that seems to unify previously disparate fields (such as archaeology, anthropology, museum studies, art history, and visual and cultural studies) is the notion of *materiality*, both in the past and in the present: the understanding that humans and nonhumans alike (including animals and objects) relate to each other and to the world though their material, physical, sensory, and embodied properties. The understanding of this phenomenon in diverse contexts and time scales has started acquiring primacy over exclusively synchronic or time-specific treatments. Aegean prehistoric societies offer some of the best examples to debate these ideas, to understand and attend to the sensory and material qualities of human experience. This will not only revitalize and rejuvenate the whole field; it will also help correct some of the 'biases' of the current debates on phenomenological archaeology that have focused almost exclusively on certain periods, material forms, and phenomena, at the expense of others. For example, the focus of such a discussion in British prehistory, and on megalithic monuments in particular, has offered many insights, but at the same time it has prioritized certain sensory qualities (primarily vision, although see Tilley 2004) and has neglected multi-sensory bodily experiences. Aegean prehistoric societies, with their complex material configurations that are at times phenomenally well preserved, can enrich the debate by providing insights into the corporeal multi-sensory reception of the world, be it the complex bodily experience of movement inside an architecturally and materially elaborate building or the multi-sensory effects of feasting and sacrifice in the enclosed space of a Mycenaean sanctuary (cf. Hamilakis and Konsolaki 2004).

Finally, if the lives of what we call prehistoric monuments have not ended with the end of prehistory but continue to the present day, then it is not outside our remit to record and understand them: to trace their entanglement with discourses of identity and to detect and analyze their political consequences and effects. This project should not be treated as a subfield, a useful but optional research inquiry: as argued above, it relates to everything else we attempt to do with the Aegean prehistoric past; no archaeological inquiry, however mundane, can escape this genealogical and political 'loss of innocence,' as several contributors to this volume have intimated. The field does not lack historiographic accounts, but how many of them go beyond the 'ancestral worship' paradigm that attempts to legitimate present and future agendas? Furthermore, how many studies attempt to focus not on archaeologists themselves but on all other groups that have taken an active interest in the Aegean prehistoric past? This archaeological project should not be seen as simply an attempt to fill the gap or even to help design a coherent research methodology;

implicit within it is an ethical dimension that is rarely discussed. I am talking about the obligation to attend to the different stories that people have told about Aegean prehistoric monuments, sites, and artifacts, in other words, to attend to alternative archaeologies, in addition to the 'official' ones in which we are implicated; also, the obligation to be at the same time attuned to the political effects and consequences of both our own and other people's stories about the prehistoric past, stories that have often offered legitimacy to various agendas and, as noted above, have a powerful political import in current developments; and, finally, the ethical obligation to be aware of the material effects of our archaeological practices, not only in terms of the 'facts on the ground' that we help to create (cf. Abu El-Haj 2001) but also in terms of the asymmetries of economic and social power that a major intervention, such as the production of an archaeological site–tourist attraction, may bring about.

Essentialist ideologies and practices such as colonialism and nationalism rely on and promote notions of homogeneous, territorially discrete, and bounded entities. The fields of representation that are created under their influence carry in them these features of homogeneity and boundedness. Aegean prehistory has been no exception in that respect. The decolonization and denationalization of that field is a prerequisite for its reinvention and its transformation into a dynamic, open-ended, and fluid arena. The reflections contained in the present volume have made considerable forays in this direction.

References

Abu El-Haj, N.
2001   *Facts on the Ground: Archaeological Practice and Territorial Self-Fashioning in Israeli Society.* Chicago: Chicago University Press.

Alcock, S. E.
2002   *Archaeologies of the Greek Past: Landscapes, Monuments, and Memories.* Cambridge: Cambridge University Press.

Andreou, S., M. Fotiadis, and K. Kotsakis
1996   The Neolithic and Bronze Age of Northern Greece. *American Journal of Archaeology* 100: 537–97.

Bennet, J., J. L. Davis, and F. Zarinebaf-Shahr
2000   Pylos Regional Archaeological Project, Part III: Sir William Gell's itinerary in the Pylia and regional landscapes in the Morea in the Second Ottoman Period. *Hesperia* 69: 343–80.

Bintliff, J. L.
2003   The ethnoarchaeology of a passive ethnicity: the Arvanites of Central Greece. In K. S. Brown and Y. Hamilakis (eds.), *The Usable Past: Greek Metahistories,*129–44. Lanham and Oxford: Lexington Books.

10   Cherry, J. F.
    2003   Archaeology beyond the site: regional survey and its future. In J. K. Papadopoulos and R. M. Leventhal (eds.), *Theory and Practice in Mediterranean Archaeology: Old World and New World Perspectives.* Cotsen Advanced Seminars 1: 137–59. Los Angeles: The Cotsen Institute of Archaeology, University of California, Los Angeles.

Davis, J. L.
    1991   Contributions to a Mediterranean rural archaeology: historical case studies from the Ottoman Cyclades. *Journal of Mediterranean Archaeology* 4: 131–216.

Gosden, C., and Y. Marshall (eds.)
    1999   *The Cultural Biographies of Objects* (*World Archaeology* 31.2). London: Routledge.

Gourgouris, S.
    1996   *Dream Nation: Enlightenment, Colonization, and the Institution of Modern Greece.* Stanford: Stanford University Press.

Gregory, D.
    2004   *The Colonial Present.* Oxford: Blackwell.

Halstead, P.
    1990   Present to past in the Pindos: diversification and specialisation in mountain economies. *Rivista di Studi Liguri* 36(1–4): 61–80.
    1998   Ask the fellows who lop the hay: leaf-fodder in the mountains of northwest Greece. *Rural History* 9(2): 211–34.

Hamilakis, Y.
    2002   'The Other Parthenon': antiquity and national memory at Makronisos. *Journal of Modern Greek Studies* 20(2): 307–38.
    2003   Lives in ruins: antiquities and national imagination in modern Greece. In S. Kane (ed.), *The Politics of Archaeology and Identity in a Global Context*, 51–78. Boston: Archaeological Institute of America.

Hamilakis, Y., and E. Konsolaki
    2004   Pigs for the gods: burnt animal sacrifices as embodied rituals at a Mycenaean sanctuary. *Oxford Journal of Archaeology* 23: 135–51.

Kotsakis, K.
    1998   The past is ours: images of Greek Macedonia. In L. Meskell (ed.), *Archaeology under Fire: Nationalism, Politics and Heritage in the Eastern Mediterranean and Middle East*, 44–67. London: Routledge.

Larsen, M. T.
    1995   Orientalism and Near Eastern archaeology. In D. Miller, M. Rowlands, and C. Tilley (eds.), *Domination and Resistance*, 229–39. London: Routledge.

Moreland, J.
    2001   *Archaeology and Text.* London: Duckworth.

Morris, I.
  2004   Classical archaeology. In J. Bintliff (ed.), *A Companion to Archaeology*, 253–71. Oxford: Blackwell.
Papadopoulos, J. K., and R. M. Leventhal (eds.)
  2003   *Theory and Practice in Mediterranean Archaeology: Old World and New World Perspectives.* Cotsen Advanced Seminars 1. Los Angeles: The Cotsen Institute of Archaeology, University of California, Los Angeles.
Papatheodorou, Y.
  2000   'Η πυκνοκατοικημένη ερημιά' των ποιητών της Μακρονήσου: Γραφές της εξορίας ['The densely populated waste land' of the Makronisos poets: writings of the exile]. In S. Bournazos and T. Sakellaropoulos (eds.), *Ιστορικό τοπίο και ιστορική μνήμη: Το παράδειγμα της Μακρονήσου* [*Historical Landscape and Historical Memory: The Case of Makronisos*], 227–44. Athens: Philistor.
Patterson, T. C.
  1997   *Inventing Western Civilization.* New York: Monthly Review Press.
Preziosi, D.
  2002   Archaeology as museology: rethinking the Minoan past. In Y. Hamilakis (ed.), *Labyrinth Revisited: Rethinking Minoan Archaeology*, 30–39. Oxford: Oxbow.
Rowlands, M.
  2004   Relating anthropology and archaeology. In J. Bintliff (ed.), *A Companion to Archaeology*, 473–89. Oxford: Blackwell.
Tilley, C.
  2004   *The Materiality of Stone.* Oxford: Berg.